Business Continuity Planning

A Project Management Approach

Business Continuity Planning

A Project Management Approach

Ralph L. Kliem, PMP, CBCP
Gregg D. Richie, PMP, CNP

CRC Press
Taylor & Francis Group
Boca Raton London New York

CRC Press is an imprint of the
Taylor & Francis Group, an **Informa** business
AN AUERBACH BOOK

CRC Press
Taylor & Francis Group
6000 Broken Sound Parkway NW, Suite 300
Boca Raton, FL 33487-2742

Printed on acid-free paper
Version Date: 20150311

International Standard Book Number-13: 978-1-4822-5178-4 (Hardback)

Library of Congress Cataloging-in-Publication Data

Kliem, Ralph L.
Business continuity planning : a project management approach / Ralph L. Kliem and Gregg D. Richie.
pages cm
Includes index.
ISBN 978-1-4822-5178-4
1. Crisis management--Planning. 2. Project management. I. Richie, Gregg D. II. Title.

HD49.K55 2016
658.1'6--dc23 2015007578

Visit the Taylor & Francis Web site at
http://www.taylorandfrancis.com

and the CRC Press Web site at
http://www.crcpress.com

To mom, Philomena, who now rests forever with my dad, Arnold—RLK

To my soul mate, Dena, who helped me become who I am today—GDR

Contents

List of Figures

Preface

We live in an unpredictable world—nothing new about that. What is new is the business environment. The complexity of global finance, advancements in technology from computing to transportation to medicine, and the rise of outsourcing and transnational companies have created an integrated and interdependent web of complexity, manifesting itself in what chaos theory would call the Butterfly Effect, a seemingly innocuous event occurs someplace on the globe and has profound impact elsewhere on the globe, possibly on the other side. Integration and interdependence have bred immense complexity with vulnerability. True, this environment affords some flexibility in response; however, the response to an event can also result in unanticipated, seemingly uncontrollable consequences.

Take, for example, the global growth and complexity of the supply chain of an aerospace firm. As complexity grew, so did the problems and events affecting it. The supply chain for aerospace products now spans the globe—the 777 and the 787 are two specific examples. Thanks to the application of Lean and Just-In-Time principles to production, immense gains have been made in simplifying flow, while at the same time increasing the interdependence and complexity of its supply chain. A hiccup, like an earthquake in Japan, can interfere and disrupt the supply chain due to the consequences of such an event. If the company is not prepared to respond, the financial, political, and social impacts can be immense. Such a company must be resilient, that is, have the ability to respond and recover from the impact of events. Business continuity (BC) is the discipline to become resilient.

Companies in aerospace, of course, are not the only ones that need to respond to and recover from an event. Much smaller companies must be resilient, finding themselves dependent on this complex business environment, being vulnerable, too, to unanticipated and even anticipated events. Unfortunately, small and middle size companies find themselves woefully vulnerable, lacking even the basics of BC.

In this book, we show how to apply project management to implement and maintain BC with a major emphasis on building business preparedness (BP) plans, enabling companies to recover their business processes from an event.

Ask yourself this simple question: If a major event such as a terrorist attack or a 7.2 earthquake hit your region, is your company prepared to recover from such an event? What if the event significantly disrupts the supply chain? Could your firm recover from such an event? Do your people understand what they have to do and what resources, for example, information, are needed to recover? Do they even know the priorities? Will your company survive or collapse like 80% of the businesses do after a significant event impact?

Only you know the answer and only you can make resiliency a way of doing business within your company. Survivability is the key, occurring only through preparation. BP is the key and PM is the door to allow your company to step into the world of resiliency.

Regardless of the size and complexity of your company, ask yourself this fundamental question: Is your company prepared to recover from a serious event?

Ralph Kliem, PMP, CBCP
Gregg D. Richie, PMP, CNP, MCTS

Acknowledgment

We want to thank our personal editor, Ameeta Chainani, for taking the time to review the manuscript and to provide insights on improving it.

Authors

Ralph L. Kliem, PMP, CBCP, president of LeanPM, LLC, has over 30 years of experience with Fortune 500 firms, including Safeco Insurance Companies and The Boeing Company. As a senior project manager for Boeing, he managed many agile and financial compliance and BC projects. Some of the BC projects he managed included building, testing, and maintaining BP plans for the 747, 767, 777, and 787 programs. He also managed a major proof-of-concept project and preparation of the corresponding business case for a web-based business analytics software application that recently won the CIO Award for Risk Management, CSO Award for Innovation and Risk Management, the Manufacturing Leadership Council ML 100, and the Manufacturing Leadership Council Project of the Year for 2014. As a former corporate auditor, he led numerous projects that evaluated the performance of major business and IT projects and programs as well as ones for Boeing's Executive Council and Audit Committee. Ralph also teaches PMP certification courses and general PM seminars and workshops and is an adjunct faculty member of City University in Seattle, a former member of Seattle Pacific University and an instructor with the Continuing Education program with Bellevue College, Cascadia Community College, and Everett Community College. He is the author or co-author of over 15 books and more than 300 articles with leading business and IT publications. He can be reached at ralph.kliem@frontier.com; (206) 963-5246; or via www.theleanpm.com.

Gregg D. Richie, PMP, CNP, MCTS, has over 35 years of experience in the project management and facilities management fields. He has managed or consulted on more than 1200 projects in the United States and other locations around the world, including Japan, Italy, Spain, the Philippines, and Guam. He is a founding member and the managing partner for P8 LLC, which is a PM training and consulting firm that specializes in Microsoft Project implementations for small- to medium-sized companies. While on active duty with the U.S. Navy SEABEES, he spent several years learning and implementing disaster recovery techniques, conducting drills, and being involved at some level in disaster recovery for the 1983 Marine Barracks attack, the 1985 Mexico City earthquake, the 1991 Mt. Pinatubo eruption, and Hurricane Iniki, which struck Kauai in 1992. Specializing in risk management approaches and techniques, the SEABEES are often called upon to help recover from manufactured or natural disasters. He holds a BS from Southern Illinois University at Carbondale in workforce education and development and has designed and delivered training programs for many organizations including the U.S. Navy and Fortune 500 companies. He has written two textbooks for John Wiley & Sons Publishing in the Microsoft Official Academic Course series on Project 2010 and 2013.

In 2006, he earned his master's certificate in applied project management from Villanova University and became a certified PMP in 2008. His current projects include Microsoft Project implementation for international companies as well as instructing for various companies in the United States and abroad. He can be reached at gregg.richie@gmail.com or by phone at (253) 255-2109.

1

Why You Need Business Continuity and Business Preparedness

As noted in the preface, commerce has become more complex, thanks in part to technology and political and social cross-fertilization—the Butterfly Effect. The flutter of a butterfly's wings can impact conditions somewhere else on the other side of the globe. Alternatively, a Black Swan event occurs, unanticipated, with devastating consequences, and being rationalized later—the impact may be immediate but the consequences linger.

WHAT ARE BUSINESS CONTINUITY AND BUSINESS PREPAREDNESS?

Business continuity (BC) is the discipline of developing, deploying, and maintaining strategies and procedures to ensure that critical business processes prevail by increasing the likelihood of responding to, and recovering from, an event crippling or threatening to destroy the existence of a business entity. In a sense, BC can be translated as "Before Catastrophe"; it makes sense to put the discipline in place in advance of events having a significant impact. Unfortunately, many companies only do so after it is too late.

Some people think that BC is nothing more than risk management. While it does require applying risk management, BC is much broader than risk management. It requires taking a systemic, holistic perspective; risk management plays an integral, salient role but not the only one.

Business preparedness (BP) is a subset of BC. It requires developing plans for a company to recover from an event having a significant impact on processes it deems critical to its survivability. These plans serve as a roadmap for guiding stakeholders, whether people or organizations, to recover from a serious event.

DRIVERS FOR BUSINESS CONTINUITY

A number of specific drivers have increased interest in BC, and rightfully so.

Global Sourcing

It is no secret that the economy has transitioned to an unprecedented global scale. For example, manufactured parts may consist of elements extracted from across the globe, from mineral resources, such as bauxite and lithium, pulled from the mines of Chile or Afghanistan, respectively. Information technology enables the spread of knowledge and data throughout the globe, too, revolutionizing the service industries, from banking to medicine. Global sourcing has also led to complex outsourcing arrangements enabling companies to deliver the necessary products and services to their customers. As products, and the processes making them, become more complex, global sourcing requires not just physical resources but also expertise to deliver the final product or service. Not surprisingly, therefore, a significant disruption can impact a company's ability to deliver its products and services.

Trans-Global Alliances and Partnerships

It is not uncommon for multinational corporations to form relationships rivaling those existing among nation states. These relationships involve two or more parties to provide goods and services not normally achievable operating alone. These relationships often involve some element of both cooperation and co-optation, meaning they are friends and rivals at the same time. Despite being competitive, it may be advantageous to work together. Nonetheless, there is a need for relying on the ability of each party to deliver. For example, if an event affecting one partner occurs, then it affects the other parties, exemplifying a symbiotic relationship. It is imperative, therefore, that the parties adopt business continuity disciplines—if for no other reason than to preclude the failure of one party to deliver.

Terrorism, War, and Political Turmoil

Let's face it: Companies that span the globe are no longer isolated from the socio-political turmoil existing across the globe. Terrorism, war, and political events not only have severe consequences locally, but also globally. Regional conflicts involving terrorism, war, and political turmoil can disrupt communications and transportation channels, for example, which cause a price rise in resources, from oil to copper. It can also make performing business difficult when a company has to escort its procurement people under armed guard in a developing country. A coup d'état or even a violent takeover of a government in a remote developing country can disrupt a company's supply chain however slightly and have a financial impact.

Regulations and Nationalizations

This driver is closely allied to the previous one. As the number of countries across the globe has multiplied over the last 20 to 30 years, the probability and the impact of an event elsewhere can affect the survivability of one or more companies. Many developing countries, regardless of location or size, may contribute labor or nonlabor resources while transitioning to a stable socio-political system. Their internal turmoil may lead to an environment not conducive to business. For example, a popular revolutionary movement can result in a regime change that demands a greater share of resources and share in the revenue if the foreign company wants to continue to operate in its country. Even in developed countries, such as the United States, the political climate can lead to greater regulation, such as International Traffic in Arms Regulations (ITAR) and Export Administration Regulations (EAR), affecting business. The consequences may impact or disrupt processes, resulting in higher prices and thereby reduce a company's ability to remain competitive.

Fragile Supply Chain

In some cases, the global supply chain has become such a complex web that assessing the impact of a significant disruption becomes quite a challenge.

Multiple tiers of suppliers can add to the challenge. An airplane part, for instance, made in India to satisfy an offset agreement, may involve a large number of multi-tier suppliers. What is the impact on a supply chain if Pakistan and India go to war? What region in India where that part is made does the conflict impact? What must a company do to continue to deliver the necessary goods and services to its customers?

Complex Transportation and Information Webs

Along with the growth of globalization of the economy comes a greater complexity. Having many varying degrees of relationships and the flattening of hierarchies comes with the challenge of knowing when a problem arises and determining its many impacts on those relationships and other entities. Ascertaining the cause can pose a challenge for a business delivering or receiving a product or service. Think of the formula often used in communications to calculate the complexity of relationships arising when adding new people or other entities:

The Number of People × (The Number of People – 1)/2

Say you have 10 people × (10 – 1)/2 = 45 communications relationships.

Now add 20 more people:

30 × (30 – 1)/2 = 435 communications relationships!

As you can see, the complexity increases dramatically. For example, someone in a relationship spreads a rumor and it spreads like wildfire among the others. Different interpretations of the rumor occur, and few people can tell the difference between the truth and exaggeration.

You can apply the same principle to transportation and information webs. Breakdowns in the delivery of a product or service can have uncontrollable ramifications. Add more business entities to the web and the consequences become more complex.

Interdependence and Integration of the Global Economy

Related to the last point, but on a more macro level, international trade is more tightly interwoven than ever before. Think of it. Before Richard Nixon became president of the United States, trade with the then Soviet

Union and Red China would have been unthinkable. Since that time, a great thaw has occurred and, in many respects, the economies among all three countries have a complex economic relationship whereby the economic weakening or collapse of one can impact businesses in the other two countries. Should the relationships deteriorate or cease, businesses that depend on such relationships need a plan to recover.

Rise of International Capital

Without getting into the polemics between capitalism and communism, Karl Marx predicted in his earlier writings that a resurgence of international capital would lead to a collapse of the world economy. Whether a collapse is coming is unknown. However, clearly international capital is flowing in and out of countries, having a tremendous impact, positive or negative. Businesses must prepare themselves for such eventualities, for example, the value of a nation's currency changes or takes flight where a subsidiary exists. Such changes can translate into a decline in business which, in turn, could impact the delivery of a good or service to another business located somewhere across the globe.

Insurance Costs

Unless they are a Fortune 100 firm, with a large financial war chest sitting in a bank somewhere, many companies lack the ability to self-insure, meaning when something negative happens they absorb the consequences. With myriad challenges and risks, from political instability to global warming, occurring in the world, many businesses assume that nothing will happen to them—that the government will bail them out or they can buy insurance to cover everything. True, they may be able to purchase insurance while premiums are inexpensive. Once the event occurs, however, these premiums often rise. The best proactive approach is not to rely solely on self-insurance or insurance but to establish plans enabling a company to recover from disaster and correspondingly reduce premiums. Many insurance companies look to having BP plans, factoring them to reduce annual premiums.

Litigation

Related to more government laws and regulations, a lawsuit is enough to put an end to companies, especially when a judgment is ruled against them. Many businesses think the likelihood of a lawsuit occurring is remote. However, there are certain areas in which they are particularly susceptible to lawsuits, such as human resource policies and manufactured goods, which, depending on the country, such as the United States and Canada, can result in severe damages to a company. BC should determine the most vulnerable lawsuits from a legal perspective to determine the risk to their firms.

There are, of course, many other drivers demonstrating the need for BC. The essence of all these drivers is, however, globalization and its reliance on an intricate weaving of technology and business processes to deliver products at an unprecedented level of speed and quality. The slightest hiccup can choke everything.

LET'S GET REAL

Unfortunately, many people believe that the business events previously described are scare tactics and hyperbole. However, consider these statistics. According to CRED International Data Base, the number and frequency of natural disasters have been increasing dramatically from just 903 in the 1970s to over 4485 in the 2000s (Hawthorne 2011).

Imagine if the "big one" hits the Los Angeles (LA) area. Can you imagine the impact, financially, politically, and socially? Not just in LA, but elsewhere in the country? LA is a major port and financial center and a disastrous impact there in the region cannot help but affect many other parts of the country, even the globe. Moreover, this potential event is imminent. The probability of a major earthquake striking LA in the next 30 years is 97% and it can happen sooner than you might expect (Matlack 2010). Here's another sobering statistic demonstrating the integration and interdependence of the world economy: According to a survey by the Business Continuity Institute, 85% of respondents said they were affected by one or more supply chain disruptions and 20% of those companies were affected by earthquakes and tsunamis in Japan and New Zealand (Spandanuta 2012).

The list of events, at various levels of scalability and magnitude, are endless. That is why good BP planning is critical for resiliency. Here is just a sample list of some natural and artificial events that could impact your business and they do not even have to occur locally; Figure 1.1 shows that

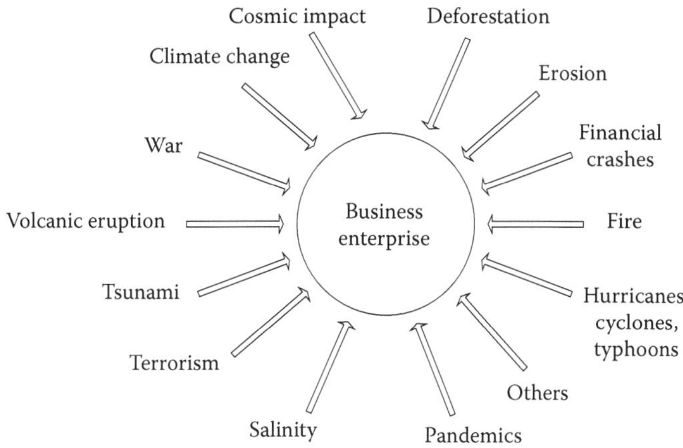

FIGURE 1.1
Potential events impacting an enterprise.

the events can come from many directions and can occur in coordination with one another.

Climate change
Cosmic impacts
Deforestation
Earthquakes
Erosion
Financial crashes
Fire
Hurricanes, cyclones, typhoons
Pandemics
Salinity
Terrorism
Tsunamis
Volcanic eruptions
War

Here are also some recent events to refresh your memory, many of them having an impact on businesses across the globe:

1991 – Mt. Pinatubo eruption
1996 – Khobar Towers

2001 – Attack on World Trade Center and Washington, D.C.
2004 – Madrid Train Bombings
2004 – Tsunami hits Southeast Asia
2005 – Hurricane Katrina
2005 – London public transportation bombing
2007 – Virginia Tech campus shootings
2008 – Unprecedented hurricane and tornado outbreaks
2009 – H1N1 Influenza global pandemic
2010 – Haiti earthquake
2010 – Eyjafjallajokull volcanic eruption
2011 – Earthquake in Honshu, Japan
2012 – Hurricane Sandy
2013 – Typhoon hitting Philippines

TIME TO PRETEND

Now take some time to imagine whether any of the events might occur that affect your business, regardless of your location. If any of these events occur, how would your company recover?

Here are just some things to toy with in your mind, to think about on how your business might be impacted by an event no matter where you are located.

A 7.3 earthquake hitting St. Louis
A 7.8 earthquake striking Caracas, Venezuela
A 7.9 earthquake wrecking the locks of the Suez Canal
A category 5 hurricane smacking into Washington, D.C.
A levee failure occurring in the Sacramento Delta of Southern California
A major drought devastating the agricultural industry of Southern California
A major drought impacting the agricultural regions of Chile
A major landslide occurring after significant volcanic activity at Mt. Rainier
A major tsunami smashing into Honolulu
A massive blackout affecting the entire Northeast

A meltdown occurring at the Diablo Canyon nuclear power plant at San Luis Obispo, California

A pandemic arising out of the Midwest United States due to a rare animal flu that mutates into a virus deadly to people

A terrorist seizing a tanker in Puget Sound and running the vessel into the Port of Tacoma, causing not only a major oil spill but also significant damage to the piers

A tsunami in British Columbia after a 7.0 earthquake in the Pacific Ocean

An outbreak of the swine flu (H1N2) occurs, originating in Southeast Asia and, due to air travel, spreads rapidly throughout the West Coast of the United States

Several large tornado cells crushing Chicago

The Po River in Italy overflowing after a heavy downpour

Alternatively, perhaps one or more mundane, immediate events such as the following can impact your company's survival:

A disgruntled employee entering your office with a high-powered rifle and killing two of your key employees

An employee diagnosed with tuberculosis (TB) coming into your office and causing other employees to refuse to come to work

An employee, perhaps intentionally or accidently, introducing a computer virus that destroys all data on your servers

You having a massive heart attack or stroke and being unable to communicate with employees on how to manage your business

Your business is destroyed by fire

A natural or manufactured area disaster causes loss of vital people and information

Naturally, most or none of these events will impact your business. However, an event is looming in the background. That is the exception rather than the rule. However, what if one of them did occur? Are you prepared to recover? No one would have thought that sale of credit default swaps would lead to a massive crash in the world's economy. No one thought the financial security breach at Target would turn the credit card business on its head. Both did. The point is not to scare you but rather to impel you to act, soon if not now, to ensure the resiliency, that is, the survivability, of your company.

ADDITIONAL INSIGHTS

Here are some additional insights to think about.

One, no guarantee exists any of the events described previously will happen and, if so, will affect your business. Neither we nor anyone else short of a clairvoyant can predict the future. Correspondingly, no guarantee exists that any of these events will *not* occur.

Two, no way exists to predict where or when such events will occur, albeit certain areas of the world have a greater proclivity for certain disasters over others, for example, earthquakes and tsunamis in the Pacific Northwest.

Three, companies that prepare for an eventual event have a greater chance of survival than companies that do not. Few companies survive a major event unless they have prepared for it through response and, just as importantly, recovery.

Four, failure to prepare is akin to relying on luck or embracing the opportunity to fail. Hoping that an event will not happen or pretending that the odds of being hit are remote is, at best, a gambler's wish. The key question is not pertaining to luck or probability, but what to do when a negative event happens.

Five, being prepared is not just for Boy Scouts. Companies preparing to respond and recover from an event have a better likelihood or probability of being in a better competitive position.

TAKING ACTION USING PROJECT MANAGEMENT

Many projects fail to meet the basic goals of completing on time, within budget, and fulfilling requirements. Some projects may meet one or two of the goals; fewer meet all three goals. Business continuity projects rarely deviate from this track record as well. Quite frequently, these projects start with only a vague idea of what to achieve in the midst of facing an unrealistic schedule and a very limited budget. In the end, the projects more often than not result in a missed opportunity for making a company or other entity more resilient. In this book, an approach is described that has proven effective in completing business continuity, specifically business preparedness, efficiently and effectively.

GETTING STARTED CHECKLIST

Question	Yes	No
1. Have you thought about how the following drivers have affected the resiliency of your company? Global sourcing Trans-global alliances and partnerships Terrorism and war Regulations and nationalization Fragile supply chain Political and military turmoil Complex information and transportation webs Interdependence and integration of the global economy Insurance costs Litigation Complexity and dynamism of the business environment		
2. Have you thought about how the following events can have an impact on your company? Climate change Cosmic impacts Deforestation Earthquakes Erosion Financial crashes Fire Hurricanes, cyclones, typhoons Pandemics Salinity Terrorism Tsunamis Volcanic eruptions War		
3. Have you assessed how your company has been impacted by previous events, for example, Hurricane Katrina?		

2

A Business Continuity Primer

In the previous chapter, business continuity (BC) is defined as the discipline of developing, deploying, and maintaining strategies and procedures to ensure the continuance or recovery of critical business processes. Business preparedness (BP) is a subset of BC, enabling an organization to continue or recover services or products during and after an event to support and service customers.

GOALS

To provide value to an organization, BC must achieve, at a minimum, three goals to demonstrate value.

Improve the Odds of Survivability

Preparing in advance for a known event negatively impacting company performance increases the likelihood of a company to respond effectively and to sustain its operations. BP plans enable a company to do just that by identifying the who, what, when, where, and why to execute if and when an event occurs. Specifically, this preparation entails understanding the financial and nonfinancial impact of an event; the type and quantity of resources needed to respond over a time continuum; recovery team membership; call trees; and workaround procedures should the key resources become unavailable. Compiling this and other information helps a company to know what to do once an event occurs and then to take action to recover.

Minimize the Impact of an Event

By knowing the processes that require attention from a BC perspective, the focus can turn to taking advance measures to enable a process to withstand or recover from an event. In other words, BC focuses on preparation and recovery rather than reaction.

Recover Critical Processes

Not all processes in an organization are equal. Executive leadership often considers processes supporting strategic goals and objectives or comprises a significant portion of the financial statement as the most important. Executive leadership can further review the processes to ascertain the ones that are most critical to the survivability of the organization. It can then decide on which processes to focus recovering from one or more events.

BENEFITS

BC offers many benefits, many going beyond the discipline itself.

Recovering Critical, or Core, Business Processes

This benefit is the ultimate purpose of BC. Response, recovery, resumption, and restoration are the four "Rs" of resiliency. If BC fails to enable resiliency, it fails to add value to an organization. All other benefits are trumped by the inability to realize this one.

Exchanging Information among Stakeholders

BC is an intensive information exercise. Ensuring greater resiliency for a process requires identifying who, what, when, where, how, and why and incorporating all datum into a plan. While obtaining and compiling the information, stakeholders engage in a dialog, requiring communication with each other, as well as acquiring a better understanding of what other people do and do not do during an event, even under normal conditions.

Building Trust among Stakeholders

Another benefit is engendering trusting relationships among stakeholders before, during, and after recovery. By preparing plans and exercises, stakeholders have the opportunity to share knowledge, experiences, and insights on resiliency. Each stakeholder garners a better understanding of the other stakeholders and can adapt accordingly during and after a disaster.

Greater Understanding of Business Processes to Include Risks and Relationships

Applying BC helps in augmenting awareness of the overall business of an organization, both at the strategic and operational levels, if stakeholders systemically view their environment. Identifying critical business processes, key stakeholders, workaround procedures, and other contents of a BP plan requires holistically perceiving how critical business processes impact the organization and the entire enterprise. It is also likely to identify significant potential vulnerabilities, perhaps affecting resiliency.

Deploying Resources Effectively

When a negative event occurs, people have a tendency to run around aimlessly or to take a shotgun approach. Both are wasteful and frequently ineffective. BC requires developing plans to determine, for example, what resources are needed in the appropriate quantity for the applicable recovery procedures. A targeted approach reduces waste and minimizes costs but also enables pinpointing accuracy when responding to an event.

Reducing Insurance Costs

Another benefit of BC, often overlooked, is that the existence of BP plans can reduce business insurance costs. BP plans demonstrate to insurers that a company takes resiliency seriously and can recover, at least to some degree, from the occurrence of known risks. Additionally, even if an unanticipated risk occurs, having such plans lays the groundwork for more effective and efficient recovery than without any preparation.

Requiring a Holistic Perspective

You need to consider the enterprise when preparing BP plans. This is especially the case for critical processes supporting an organization's strategic goals and objectives. Critical business processes often transcend a single business entity, such as a department, subsumed under a bigger one. Developing effective BP plans requires knowing what other organizations, such as a department in an enterprise, can provide in terms of support and resources if a negative event occurs.

Leveraging Areas of Commonality

When developing multiple BP plans, it behooves you to identify common areas among critical business processes. These common areas not only demonstrate value from a resiliency perspective but also pinpoint where stakeholders in different processes will likely contend for support in recovery. Key stakeholders from each of the critical business processes can then determine priorities if an event occurs.

Identifying Strengths and Weaknesses

When developing BP plans for critical processes, discussions will likely reveal which stakeholders can be relied upon to respond to an event and who will likely struggle to do so. It is not uncommon for discussions over the adequacy of resources, in terms of quantity and quality, to arise and where, other than under normal operations, to procure them. The very act of building BP plans causes stakeholders to raise such issues. This analysis indicates what resources and expertise to apply on workarounds and what areas to improve, and this is important, before an event occurs.

Demonstrating Due Diligence

Failure to prepare for an event may be construed by legal professionals and stockholders as a failure on the part of executive leadership. This situation is especially the case where executive leadership fails to act to become resilient when an event has a likelihood or probability of occurrence. By providing BP plans in support of a BC program, executive leadership addresses this issue as best it can in advance, even if its results turn out catastrophic, such as an Act of God or Black Swan.

TERMINOLOGY

Like all disciplines, BC has its own set of terminology.

A *BP Plan* is a document guiding the recovery and ultimate restoration from an event having a significant impact on those processes deemed critical to its survivability. It documents its scope, recovery team membership, procedures and accompanying resources and workarounds, timeline for full restoration to normal operations, and call tree instructions. One or more plans may support restoring a critical process.

A *Critical Business Process* is a series of procedures and activities key stakeholders have identified as vital to the survival of an organization. A critical business process can have one or more BP plans supporting it. Processes often transcend an organizational silo. Each process or function has an owner, usually at the executive leadership and senior management levels (refer to Figure 2.1).

Due Diligence is a legal concept meaning an organization or person must take reasonable actions to protect people and property under a set of circumstances. Frequently used interchangeably with due care, failure to

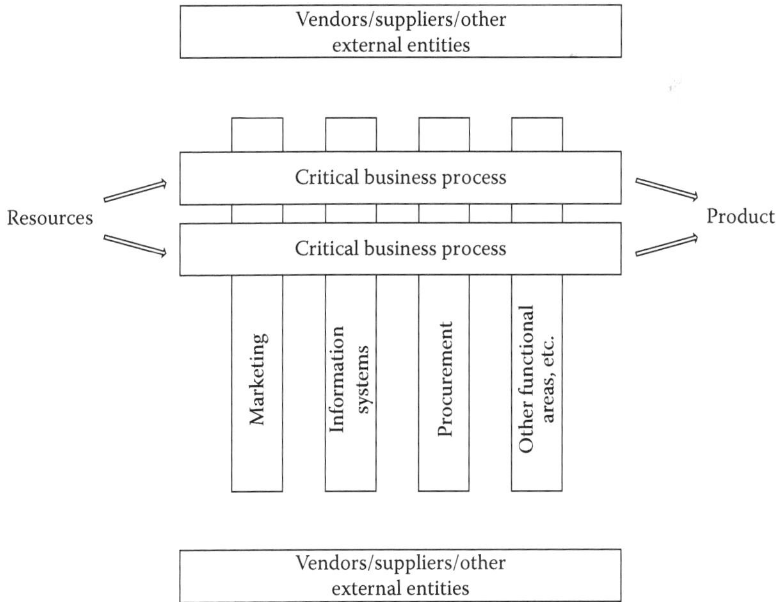

FIGURE 2.1
A critical business process.

exercise due diligence can have legal ramifications, especially if damages arise resulting from plain neglect. An example of due diligence is having BP plans for all critical business processes.

An *Event* is the occurrence of an incident impacting a critical business process. An event can range in intensity and impact, such as very mild to catastrophic. An example of an event is an earthquake in Japan affecting the delivery of a key component to a manufacturing facility on the other side of the globe. There are several types of events that can occur, as shown in Figure 2.2 and described in the following paragraphs.

A *Catastrophe* is a crisis that exceeds the ability and capability of a company or other entity to respond and recover from an event, leading to devastating consequences.

A *Crisis* is an event far exceeding normal expectations of disruption and necessitates recovery actions, which if not taken, threaten the survivability of an organization. An example of a crisis might be a major dam downriver, potentially flooding the area around a key production facility unless barriers are in place to prevent destruction.

A *Disaster* is a sudden, unexpected event having severe consequences on a critical business process for a considerable time unless a recovery team takes immediate action. An event can have serious operational, financial, or legal impacts, to name a few, requiring immediate attention, such as after a boiler explosion in a manufacturing facility.

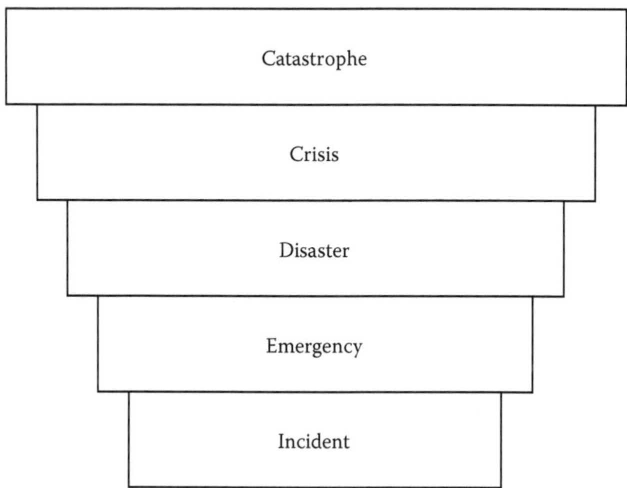

FIGURE 2.2
Hierarchy of events.

An *Emergency* is an event threatening life, safety, and property, requiring immediate attention. It may not be a disaster quite yet, but does require attention to preclude becoming a disaster or catastrophe. An emergency usually requires a response and may require additional attention. An example of an emergency is someone getting hurt or a fire erupting in the workplace.

An *Incident* is an event impacting a process. People often use "incident" and "event" interchangeably; however, a slight nuance exists. An event impacts a critical process; an incident impacts a process, not necessarily a critical one, and inconsequentially.

Normal Operations, also known as business as usual, is the state of business operations prior to the occurrence of an event. An example might be the daily performance of developing and delivering products and services for internal or external customers.

A *Recovery Team* is a group of individuals responsible for recovering a critical business process after a disruptive event. Each BP plan should have a recovery team with specific responsibilities as well as listed on a call tree.

A *Recovery Time Line* is a sequence of activities when recovering business process operations over a time continuum. All activities, or procedures, fall on what is sometime referred to as a critical path, such as from 4 to 12 hours, whereby certain activities must occur using the requisite resources or dependencies. Cumulative resources are distributed over this time continuum to facilitate recovery and restoration.

Resilience is the ability of an organization and its accompanying critical business processes to withstand or recover from a business interruption. Resilience requires knowing who the members of the recovery team are, their contact information, procedures to perform, and the resources required for recovery. There are four components of resiliency (refer to Figure 2.3).

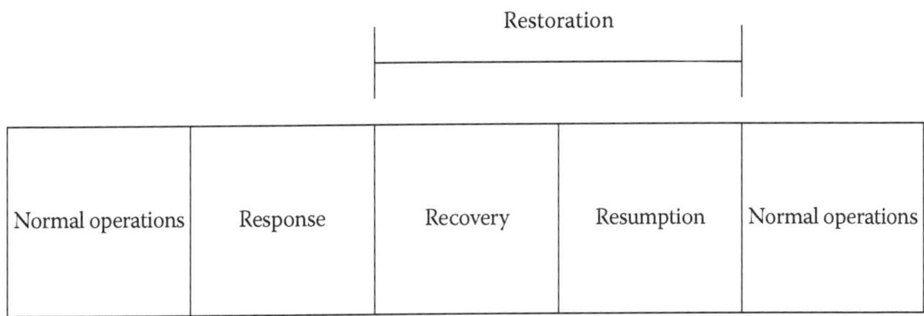

FIGURE 2.3
The four Rs of resiliency.

Response is applying processes, procedures, and actions as quickly as possible to prevent, mitigate, or avoid the impact of a negative incident. A response is often immediate to preclude an incident turning into a significant event. An example is company security responding to an incident of workplace violence.

Recovery is the actions taken by a team that will lead to the resumption of a business process and, ultimately, to a return to normal operations.

Restoration is the process, procedures, and actions taken to return a critical business process to normal operations, or business as usual. It includes recovery and resumption. Hence, restoration equals recovery plus resumption.

Resumption is the processes, procedures, and actions to restart a critical business process when recovery actions are completed after a disruptive event. It entails getting a critical process back on its feet; in other words, recovery begins after the response has adequately dealt with the incident or event and deliveries are made to the customer.

A *Single Point of Failure* is a specific breakdown in a sequence of activities, impacting a critical business process. An example is a specific supply chain affected by an incident impeding the development and delivery of a product or service to a customer. A single point of failure impacts all subsequent activities downstream, much like the derailment of a railroad car.

Reasonable Assurance is often associated with auditing but is applicable to BC, meaning no one can guarantee 100% that something will prevent an event from happening. From a BC perspective, because of the unpredictability of events and their accompanying impacts, no plan can ensure a critical business process can be completely resilient, only that measures are in place to enhance resiliency with some level of confidence.

A *Reliance Statement* describes why a critical process needs a specific resource for recovery. It provides a high-level description of the resource with an accompanying reason. Every procedure contains a reliance statement and one or more workarounds.

A *Workaround* is a set of activities to execute a procedure if a specific resource is unavailable during recovery. Resources can include people, supplies, equipment, labor, suppliers, etc. For example, if a key software application is unavailable, a recovery team member can perform other actions to improve restoration until the software is available.

KEY CONCEPTS

For BC to become accepted and deployed on a sustainable basis, you need to keep several concepts in mind.

Obtain Buy-In from Key Stakeholders, Initially at the Executive Level

An executive champion should provide the political clout to help address resistance to change. Naturally, a champion will not eliminate all resistance but will demonstrate the seriousness of the support.

Determine Priorities When Implementing BC

Not all processes are critical; the ones deemed so will likely not be able to be done all at once. Executive leadership should determine which ones have the highest priority, derived from a business impact analysis (BIA) to determine the firing order. The results should be based upon the impact to the financial statement as well as the strategic goals and objectives of the company.

Institute a Governance Program for Implementing BC

The reality is that some kind of a support organization is required to provide the necessary expertise and resources to implement BC. This support organization should provide tools, expertise, and assistance to owners of critical processes, for example, when developing, testing, and maintaining BP plans. Its support should also include expertise in BC and BP, risk management, tool utilization, and project management.

Apply Good Project Management Tools and Techniques

The best approach is for the governance program to manage BC projects and let the critical process owners take ownership of it, meaning the recovery teams take on responsibility to build and maintain the BP plans. This approach will generate ownership in the BP plans and limit the amount of pushback simply because the responsibility for success rests with the critical process owners.

Build Trust

The BC governance program exists to seek buy-in for BC, not to act as a police force. It provides the necessary support, as discussed in the previous paragraphs, and flexibility in accommodating the needs of the critical process owners in building their plans. By tracking performance in completing and maintaining plans, it provides the necessary visibility on progress to date and any obstacles requiring attention from executive leadership and senior management. Only on rare occasions should executive leadership and senior management exert negative pressure to comply with resiliency requirements.

Document and Distribute All BP Plans

BP plans residing in someone's head or documented but not distributed serve little or no value. A plan must be documented and reviewed periodically for content accuracy. Recovery team members and other stakeholders will require a copy during the recovery of a critical business process. Keep in mind that distributing a plan should be done with discretion. A plan often contains sensitive, proprietary information and released to the wrong people can prove troublesome.

Subscribe to a Holistic, Multi-Disciplinary Perspective

BC and BP require taking a broad perspective on recovery. Too often stakeholders think that BC and BP are restricted to facilities and information technology. Albeit important, both are not the focus; concentration should be on recovering the business side of a critical process. Facilities and information technology should be considered on how to further the business side of BC, not the other way around. The real purpose of BC and BP is building and maintaining resiliency of a critical business process.

Establish and Solicit Communication and Feedback

BC is about communication among stakeholders to enhance involvement in the resiliency of a critical business process. If communication fails, recovery will fail. Communications spans a wide range of approaches and media; any obstacle can lead to miscommunication, thereby impeding recovery. The larger the number of stakeholders involved in the recovery of a critical process, the greater the chances for communication failure resulting from misinformation or inaccurate information; communication failure, in turn, affects recovery from an event.

Maintain Viability and Readiness

Building a plan is important; however, the environment often changes, and when that occurs, the BP plan supporting a critical process also changes. Not updating a plan to reflect such changes weakens its relevancy. Ongoing effort is needed for plans to remain accurate and useful. Consider, for example, a periodic, perhaps semi-annual, review to update the content of a plan and then to redistribute it to applicable stakeholders.

Demonstrate Value

BC must show that it contributes to the success of an organization. This aspect is quite challenging because the payback is not realized until after an event occurs, just like insurance. Even then, depending on the magnitude of an event if it occurs (and it may never occur), the value of BC may be difficult to demonstrate. Its benefits are often intangible, for example, improved communication and collaboration. Regularly scheduled exercises can help alleviate this difficulty. Through regular exercises applying a plan to a scenario, such as an earthquake, stakeholders can see the value more clearly than after the event occurs.

Establish and Maintain Awareness

BC is not something in the forefront of people's minds. People are focused often on what is deemed important at the time, such as maintaining operations, rather than what might happen in the future. The BC governance infrastructure can prove invaluable in this regard by making special effort to ensure people have an understanding and awareness of what BC is and what their role is in its successful deployment. Perhaps the best way to establish and maintain awareness is to conduct regularly scheduled test and maintain practices combined with presentations explaining the importance of BC and BP.

Encourage Ownership

An effective BC governance infrastructure guides and directs but does not dictate; key stakeholder participation is important to the recovery of critical business processes. Participation in building and maintaining BP plans is crucial for buy-in and plan relevancy. They also gain a greater appreciation of BC, as well as know when and where to apply concepts and plans during recovery. Without participation, BC will find it harder to demonstrate its value; BP plans simply become another placeholder on a shelf populated with other plans, satisfying only compliance auditors.

CHALLENGES

Despite the advantages of BC, like all other disciplines, challenges exist when implementing them.

Awareness and Education

BC is often not a topic on the forefront of people's minds. Their concentration is on the here and now, not on something possibly happening in the future. Most people, too, have little or no experience with BC. Executive leadership and senior management need to designate an owner to emphasize and reemphasize the importance of resiliency. This emphasis on awareness can be tangible, such as funding, and intangible, such as political support. Education is generally weak in organizations. Executive leadership and senior management need to demonstrate their commitment. Because BC deals with events happening infrequently, BC training seems inconsequential or irrelevant until something imperiling an organization happens. Through education, organizations will be more aware of the need for BC and be ready for an event.

Critical Business Process Identification

This challenge is tougher than what you might think. All organizational units and their leadership think their process is critical. After all, if not critical, then when budget cuts come they become a target for cost cutting.

BC helps to determine what processes are critical within an organization, being vital to its survivability. Executive leadership and senior management focus on the criteria and requirements for determining what processes are necessary for recovery.

Daily Operations Priorities

Let's face it: BC is not the number one priority for people involved in daily operations. They focus on delivering a product or service fulfilling the needs of the customer. They do not continually think about an anomalous event or even a disastrous event with a high probability of occurrence. This is even more reason to stress the importance of awareness and education. Executive leadership and senior management need to keep reminding people up and down the chain of command of the necessity to become more resilient, should an event occur.

Different Mindsets

Not everyone thinks the same way. Mindsets, or paradigms, make it difficult to come up with BP plans adequately addressing the needs of an organization. Some prefer a high-level approach, while others prefer a detailed plan. In the end, of course, people make a judgment call regarding the adequacy of a plan, largely based on their mindsets of how the world operates. These mindsets sometimes make it difficult to achieve consensus or agreement on a plan to enhance the resiliency of an organization. For example, their risk attitude and tolerance affect whether they embrace or avoid risk, affecting whether a BP plan is necessary or is overkill.

Integration

BC is one of those disciplines requiring the participation of other disciplines. For example, a critical process in the supply chain may require the participation of people from Information Systems, Legal, Facilities, Finance, and other functions and disciplines. A holistic perspective, therefore, becomes critical for building a reliable BP plan. The challenge is often breaking and integrating the mindsets of specialists resulting in silo thinking—only what is within their discipline becomes important. When it comes to developing and finalizing a BP plan, executive leadership and senior management can play a key role in reconciling these differences.

They, along with project managers, are the one group of people who must have the opportunity to see the big picture.

Funding

In the business world, there is never enough money even in the midst of plenty. Funding follows what key decision makers consider higher priorities; the challenge is having them determine BC as one of those key priorities. Often, it is not. They will say BC is important; however, they view preparing and maintaining BP plans, for example, as overhead, consuming funds that should be allocated to more immediate concerns. Ideally, BC should receive all the funding to ensure resiliency; however, reality often reflects otherwise. This is even more reason BC often needs to have a champion in the senior ranks to keep BC in the forefront of all key stakeholders.

Globalization

The world is economically integrated and interdependent to an unprecedented level. The number of key stakeholders, organizations and individuals alike, has multiplied dramatically. This circumstance adds more complexity, making it difficult to ensure adequate BP plans are in place for all critical business processes. For a Fortune 100 firm, such an effort can become monumental, especially when integrating with partners, suppliers, subsidiaries, and other entities. For example, as the number of suppliers and their supporting tiers expand in the supply chain, it becomes more difficult to determine the resiliency for all key stakeholders. Executive leadership and senior management must continually remind these stakeholders of the importance of BC and hold them contractually liable for failing to comply. Otherwise, a critical process becomes only as strong as its weakest link.

Integration with Other Recovery Plans

Rare is the company having only one critical business process. Often, two or more critical business processes exist, resulting in creating multiple BP plans. These plans frequently overlap, resulting in duplicate, uncoordinated effort and impeding recovery efforts. If an event occurs, for example, the workaround procedures within each plan may tax key decision makers, and paralyze recovery efforts. At such times, some decision makers find themselves unable to respond, competing with others for important resources. By integrating BP plans, such as establishing a firing order of those plans, recovery can occur more efficiently and effectively.

Internal and External Exposures Identification

Due to globalization and the accompanying integration and interdependence of business entities, the number, complexity, and magnitude of risks becomes greater and less predictable. A critical business process rarely exists unto itself. An unknown risk exists somewhere inside or outside an organization, imperiling a critical business process. This situation exemplifies the Butterfly Effect, whereby something so innocuous in one place can have a dramatic impact in another. The mere act of building solid, integrated BP plans can help to address even unanticipated events.

Organizational Resistance to Change

This challenge is ubiquitous when implementing something new in an organization. For many organizations, implementing BC is new and can be threatening for one reason: it encourages breaking down the silos that plague medium and large companies. Critical business processes transcend functional boundaries, thereby causing organizations to question their current mode of business and to increase awareness of their value under normal operations and during an event. It also requires a working community with other processes that, frankly, did not previously like to do so in the first place. As a result, many organizations reluctantly engage in serious BC discussions.

Information Technology Focus

Undoubtedly, most firms today rely on information technology to create and deliver products and services to their customers. If hardware and applications crash, firms can find themselves hampered in performing basic processes. However, the issue people are forgetting is that a company is more than just technology. To execute, processes and procedures also exist and are required to maintain the resiliency of a company, including those related to, for example, financial, legal, design, engineering, and marketing. Unfortunately, BC often is narrowly construed as solely an information technology initiative, leading to an incomplete BP plan. Instead, stakeholders should view information technology as a means of supporting the resiliency of a critical business process, not the other way around. A holistic perspective when building BP plans is a way to achieve a balanced view. In fact, it may even help to identify opportunities for trimming the fat that often plagues information technology, such as support for outdated legacy systems.

Resource Availability

In many organizations, pressure exists to lower labor costs, especially overhead. BC is often viewed as overhead because it lacks the immediacy associated with the daily production environment. Asking an organization to divert scarce resources to support building a BP plan, for example, is viewed as costly and interferes with performing "real work." Unless strong executive sponsorship is behind the building of BP plans, some stakeholders may exert considerable pushback if an organization has to absorb the costs for building and maintaining the plan using their own budget.

Scope Determination

Determining the boundaries of a critical process can be quite difficult if the number of stakeholders increases. This is often the case for medium to large companies, whereby multiple processes and functions intersect and collaborate on multiple levels. The best approach is to map out what processes are considered critical and then to eliminate what key stakeholders consider not key for maintaining the resiliency of the company. If an organization has embraced Lean, a framework for delivering value to the customer, such an effort becomes easier to review documented processes and to determine the ones requiring attention. However, if no Lean initiative occurred, then it behooves executives and senior managers to agree on the critical processes supporting the strategic goals and objectives and impact to the financial statement, document them, and then eliminate nonessential ones for consideration from a recovery perspective.

Stakeholder Acceptance, Involvement, and Ownership

After identifying critical business processes, key stakeholders should develop a BP plan. Due to their knowledge and experience with critical business processes under normal conditions, the people who execute the critical business process should play a leading role in developing the plans for recovery. Stakeholders will have a sense of ownership, too, in their plans; the plans are not something imposed upon them. They will also be more inclined to test and maintain the plans later.

Time Availability

Faster, better, and cheaper is the mantra of business today, leaving very little time to do anything else other than delivering goods and services. With priorities coming from multiple directions, and seemingly having equal importance, the very idea of devoting time to BC seems somewhat absurd, at first. Dealing with the here and now is the focus of many stakeholders, not something that might happen, and, if it does, only in the future. BC is like life insurance; you may never have to collect it but, if for some reason you have to, you are glad you have it; if nothing happens, then it seems like a worthless investment and you could have spent your money on more valuable endeavors. Executive leadership and senior management need to convey the importance of BC, not only from the perspective of an investment in the survivability of the organization, but also among its members. If the organization fails, then employment will decline. Executive leadership and senior management need to set the expectation that stakeholders in a critical process must make time available for BC.

DELIVERABLES

BC has three principal deliverables (refer to Figure 2.4). These deliverables have a tight inter-relationship.

The infrastructure is the organizational apparatus in place to support the development and deployment of BC and BP throughout an organization.

The first deliverable, the infrastructure, provides the organizational structure and guidance to support the conduct of a BIA. The second major deliverable, the BIA, helps to determine what business processes are critical for the resiliency of a company or other entity.

The BP plan provides the direction needed to achieve recovery and resumption of a critical business process identified by key stakeholders in the infrastructure and the BIA.

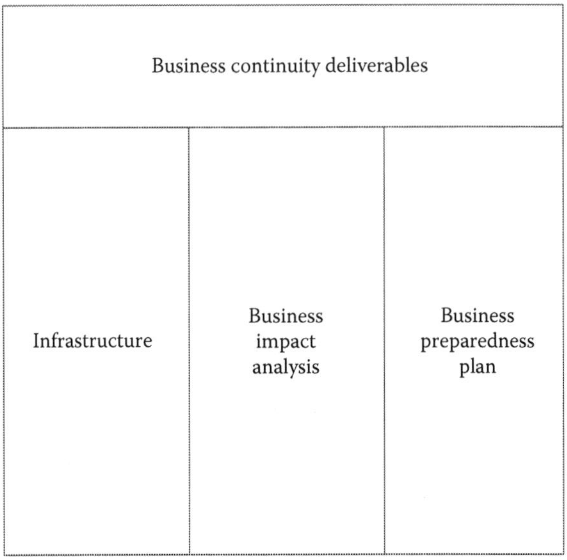

FIGURE 2.4
The BC deliverables.

STAKEHOLDERS

A number of stakeholders are involved in each of the three deliverables as shown in Figure 2.5.

Senior leadership of an organization plays a critical role in establishing the infrastructure by setting strategic direction and policy and in providing in-kind support. These stakeholders include members of the board of directors (BoD), senior executives, and managers who belong to the steering committee and working group of senior managers. The project manager or program manager is kept apprised of what has occurred or decided among other parties. Audit, customers, and shareholders may be kept abreast of decisions and actions.

The BIA will likely involve risks at the executive level in an operational environment, not so much at the strategic levels of the organization. These executives and senior managers understand their business processes, sometimes from a cross-functional perspective. They capitalize on the results of the enterprise risk assessment performed at the strategic levels of the organization as well as ensure compliance with strategic policies, procedures, and other high-level guidance from the BoD, audit committee, or senior

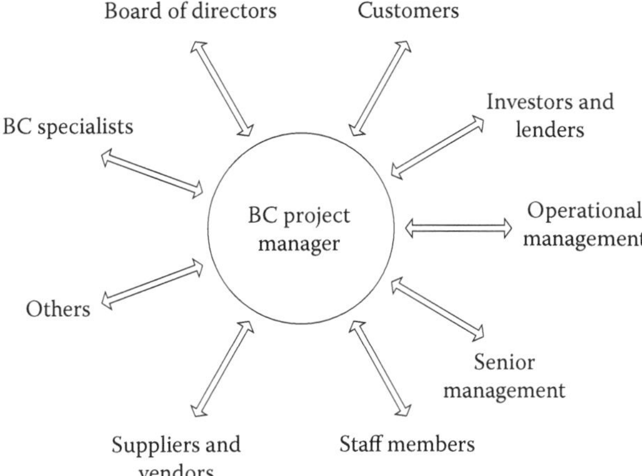

FIGURE 2.5
Stakeholders and the project manager.

executive leadership. The BIA, incidentally, is conducted at the strategic and operational levels with the latter capitalizing on the output of the former.

The BP plan is the third major deliverable. One or more plans are developed for each critical process. Both the recovery team leader and the recovery team members perform the work. These stakeholders provide the content of their relevant plan. The content provides the necessary guidance for recovery. In some cases, vendors and customers are requested to participate in developing a plan while other entities, such as Audit, are notified of the results. The responsibilities can be identified in a responsibility assignment matrix (RAM) in the form of a responsible, accountable, consult, and inform (RACI) chart (refer to Figure 2.6).

FINAL THOUGHTS

BC and the accompanying BP plans play key roles in the resiliency of an organization. If a significant event does occur, it impacts one or more critical processes, and a company fails to recover, survivability becomes questionable. The consequences include people losing their jobs, stock price plummeting, losing market share to competitors, experiencing high turnover of key personnel, and, ultimately, becoming nonexistent. It is in a company's best interest to follow the old English proverb, "Hope for the best but prepare for the worst."

Role / **Tasks**	Board of Directors	BC Steering Committee	Business Continuity Working Group	BC Project Manager/Program Manager	BC Specialists/Staff Support	Business Process Owner/Senior Management	Recovery Team Leader (Operational)	Recovery Team Members (Operational)	Audit	Customers	Suppliers/Vendors
Deliverables											
Infrastructure	R	A	A,C	I	I				I	I	I
Business Impact Analysis	I	A,I	A	R	C	C,I,A			I		
Business Preparedness Plan		I	I	R	A	A,I	A	A	I	C	C

Legend
R = Responsible
A = Accountable
C = Consult
I = Inform

FIGURE 2.6
RACI chart for the three BC deliverables.

GETTING STARTED CHECKLIST

Question	Yes	No
1. Have you thought about:		
Ways to improve the survivability of your company?		
Minimizing the impact of an event?		
2. Have you identified and thought about addressing these challenges when improving the resiliency of your company?		
Awareness and education		
Critical business process identification		
Daily operations priorities		
Different mindsets		
Integration of multiple disciplines		
Funding		
Integration and interdependence due to globalization		
Integration with other recovery efforts		
Internal and external exposures		
Organizational resistance to change		
Tendency to emphasize information technology at the expense of business recovery		
Resource availability		
Scope determination		
Stakeholder acceptance, involvement, and ownership		
Time availability		
3. Has your company built, or thought about putting together, a BP plan?		
4. If you decide to implement BC, more specifically BP, have you considered how you will:		
Obtain buy-in from key stakeholders, initially at the executive level?		
Determine priorities when implementing BC and BP?		
Institute a governance program for implementing BC?		
Apply good project management tools and techniques?		
Build trust?		
Document and distribute all BP plans?		
Subscribe to a holistic, multi-disciplinary perspective?		
Establish and solicit communication and feedback?		
Maintain visibility and readiness?		
Demonstrate value?		
Establish and maintain awareness?		
Encourage ownership?		

3

Apply Project Management

Business continuity (BC) adds value. However, it cannot just happen on its merits alone. It requires good program and project management (PM) to ensure that value is demonstrated before and after an event occurs. Cost, schedule, scope, and quality all play an integral part in making an organization and its accompanying critical business processes resilient.

THREE KEY DELIVERABLES

A BC program or project has three deliverables (infrastructure, business impact analysis, and business preparedness [BP] plans) to develop and deploy if it is to add value to an organization. PM plays a key role in ensuring these deliverables become a reality rather than a wish list or a talking point around a conference table.

Infrastructure

This deliverable pertains to the management and leadership sides. It consists of two components. The first component is applying the necessary program or PM disciplines. It includes establishing a common infrastructure; defining the goals and objectives of the program; identifying the strategies to achieve them; managing risks; establishing the budget; developing and deploying a schedule for building, testing, and maintaining BP plans; assigning roles and responsibilities; and tracking and assessing performance in achieving the goals and objectives. The other component is providing ongoing education and awareness, such as communicating about BC and its value to an organization by making its critical business processes resilient.

Business Impact Analysis

Business impact analysis (BIA) determines the priority of business processes based upon the qualitative or quantitative impacts of disruptions. It is an action that requires analyzing all the operations within an organization to identify critical business processes and the impact of realized risks, or threats, upon them. Executive leadership and senior management consider the strategic considerations of an organization or critical business process, risks, and key stakeholders. With this information, the BIA lays the foundation to determine what critical business processes require one or more BP plans to guide recovery.

BP Plans

These documents provide guidelines for recovery and restoration from an event. They define the scope, designate roles and responsibilities of the recovery team, identify members of a call tree, delineate the actions needed to enhance resiliency, and determine essential resources and their quantity over time. These documents are not a one-time affair. They require ongoing care and maintenance; otherwise, they will lose their value over time.

PM, THE CATALYST

These three deliverables—BC program/project infrastructure, BIA, and BP plans—are essential for enhancing the resiliency of critical business processes. PM plays an instrumental role in ensuring their development and deployment, as shown in Figure 3.1.

PM consists of the tools, techniques, methods, and concepts to deliver a product or service on time, within budget, and in scope. It consists of several key processes: leading, defining, planning, organizing, executing, monitoring and controlling, and closing. PM is the means to develop, deploy, and maintain the three BC deliverables. It achieves that by systemically executing seven actions:

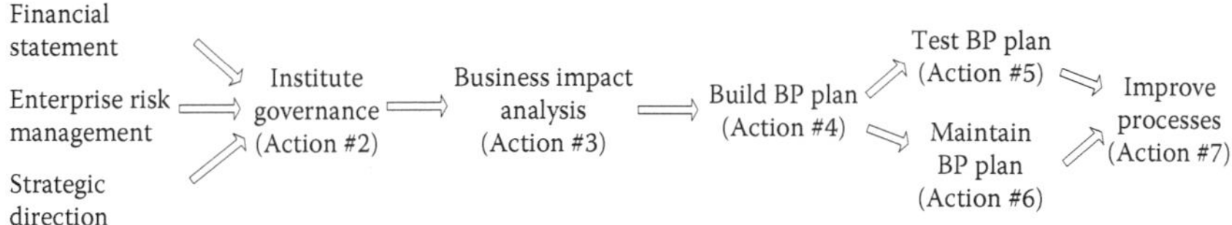

FIGURE 3.1
BP actions and their relationships.

- Action #1: Apply PM
- Action #2: Institute governance
- Action #3: Conduct BIA
- Action #4: Build BP plans
- Action #5: Test BP plans
- Action #6: Maintain BP plans
- Action #7: Perform process improvement

Action #1: Apply PM

This action involves applying PM to establish a BC program or project. It establishes, implements, maintains, and improves the other actions by leading, defining, planning, organizing, executing, monitoring and controlling, and closing each BC process (refer to Figure 3.2).

THE OTHER ACTIONS

Action #2: Institute Governance

This action entails putting together the infrastructure for supporting the development and deployment of BC. It also includes the training and awareness among key stakeholders, such as high-level executive management of an organization or at the critical business process level. Specifically, it requires conducting such steps as developing a business case, determining strategic direction and guidance, identifying and engaging key stakeholders at the highest executive and managerial levels, performing

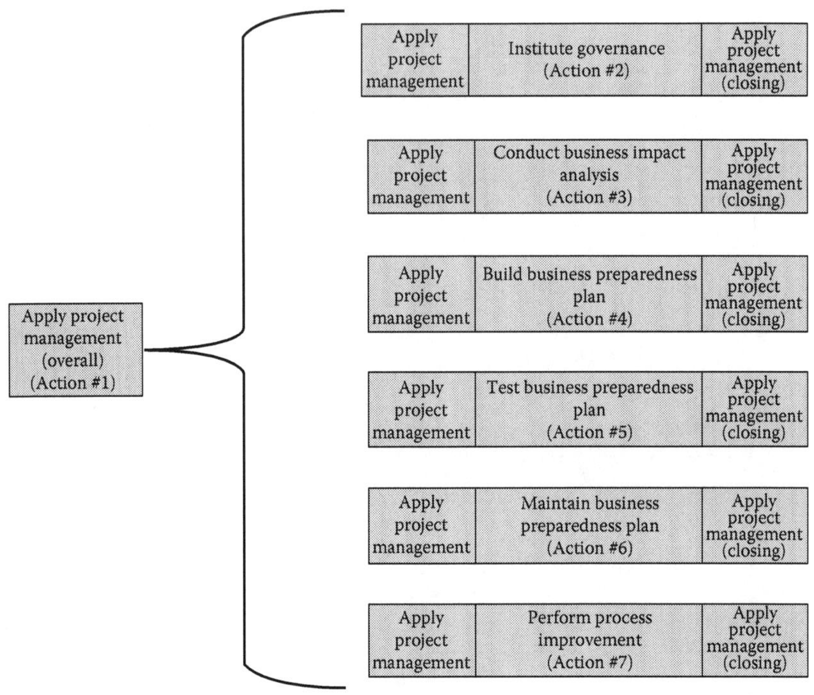

FIGURE 3.2
PM application applied to other actions.

enterprise risk management, preparing policies and procedures on implementing projects, establishing an organizational structure, defining roles and responsibilities, and keeping BC in the forefront of people's minds.

Action #3: Conduct BIA

With the enterprise risk management complete, the BIA takes risk management to a lower level to determine the impact of various events on a critical business process. It also determines what and how many BP plans are required. Specific deliverables include identifying critical business processes, a listing of risks applicable to each critical business process, their impact, and the specific BP plans to develop for each critical business process.

Action #4: Build BP Plans

A major deliverable of BC is the plan or plans needed to recover from an event. Like all plans, these serve as a guide because of the impossibility of anticipating what will happen. BP plans should contain the essential elements of information for recovery. The content includes roles and responsibilities of the recovery team, key procedures containing workarounds for recovery, resource requirements over time, and a call tree.

Action #5: Test BP Plans

BP plans require testing to ensure the relevancy and accuracy of content. Testing, a major step for this action, takes the form of an exercise, such as a tabletop or a drill. After testing, you can revise the plan to reflect reality. The plans should be practical, demonstrated via an exercise. Additional steps include a report on the results of a test and recommendations for improvement.

Action #6: Maintain BP Plans

This action is keeping BP plans current to be of value to key stakeholders. Nothing is more wasteful than a plan sitting on a shelf, getting dated, and being unread; its only purpose becomes, for example, serving the needs of auditors. Maintenance also includes enabling key stakeholders to access the most current plan.

Action #7: Perform Process Improvement

All the other actions mentioned previously need revision from time to time. This action involves keeping the actions and their corresponding steps Lean by eliminating waste and providing value to key stakeholders. A business environment is continually in flux and the processes operating in such an environment require a revisit to ensure that all BC actions add value. A significant step for this action is a situation target proposal (STP) and an implementation plan for improvements.

HOW THE ACTIONS INTEGRATE

Keep the following points in mind. All the actions, including one for PM, apply to these elements of PM: leading, defining, planning, executing, organizing, monitoring and controlling, and closing. The only difference is the level of perspective determines the breadth, depth, and perspective of each; for example, Action 2.0 Institute Governance and Action 7.0 Perform Process Improvement require more of a high-level strategic orientation than the others but still require the same application of the functions of PM.

Apply PM

This action ensures that all actions receive the necessary guidance and directions for their execution and that sufficient progress reporting and feedback occur. It also helps to ensure all the actions interact in a coordinated manner to maximize efficiency and effectiveness. All the standard PM deliverables are created for each action.

Institute Governance

This action provides the infrastructure to institute and oversee BC in a company. It is the strategic side of BC, by looking at the company from a broad perspective. Key stakeholders, usually from the executive leadership and senior management levels, provide the necessary guidance and direction, enabling the company to put in place an effective infrastructure supporting the execution of other actions.

Conduct BIA

Using the risk information and the critical business processes identified, this action determines the impact on those processes to ascertain what BP plans to develop.

Build BP Plans

Using the information from Action 4.0, one or more plans are developed guiding the recovery of a critical business process. Before becoming final, one or more plans go through several iterations after data is compiled and converted into information.

Test BP Plans

The plan or plans built for a critical business process in 5.0 are now tested for accuracy and reliability during a hypothetical event. Also known as an exercise, a test can take several forms, such as a tabletop or drill. Tests often result in revising one or more plans and determine how the recovery team can recover more efficiently and effectively from an event.

Maintain BP Plans

All plans must be kept current and accurate to enhance the resiliency of critical business processes and the entire firm. Plans must be updated periodically, such as twice a year, to capture any changes affecting a business, for example, a merger or outsourcing.

Perform Process Improvement

During, or after completing all, the critical business processes, the actions to build, test, and maintain them should go through a periodic evaluation. The purpose is to remove any defects occurring while executing the actions processes as well as removing other waste not demonstrating any value to the customer. The results of this evaluation are fed back to institute BC governance.

MAKING PM HAPPEN

Applying PM for BC and BP involves the following tasks, which are shown in Figure 3.3.

DEFINE VISION, GOALS, AND OBJECTIVES FOR PROJECTS

Identify Key Stakeholders

BC often has many stakeholders having a direct or indirect interest in the outcome of a project. The cross-functional perspective often needed to recover a critical business process requires the participation of individuals and organizations from many backgrounds to work together to achieve resiliency. These stakeholders are at the strategic and operational levels.

ID	Task Name	Predecessors
2	1.1 Manage projects	
3	1.1.1 Apply project management	
4	1.1.1.1 Define vision, goals, and objectives for the projects	
5	1.1.1.1.1 Identify stakeholders	
6	1.1.1.1.2 Build charter	5
7	1.1.1.2 Plan the project	
8	1.1.1.2.1 Build work breakdown structure	6
9	1.1.1.2.2 Construct network diagram	8
10	1.1.1.2.3 Estimate times	8
11	1.1.1.2.4 Estimate costs	8
12	1.1.1.2.5 Determine resource requirements	8
13	1.1.1.2.6 Make assignments	8
14	1.1.1.2.7 Perform risk management	9,10,11,12,13
15	1.1.1.2.8 Build schedule	9,10,11,12,13,14
16	1.1.1.2.9 Baseline performance measurement criteria	15
17	1.1.1.3 Organize the project	
18	1.1.1.3.1 Establish configuration management	6
19	1.1.1.3.2 Establish change management	6
20	1.1.1.3.3 Establish requirements management	6
21	1.1.1.3.4 Establish communications management	6
22	1.1.1.3.5 Establish quality management	6
23	1.1.1.3.6 Identify tools	6
24	1.1.1.3.7 Create project procedures	6
25	1.1.1.3.8 Determine reports	6
26	1.1.1.3.9 Determine organizational structure	6
27	1.1.1.4 Execute the project	
28	1.1.1.4.1 Manage project activities	16
29	1.1.1.4.2 Procure resources	16
30	1.1.1.4.3 Make adjustments, e.g., corrective action or replanning	32,33
31	1.1.1.5 Monitor and control project	
32	1.1.1.5.1 Collect status	16
33	1.1.1.5.2 Verify scope	16
34	1.1.1.6 Close the project	
35	1.1.1.6.1 Validate schedule performance	
36	1.1.1.6.2 Validate cost performance	28
37	1.1.1.6.3 Validate quality performance, e.g., satisfy requirements	28
38	1.1.1.6.4 Perform administrative closure	35,36,37
39	1.1.1.6.5 Performance financial closure	35,36,37
40	1.1.1.6.6 Perform contractual closure	35,36,37

FIGURE 3.3
WBS for applying project management.

Without the participation of a key stakeholder, resistance or lack of cooperation can impact the quality of a BIA or a BP plan.

Build a Charter

The charter is essentially an agreement about the overall mission and approach for a project. It requires key stakeholders, usually ones who will be responsible for building, delivering, and receiving a product or service. From a BC perspective, a charter should be developed and agreed on by stakeholders when instituting a governance infrastructure, conducting a BIA at the executive level, and building a BP plan. Depending on the scale and complexity, each major deliverable, for example, build BP plan or conduct BIA, should have a charter, whether or not formally signed. Failure to start any BC activities without a charter is a warning sign to a project manager that negative conflict is looming in the sidelines and will surface sometime during the lifecycle of the project, potentially due to misunderstandings, miscommunications, and disagreements over what to expect from the project.

PLAN THE PROJECT

Build Work Breakdown Structure

The work breakdown structure (WBS) is an expansion in detail of the work to perform. It serves as a basis for building the BP plan to manage a project and tracking, as well as monitoring performance. As with the charter, no BC project should begin without a WBS. Again, depending on the scale and complexity of the project, the WBS should be sufficiently detailed enough to allow developing a meaningful plan for all actions, for example, institute governance or build BP plans.

Construct Network Diagram

The network diagram reflects the logical sequence of the tasks at the lowest level identified in the WBS. It enables building a meaningful schedule. Too often, BC projects simply put together a to-do list that serves as a checklist. The logical sequence of those tasks, however, is missing, thereby losing the visibility of the impact of one or more tasks not being performed or some being completed early. For example, a failure to perform a BIA may lead to not building BP plans for a critical business process, resulting in applying resources to areas not furthering the resiliency of the company or organization.

Estimate Times

Using the WBS, the project manager, with other stakeholders, determines the amount of time to complete each task. For instance, determining what kinds of people with specific expertise in BC are needed to complete a certain task. This information is then used to assign responsibilities, determine costs, and develop a meaningful schedule.

Estimate Costs

Again, using the WBS and the time estimates, the BC project manager can calculate the costs for instituting governance or, for example, conducting process improvement. He or she can then determine whether the estimates fall within the amount identified in the charter. This task is usually done in parallel with estimating times, determining resource requirements, and making assignments.

Determine Resource Requirements

The BC project manager determines the resources needed to perform the tasks. These tasks require looking at the skills, expertise, and experience of labor and the availability of nonlabor resources. Often for BC projects, such determinations depend on labor availability and their requisite background.

Make Assignments

This task requires assigning people based on the availability of resources. The BC project manager and key stakeholders determine whether the resources are available internally, for example, or whether to procure them outside the company or organization. This task is often done in parallel with estimating costs and perhaps also with tasks like building the schedule.

Perform Risk Management

Few, if any, projects occur without facing some degree of risk. A risk is something that may happen in the future. Performing risk management entails more than simply identifying risks, however. It also requires determining their probability and impact to all or selected aspects of a project. For example, lack of participation of a key stakeholder when instituting governance infrastructure may impact the effectiveness in policy making and completing a charter. The BC project manager must determine the responses to take should a specific risk arise.

Build the Schedule

With the resource assignments, time and cost estimates, logical sequence, and any constraints identified in the charter, the next task is to build a schedule that serves as a roadmap for leading and managing the BC project. Like all the aforementioned tasks, several iterations of a schedule may be necessary before stakeholders buy in to it as well as ensuring that it fits within the constraints identified in the charter.

Baseline Performance Measurement Criteria

With the cost estimates complete, the requirements identified by senior leadership, such as the high-level ones reflected in the charter, and the schedule ready, the BC project manager can baseline all three to create a baseline performance measurement criteria. These baselines, predicated on the output of all the previous tasks, serve as the basis for focusing on the mission for the project and ascertaining progress toward achieving it.

ORGANIZE THE PROJECT

Establish Configuration Management

This discipline ensures the integrity of the deliverables being produced on a project. It ensures the configuration, or baseline, of the deliverable is captured and that any changes to a deliverable baseline are recorded and audited. From a BP perspective, for example, a signed BP plan is placed under configuration management and a history of any approved changes is kept. No changes are allowed until formally approved. Establishing configuration management is often done in concert with establishing change management.

Establish Change Management

This task involves setting up administrative disciplines to ensure no changes are made to the performance measure baseline or any deliverables unless formally approved by specific stakeholders, such as a change board or a sponsor. For example, no changes can occur to the scope, schedule, or cost baselines unless formally approved by an established change management process. This task is often performed in parallel with establishing configuration management.

Establish Requirements Management

Requirements can take many forms, such as graphics or narrative formats. BC project managers and other stakeholders realize that satisfying requirements is the way toward achieving customer satisfaction. The degree of rigor in developing requirements depends on the scale, complexity, and visibility of a project. Once bought off by key stakeholders, such as a BC steering committee, requirements become "baselined" like all other deliverables. The requirements, too, are placed under configuration management and any revisions require going through a change management process. A prime example is the requirements that must be addressed in a BP plan. These requirements are bought off by key stakeholders. Then, the requirements are incorporated in a document, which is placed under configuration management. Any changes to the requirements require proceeding under the change management process.

Establish Communications Management

Communications is the lifeblood of BC and a key determinant of success on any project. This task requires, from a PM perspective, to determine who needs what information at a specific time in the right amount. The idea is to strive to give only what is required to a specific stakeholder, no more and no less. A communications management plan is the major deliverable of this task.

Establish Quality Management

The common definition of quality has evolved over the years since the quality movement took on momentum in the mid-1980s to now. The current definition is satisfying the needs of the customer, such as ones identified in a requirements document. The old notion of exceeding those requirements and expectations has declined due to the negative effects on the performance measurement baseline. In BC, quality is difficult because often it requires a judgment call by key stakeholders, for example, when a BP plan or a BIA is complete. Walkthroughs and testing are two ways to determine whether quality requirements have been met and whether they satisfy expectations.

Identify Tools

This task requires identifying the tools to use on a project. Often these range from graphic packages to building bar charts to using software to construct and calculate a schedule. From a BC perspective, tools may also include templates for building BP plans and applications for compiling data and generating information for analysis, such as the number of plans built and their touch points.

Create Project Procedures

This task requires developing procedures on managing a project. These procedures cover a wide range of project topics to include collecting status, conducting change board sessions, reviewing quality of deliverables, and much more. Depending on the size and scale of a project, these procedures can be incorporated into one document or each topic is treated as a stand-alone procedure.

Determine Reports

This task is closely linked with the communications management plan. The content, purpose, and audience for reports are determined and then periodically distributed according to the communications management plan. A BC project manager and key stakeholders work together to define the reports so that people and organizations receive the information that they need. These reports cover not just project performance but also ones related to BC, such as reports resulting from a BIA and a burn down or burn up count of deliverables generated.

Determine Organizational Structure

The project should have an organizational structure that displays the roles and relationships among the stakeholders. The BC project manager, along with the BC steering committee, often determines and approves this structure. Additionally, the roles, responsibilities, and authorities are defined during the execution of this task.

EXECUTE THE PROJECT

Manage Project Activities

Once the plan has been approved, the time comes to execute. This task involves deploying the plan and taking the necessary actions to follow it to achieve the vision, mission, goals, and objectives of the BC project in respect to BP.

Procure Resources

This task involves obtaining the resources needed to execute the plan. These resources may be labor or nonlabor, and they can come from internal or external sources. In reality, this task may occur before executing the plan to ensure timely availability. This task, therefore, can occur during organizing the project as well as during executing. For example, bringing on board BC specialists may be necessary before even establishing a governance infrastructure.

Make Adjustments

The availability of reliable data and information is vital in executing this task. Not surprisingly, this task is closely tied to two others—collect status and verify scope (described next). Adjustments are based on the confidence in the data and information received from different sources and the impacts on the performance measurement baseline. Corrective action may not require going through a change management process; replanning would require taking the necessary action to refocus on a BC project's vision after going through change management.

MONITOR AND CONTROL THE PROJECT

Collect Status

This task is important to determine how well a project is progressing toward its vision, goals, and objectives. The key for successfully executing this task is to perform it persistently and consistently; that is, to ensure that the status data comes from the same sources and is "scrubbed" and collected regularly. At a minimum, status data should be on the components of the performance measurement baseline—cost, schedule, and quality.

Verify Scope

This task requires ensuring that the project focuses on the vision, goals, and objectives. Periodically, and more often than not, the scope, both work and technical, are integrated. Any significant changes should be clearly documented, evaluated, and decided upon according to the change management process. Too often scope creep occurs without any corresponding assessment on the performance measurement baseline. For example, the scope of a critical business process could expand during the development of BP plans. The scope of the work may increase; without configuration and change management, however, the schedule and budget may no longer be practical while people work under the assumption that it is.

CLOSE THE PROJECT

Validate Schedule Performance

All projects end for one reason or another. We hope that they end because they reach the vision, goals, and objectives as described in the charter and according to the performance measurement baseline. This task focuses on the schedule and can be done concurrently with validate cost performance and validate quality performance. For this task, a review is conducted to ensure that all tasks in the schedule are complete and all milestones have been met. Any deviations are noted and any relevant data compilation and information generation are noted and assessed to determine if any additional work is necessary.

Validate Cost Performance

This task requires reviewing the cost performance for the project, noting how well compliance with the baseline occurred. It also identifies any deviations from the baseline and relevant data compilation and information generation are noted and assessed to determine if any outstanding costs exist.

Validate Quality Performance

Satisfying requirements is critical to ensure customer satisfaction. A project can still meet cost and schedule targets and still fail simply because the quality of the deliverables, especially the final product, is less than what is expected by the customer. Therefore, this task requires looking for shortcomings in quality and ensuring that the release of defective products or services does not occur beyond what could reasonably be expected by the customer. Validating quality performance is difficult for BC projects because of the subjective nature of the work. That is why walkthroughs and testing are so important to ensure deliverables meet expectations and to address any minimum requirements established, for example, by the BC governance infrastructure.

Perform Administrative Closure

This task requires compiling all the data and information about the project. The data and information include, but are not limited to, formal documentation like the charter, cost and schedule, performance history, contracts, reports, and much more. The goal is to capture and then archive data and information so future projects can reuse or capitalize on the experience, provide an audit trail for reviews and inquiries, and sometimes satisfy legal requirements. The degree of compilation and archiving depends on the scale, complexity, and criticality of the project. Due diligence is very important regarding business continuity; data and information compilation and archiving, therefore, make this task very important to complete.

Perform Financial Closure

Financial matters should not be left outstanding on projects for the simple reason that they can lead to legal complications. This task involves "closing the books" by ensuring all payments are made, such as to vendors performing work or those obtaining training.

Perform Contractual Closure

The terms and conditions, known as Ts and Cs, should be reviewed throughout the lifecycle of a BC project. Toward the end of the project, however, the BC project manager needs to ensure that all terms and conditions have been met and that any deviations are duly documented. Otherwise, legal disputes may arise and, if no audit trail exists, it could have a severe financial impact on the company or organization.

HOW THINGS CAN GO AWRY

The flow of data throughout the diagrams is akin to blood flowing throughout every organ of a living creature to stress the importance of integration. You can understand this perspective by equating data as blood cells. If those cells are tainted in any way, the bad data, like bad cells, affect the rest of the body, like its organs, which, in turn, can have dysfunctional, deleterious results.

Take the following example directly related to BC. A number of stakeholders agree that BC is necessary; however, they disagree vehemently over the approach to take and the extent of its deployment. A project manager is assigned to apply PM. The project manager is told to establish a BC program throughout the company, and to institute governance. Once again, key stakeholders cannot agree on a strategy or direction, yet pressure the project manager to put something in place. After a while, despite the lack of a charter, for example, and the lack of guidance and participation of key stakeholders, a makeshift governance infrastructure is put into place. Some key stakeholders do not even adhere to the requirements of the BC governance infrastructure. Nevertheless, some key stakeholders agree to perform an enterprise risk analysis. Again, without participation of other key stakeholders and guidance or direction, the results of the enterprise risk management are marginal, at best. Next, the inadequate BC governance infrastructure, money, or political support set the project manager up for failure, surfacing early, such as during a BIA. The result is inadequate because not all the key stakeholders agree on the enterprise risks and the list of critical processes. The project manager, with his team, nonetheless marches forward by meeting with the leadership of the critical business processes designated to build one or more BP plans. Some leadership does not embrace the effort with much enthusiasm. They provide minimal support in terms of time, effort, and data for build BP plans, resulting in one or more plans simply filling space on a shelf and adding no value. After publishing the plans, some time passes, and then testing and other actions occur. Once again, the combination of lack of support by key stakeholders and the dearth of information to build one or more BP plans impacts the testing and makes the exercise simply perfunctory. Maintenance of the plan simply becomes another perfunctory endeavor, treated as if administrative scatology. Finally, sometimes before it is too late, such as a significant negative event, executive leadership is reluctant to kill the program or project.

DELIVERABLES

A BC project needs to produce several PM deliverables if it is to be completed efficiently and effectively. These deliverables should be developed for every action described in this book for increasing the resiliency of a critical business process, both at the strategic and operational levels. While they do not guarantee success (poor leadership can destroy the advantages gained from these deliverables), they increase the likelihood of success. These deliverables are:

- Charter
- Work breakdown structure
- Responsibility matrices
- Performance measurement baseline
- Procedures

- Reports
- Communication management plan
- Configuration management plan
- Change management plan
- Risk management analyses and responses

These are the minimum basics for effectively and efficiently managing projects, let alone BC projects. The degree of development and implementation of these deliverables depends, of course, on the size, complexity, and criticality of a BC project, and, in some cases, programs.

STAKEHOLDERS

Just think about the number of stakeholders that have an interest in BC (refer to Figure 3.4). This list is only partial:

- BC project managers and specialists
- Board of directors (BoD)
- Consultants
- Customers
- Investors and lenders

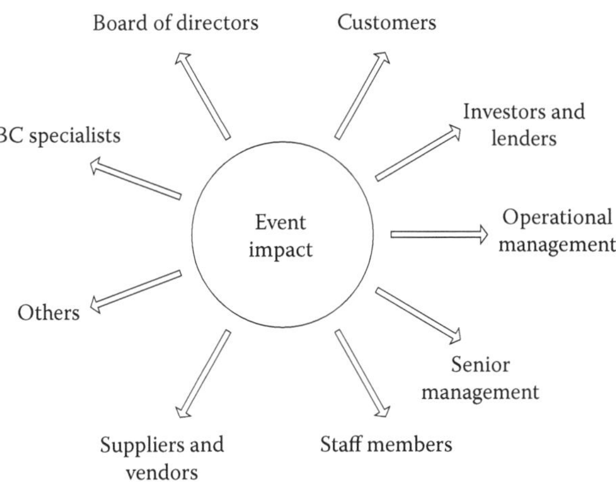

FIGURE 3.4
BC stakeholders.

- Operational management
- Senior management
- Staff members from various disciplines, for example, information technology, security
- Suppliers
- Vendors

The degree of stakeholder involvement depends on what level a BC project occurs in a company or an organization. At the strategic level, the BoD, other executives, the project manager, and some team members will likely be more engaged than will people in the operational levels. This situation might exist when initiating a BC governance infrastructure or conducting a BIA.

However, at the operational level, consultants, customers, senior managers, suppliers, and vendors will likely be more involved and the stakeholders at the strategic level are mainly kept abreast on progress. This situation might be the case when building BP plans.

INCREASING CHANCES FOR SUCCESS

In the remaining chapters of this book, we provide you with the knowledge, tools, and techniques of PM to avoid the scenario previously described. If such a scenario does arise, however, you can apply the very same knowledge, tools, and techniques to turn the project around.

GETTING STARTED CHECKLIST

Question	Yes	No
1. To increase the resiliency of your company, have you considered building and implementing these deliverables?		
BC governance infrastructure		
BIA		
BP plans		

2. Will you implement these actions?
   Apply PM
   Institute governance
   Perform enterprise risk management
   Conduct BIA
   Build BP plans
   Test BP plans
   Maintain BP plans
   Perform process improvement
3. Have you identified the stakeholders having an the resiliency of your company, including:
   BC project managers and specialists?
   BoD?
   Consultants?
   Customers?
   Investors and lenders?
   Operational management?
   Senior management?
   Staff members from various disciplines, e.g., information technology, security?
   Suppliers?
   Vendors?

4

Project Management 101

This chapter provides a basic understanding of what project management (PM) is and a framework to implement it. Understand that a framework is not a usable methodology. Use the information contained in this chapter to develop specific processes and approaches to lead and manage business continuity (BC) projects, especially those for building, testing, and maintaining business preparedness (BP) plans.

FUNDAMENTALS OF PROJECT MANAGEMENT

PM, in its most basic form, is a set of processes that enables a team to progress from point A (the start of the project) to point B (the final product, service, or capability, also known as deliverables) efficiently and effectively. Avoid confusing the use of a software tool as a process of PM. PM requires people, intuitive thought, and money. Bear in mind that PM processes can differ greatly from industry to industry and from company to company even within the same industry or company. PM offers enough flexibility to adapt to any industry or company. However, this variability provides a downside: the need to learn a new set of processes and terminology.

Modifying the processes to fit the needs of each project is a key, critical element for success. For example, not every project will require a highly detailed list of stakeholders or a procurement management plan. For some projects, managing the stakeholders may be just fine with a general list of categories of stakeholders. Applying a specific, defined set of processes for each project will greatly enhance the probability for success.

Each project will go through a series of phases. A project manager's primary responsibility is to manage the work of the project to produce deliverables that meet requirements. With each project being unique, even within the same industry, a project manager should avoid being complacent when working on projects, even those of a similar nature to past ones. Each project has its own unique sponsor, risks, quality requirements, communications quirks, and team members. Actively planning a project defines these differences and results in a project-specific plan.

Each project should have a single person assigned, who has the title, role, and responsibility of project manager, to oversee the project. Contrary to popular belief, a project manager does not need to be the technical expert on a project. Every project manager should have a working knowledge of the application area, but he or she should not be the chief expert on the project. The project manager's job is to lead and manage the team through the PM processes, not to perform the technical work. To do otherwise can result in scope creep, budget over-runs, schedule delays, and missed requirements.

Along with an assigned project manager, each project should have a project sponsor. The sponsor is the person or group of people who "champion" the project. The person or group should agree with the purpose of a project and support the accompanying change that it brings. The sponsor should be someone high in the parent organization having the political clout and authority to make strategic decisions. The sponsor also ensures that the organization realizes the benefits of the project. If a project to develop a new payroll system is complete, tested, and is deployable, the sponsor ensures the system is implemented and the organization realizes its benefits.

Finally, in professional PM, the project manager does not do everything alone. He or she should have a staff to assist in managing the project. Generally, this staff consists of a group of people from the organization having a high level of subject matter expertise and an understanding of the "big picture" of the project and how it fits within the organization. This staff, along with the project manager, is called the PM team.

One major factor, which can have an enormous impact on the success of a project, is known as organizational PM maturity. Organizations go through phases, becoming more mature as they grow. In regards to PM, some organizations lack PM maturity despite the organization having existed for many decades. PM maturity is usually described in five stages and may have various names in various industries. Let us examine the five levels. Figure 4.1 will assist in understanding this concept.

Very low maturity level organizations lack predefined PM practices, or do not recognize the benefit and duties of a professional project

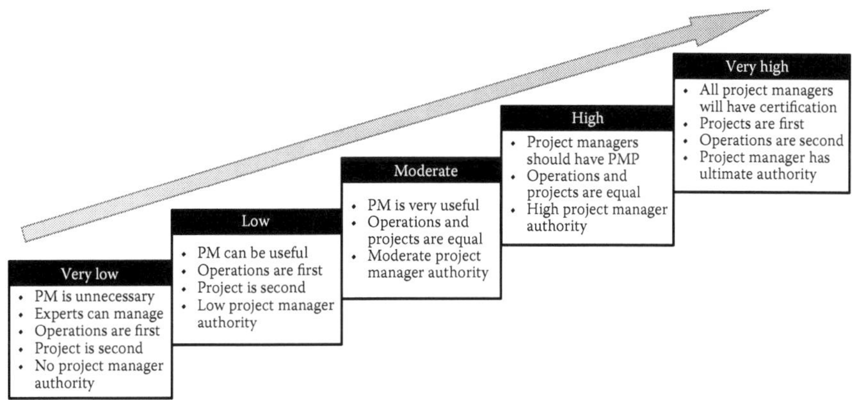

FIGURE 4.1
PM maturity levels of organizations.

manager. Low maturity level organizations recognize PM as beneficial, but fail to take full advantage of it, seeing PM as a "part-time job." Moderate maturity level organizations have varying degrees of PM implementation and may even have formalized PM procedures. They see the job of the project manager as beneficial but they also fail to take full advantage of its benefits, again seeing PM as a part-time job. High maturity level organizations take full advantage of the benefits, seeing PM as a method to achieve objectives efficiently and effectively and providing a real payback in having a professional project manager run their projects. Organizations of this category usually have a separate unit within a company having sole responsibility for managing projects. This unit is sometimes called a project management office (PMO). Depending on the type of PMO, it provides support for and expertise on managing projects.

The last category is the very high maturity level organizations. These are structured around projects, whereby managing projects is all they do. At this level, project managers have ultimate authority over projects. These project managers do not have to negotiate and coordinate with functional managers to obtain resources. Such organizations are rare and the senior management staff must have excellent leadership capabilities. The downside is that business opportunities must constantly flow into a company; otherwise, project teams may have to reduce headcount. Only certain industries have organizations in this category, such as architectural and engineering firms and software design houses.

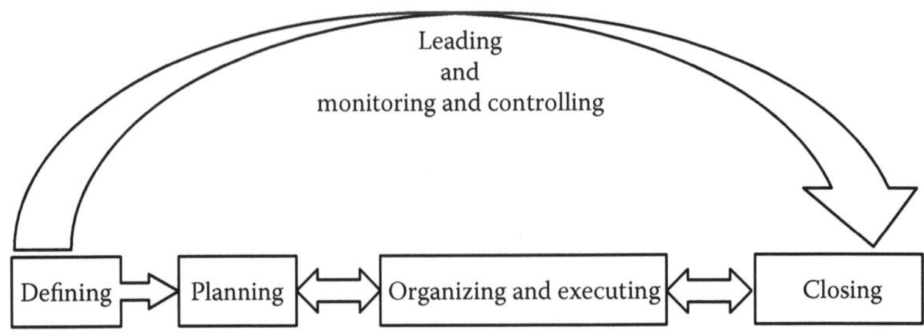

FIGURE 4.2
The interaction of the major processes of PM.

MAJOR PROCESSES OF PROJECT MANAGEMENT

PM can be viewed as six concepts, or groups of processes, consisting of leading, defining, planning, organizing, and executing, monitoring and controlling, and closing. Each area requires specific attention to a set of processes and procedures that lead to a specific outcome. For example, the planning processes lead to an outcome called a PM plan, a document guiding a team's efforts to create the outcome of a project. These processes are not always performed individually as many must be performed iteratively to reach the outcome. They are also not necessarily performed in a specific order. Figure 4.2 assists in understanding this concept.

LEADING

Leadership is a quality that can and should be learned by everyone who fills the position of a project manager. The definition of leadership we will use in this book is the act of inspiring a group of individuals to reach a common goal or outcome through the effective use of interpersonal skills. Leadership and management are not the same. Leaders are vision oriented; managers are task driven. Leaders inspire others to do things while managers direct others to do things. Leadership is a character trait that all effective project managers must possess. Leadership should be employed from start to finish on each project.

Benefits

The benefits that a project and a project manager receive by employing leadership are numerous, both tangible and intangible, and in some cases, immeasurable. Benefits can range from less conflict that a project experiences to a project that completes well ahead of schedule and under budget. Project managers possessing leadership traits gain buy-in from the team, helping them understand the reason for the project, and building a sense of team unity and identity. By building a team, they create conditions that increase team cohesion, resulting in an efficiently executed project.

Challenges

The challenge most project managers face when leading is lacking authority. Great leaders have led without authority in the past, but most had the necessary authority. Leadership does not require authority to be effective; however, to be an effective leader, having authority is necessary. Other challenges include projects where the team is geographically dispersed, such as a virtual team. Such teams rarely, if ever, meet face-to-face. Project managers must handle this situation carefully and quickly build team cohesion.

Responsibilities

In the realm of professional PM, the ultimate responsibility of leadership lies solely with project manager. They are also expected to develop leadership in others. In most organizations, during project selection (usually not considered part of the PM processes), senior management is responsible for selecting a project manager. One of the key traits they should consider is the project manager's leadership abilities. The project manager has a responsibility to sharpen and improve his or her leadership abilities.

DEFINING

Defining a project involves three basic steps: (1) creating the authorizing document, (2) performing stakeholder identification and analysis, and (3) defining roles and responsibilities for PM.

Creating the Authorizing Document

When creating the authorizing document, consider the overall goal or objective of the project, the deliverables (the product, service, or capabilities), the expected benefit, why it is being done, who will be impacted, who will be involved, the expected costs, and the expected finish date. The authorizing document is sometimes called the "project mission statement," "project overview statement," or the "project charter" and all of the key stakeholders should sign it. The charter authorizes the project to exist and provides the project manager with the authority to complete it. When written properly and completely, the charter helps to ensure a project stays on track to deliver its expected benefits.

Stakeholder Identification and Analysis

Part of defining includes identifying and analyzing project stakeholders. A stakeholder is any person, organization, or thing that is involved in the project or could be impacted (either positively or negatively) by either the execution or completion of a project; someone or something that could influence or impact the project's planning, the project team, or the success of a project.

Stakeholder identification is a straightforward process. A project manager and the planning team (sometimes called the PM team) meet briefly to identify all the groups, organizations, and individuals that will be involved, impacted by the execution or completion of a project. The information the team collects and records about each stakeholder depends on several factors, such as the project's duration, type, cost, and importance. Some stakeholders will be easily identified, while others may be identified only by speaking with already identified stakeholders.

The process of stakeholder analysis involves identifying all stakeholders, assessing their interest and influence on a project, and documenting their reaction to certain situations, such as reducing or adding to the scope or changing the level of quality delivered. Not all stakeholders will have the same interest nor will they have the same level of influence. For example, a chief operating officer and the facilities manager may be stakeholders on a project. Depending on the type of project or the specific deliverable, the facilities manager may have more influence and even more interest in a project. Titles and positions alone do not dictate the degree of interest a stakeholder may have in a project.

Defining Roles and Responsibilities

Defining roles and responsibilities for managing a project should occur during project definition. Prior to stakeholder identification, a project manager should have available a team to assist with project planning and management. This PM staff with the project manager is called the PM team. All team members should have clearly defined roles, such as only one person accountable for risk, for quality, etc. Clearly defining roles and responsibilities early on can reduce conflict, promote clear communication, and assist with creating a cohesive project team.

Challenges

Project managers face a wide variety of challenges on projects. Several factors impact project definition including the organization's political environment, structure, views of authority, and available resources. For example, during project definition, the executives may face internal turf wars or "disagreements" over benefits of a project, such as over its real need. The best practice to deal with such a challenge is to have clearly defined objectives and goals as well as a sponsor having sufficient political clout.

Deliverables

The deliverables from this set of processes are two documents: a project charter and stakeholder register. The project charter rarely changes and, if it does, it is usually cancelled and reissued. The project manager often begins at this point to start a project notebook, which includes many documents. This notebook could be an actual three-ring binder or electronic, such as a shared network drive or document repository.

The other document to add to this notebook, and one of the deliverables for project definition, is the stakeholder register. This document differs greatly from the charter, serving more as a reference and updated more frequently. In some situations, a project manager may have two notebooks, one for the documents that rarely change, such as the charter and the PM plan, and one for documents that change often, such as a stakeholder register, change log, risk register, and issue log, all discussed later in greater detail.

PLANNING

Planning a project means completely defining the scope of a project. Most of the PM effort should focus on planning, especially early during the life-cycle of a project. Without a plan, the project team and its project manager will likely react to situations rather than be proactive.

Benefits

The benefits of planning include better estimating the total duration, effort, and cost of a project; identifying possible risks and proactively planning for them; having a clear communications plan (e.g., who communicates what to whom, when, where, how, and how often); developing an approach to handling stakeholders; clearly defining the level of quality required for the final deliverable; and deciding on what to buy from outside vendors.

Challenges

The biggest challenge for most project managers when planning a project is the level of support from senior management. The biggest challenge for senior management, in turn, is to understand that planning is necessary. As an old saying about planning goes, if you fail to plan you are planning to fail, regardless of industry. Project managers must use every skill in their arsenal to convince management that planning pays huge dividends to start a project.

This challenge usually manifests itself as a lack of resource availability to plan a project, often according to senior management's view. Some members of senior management say, "I can let you have this person for when the project begins but I cannot afford to have them gone just for planning." Such a perspective often results in a slower planning process and poor estimates, resulting in blown budgets and schedules.

Deliverables

The primary deliverable in this process is a document called a PM plan. This document outlines how all aspects of a project will be planned, managed, monitored, controlled, verified, and closed. It includes a description of the entire scope of work and the specific deliverables to produce. The major sections of a plan can/should include:

- Baseline information (approved versions)
- Communications
- Cost estimating and budgeting
- Human resources (obtaining and releasing)
- Management of stakeholders
- Process improvement
- Purchasing
- Quality requirements and processes
- Risk
- Schedule
- Scope (both product and project)

Once complete, a PM plan should be signed-off, or approved by, the project sponsor, project manager, project team members, and other key stakeholders. This action gains commitment from all parties by providing a common understanding on how to plan, manage, monitor, control, and close a project. After receiving approval, the project plan is "baselined." Baselining makes official the approved version from which to measure project performance. Most projects contain three baselines—schedule, cost, and scope. All baselines should be included in the PM plan. Once the entire PM plan has been approved, any element requiring a change should go through the change process (also defined in the plan) for approval.

Responsibilities

It is the project manager's responsibility to assemble the most complete and accurate PM plan possible. The project manager, however, rarely has all the knowledge or expertise to address the specifics needed in a PM plan. To ensure correctness and accuracy, senior management provides the project manager with enough resources to plan the project. Senior management is responsible for the overall quality policy of the organization, to include ensuring a project has adequate resources.

The members of the PM team usually participate in the early stages of planning by working with the project manager to develop the plan, giving adequate weight and attention to its content, and ensuring all aspects are thoroughly planned, discussed, and documented. The PM team is responsible for the initial understanding of the project scope, developing the PM plan, assessing overall team effectiveness, and leading and directing future team members during execution.

ORGANIZING

Organizing is the act of bringing together all aspects of a project, including gaining final commitments for the human resources, setting up the infrastructure, conducting a kick-off meeting, and overseeing its start. Not necessarily done all at once, organizing may be completed in steps, iteratively. An example is gaining commitments for the project's resources from resource or functional managers at different times rather than all at once.

Benefits

Organizing a project has obvious benefits, such as knowing who reports to whom to reduce communications errors. Other benefits are not as readily visible. For example, conducting a kick-off meeting is a way to disseminate project information to all key players, reducing the number and probability of subsequent change requests. The overreaching benefit of organizing, however, is having a clear plan for a project and communicating its contents to the team, resulting in a better understanding of the reason for its existence.

Challenges

Depending on the structure and culture of the organization, challenges during organizing can be minimal to overwhelming. If the organization has a very low or low maturity level, a project manager may have extreme difficulty in acquiring resources, setting up meetings with a good attendance ratio, and having the organization take them seriously. Moderately mature organizations may cause time management challenges for a project manager because the job is viewed as part time. Friction between the project manager and functional managers can arise, such as over issues related to the overall interests of the project because project managers may report to the latter. In highly and very highly mature organizations, the challenges exist but a project manager has more authority over project priorities relative to other considerations.

Deliverables

The deliverables from organizing vary depending on a project's size, type, duration, cost, and objectives. Generally, a deliverable manifests itself in the form of a well-operated project that meets the objectives for which it was undertaken as well as completing on time and within the budget. Having a kick-off meeting notifies all the key participants of the project name and purpose, the outcome, schedule, and budget, and sets the tone for managing the project, such as who reports to whom.

Responsibilities

A project manager has the ultimate responsibility for organizing a project to include the PM team to complete the project within constraints and other parameters. A project manager has sole responsibility for a project's success or failure.

EXECUTING

Executing means implementing the PM plan completed during planning processes. The plan includes a schedule, a list of the team members, a detailed description of the work to complete, the level of quality to achieve, the total cost, and the timeline. Executing may also include finalizing procurements, such as purchases from outside an organization, to include signing contracts with vendors.

Benefits

The benefits of execution are realized as work completes. The goals and objectives of the project will be met and, ultimately, the final deliverable or outcome will be achieved. All projects have a desired outcome (either tangible or intangible) that is expected to be completed smoothly.

Challenges

The biggest challenge during execution is managing change and ensuring a project adheres to baselines. Yet, all projects change. A change-free project is extremely rare and very challenging especially in organizations that have very low, low, and even moderate maturity levels. Senior management in these structures feel that change is "easy" and something not harmful to a project. The lack of a disciplined way to manage change causes the greatest harm to a project. When change management is performed properly and in an integrated fashion, it is beneficial and "easy." However, many organizations have very little patience for conducting change management properly.

Deliverables

From a PM perspective, the deliverables are raw data or information about work performance. The project manager collects the data about the work, directs and oversees the work, proactively manages change, and tries to prevent problems before they arise.

Responsibilities

The responsibilities for executing are assumed by all members of the project team; however, the project manager has sole accountability for completing work. In other words, the project manager manages the project work to create the final deliverables without doing the technical work. The actual work the project manager does is leading and directing the team, communicating, anticipating issues before they become major problems, developing the team by providing feedback to individual team members on their performance, and finalizing procurements.

The PM staff (individuals having a leadership role on the project) assists the project manager with their respective areas of responsibility. However, they are also responsible to assess team effectiveness (to include input from the project manager). As mentioned earlier, the PM staff, along with the project manager, is called the PM team.

The project team includes the project manager, the PM staff, and other team members who perform the work to complete the project deliverables. The team members also have responsibilities for executing the project. These responsibilities include communicating with other team members when necessary, notifying the PM team when issues arise, and ensuring the work is within quality parameters as well as cost and schedule constraints. While the project manager is ultimately responsible for the overall work of the project, the team members check their own work and only deviate from the plan when approved to do so.

MONITORING AND CONTROLLING

Monitoring and controlling (M&C) a project has essentially two different facets. In monitoring, the project manager is observing, measuring, assessing the situation, and watching for areas causing some concern. Controlling, on the other hand, is taking action—either to ensure future project performance stays within the baseline, called a preventative action, or taking action to correct a problem that has already happened, called a corrective action. M&C is performed throughout an entire project.

Benefits

The benefits realized from M&C include the ability to see the status of a project vis-à-vis what was planned up to a given point in time. In other words, the organization can see how well the project is performing. The project manager can employ various techniques to collect data and measure progress, allowing the project manager to forecast cost and schedule performance. M&C allows the project manager to make mid-course corrections to ensure a project finishes within the planned schedule and budget, within the allowable variance thresholds.

Challenges

M&C presents unique challenges to the project manager for the exact same reasons as organizing. However, at this point, the challenges actually manifest themselves. When a project manager seeks status information from people not reporting directly to him or her, this can result in friction and conflict. Sometimes, team members may take exception to the project manager asking them how much work they have done. Team members may view the project manager as "looking over their shoulders," rather than a genuine inquiry to ascertain the work status of a particular section of work so the project manager can meet schedule constraints.

Depending on an organization's maturity level, controlling can be difficult, necessitating the project manager to take action. For example, if a corrective change is necessary, such as replacing a poor performing team member, some people may view that request as too harsh and, therefore, it may receive less attention.

Deliverables

Some deliverables are easily identifiable and measureable, while others are not. The specific, tangible, PM deliverables from M&C are status reports. These usually are in the form of a table, chart, or graph that the project sponsor uses to view overall project progress. Some status reports cover cost only, while others may include cost, schedule, scope, quality, and technical information. The specific information contained within the status reports is based on the needs of the project sponsor or whoever receives the status report.

Other deliverables will include status meetings, approved and rejected change requests, measurements of the quality of the project's product (the project deliverables themselves), reports of the vendor's progress on a contract and, of course, acceptance of a project's deliverables.

Responsibilities

The primary person responsible for M&C is the project manager but, as mentioned earlier, some duties can be delegated to other members of the PM team. The project team members also have the responsibility to review their own work and report status about the deliverables to the project manager, upon request. If the project utilizes the resources of a quality assurance (QA) or quality control (QC) department, then it is responsible for conducting the QA and QC activities. The project manager may use these resources, but this does not abdicate his or her accountability for quality.

CLOSING

Closing a project is defined as the actions taken to complete all activities and tasks and to bring the project to a formal close. This entails finishing any remaining administrative activities and informing the stakeholders that the project is closed. During this period, final acceptance of any remaining deliverables or the entire project are obtained, all contracts are closed, any outstanding lessons learned are recorded, all records are archived for future use, the project team is released, and, when required, a project closure report is generated and sent to upper management.

Benefits

Benefits from closing will be realized while completing the closure activities. For example, the team may identify any missing components the project should have had, or the contracts may be missing elements to complete to avoid a breach of contract. However, benefits can also be realized in future projects by collecting and recording lessons learned and trying to avoid repeating the same mistakes on another project.

Organizations having many projects need a storage system to save and search records and documents from previous projects. Having this capability enables project managers to look at previous work and to assess work performance, identify problems or issues that arose and were then resolved, capture risks and their impact, review risks that were not identified but occurred, and look at budget performance on the past projects.

Challenges

One of the biggest challenges for project managers during project closure is to obtain commitment from the team to take time to discover and discuss any remaining lessons learned. In today's fast-paced world, once a project is complete, the project manager and team members are immediately off to the next project, without regard for capturing this valuable information. This situation is especially true for organizations that have projects for paying customers. Upon paying the final bill, senior management does not want anyone to put time against a project without an invoice. This is a shortsighted approach without regard for improving going forward. The definition of insanity is doing the same thing repeatedly, and then expecting a different result.

Closing any procurement, such as a contract, is part of closing a project. Another challenge includes claims made against a contract. A claim is a dispute between the two parties of the contract. Most claims are started by the seller and often result in additional work or failure to fulfill the terms and conditions. This circumstance can create confusion over whether to close the contract; in most states, a contract can be closed with outstanding claims that lack resolution.

Deliverables

The primary deliverable of closing a project is the formal transition of the product or service of the project. Generally, the product or service is transitioned to:

- The client, customer, or sponsor
- The next phase of the project
- Operations and maintenance

Other deliverables may include a final project closure report or a formal presentation given to senior management. This report includes subjects like key objectives of the project, actual deliverables, issues, risks, lessons learned, and any others needed by senior management.

Responsibilities

The ultimate responsibility for project closure belongs to the project manager. However, the work to complete project closure is mainly performed by team members. For closure of contracts, the purchasing, contracting, or legal organization may perform the duties. During the early stages of closure, a project manager, along with the rest of the PM team, should plan how to close the project. These activities should be developed, recorded, and responsibilities assigned.

FINAL THOUGHTS

Implementing BC and BP, by definition, is a project. Each BC and BP project is temporary and results in a unique product or service. As you have read in this chapter, PM can be quite an undertaking. In the event of business disruption, you probably will not have the time to select a sponsor, project manager, and project team. However, prior to an event, PM can be used to establish and deploy disciplines that enable efficient and effective recovery from an event.

For example, prior to an actual event occurring, an organization should look at it based on likely events that could occur, and establish test and recovery procedures to enhance resiliency. PM can be used to provide the necessary structure to ensure plans and risk assessments occur so that an organization can respond effectively to an event. However, BC and BP planning is only a part of attaining resiliency. The effectiveness of BC and BP must be tested and PM is the discipline that can help.

5

Enterprise Risk Management 101

The process of enterprise risk management (ERM) is imagining what could go wrong or looking for opportunities to seize during a project, program, or business initiative. Project managers need to know and understand a wide assortment of definitions, key actions, benefits, and processes for performing risk management at the enterprise level. ERM means applying risk management processes at the strategic level.

KEY CONCEPTS

Risk management is the art and science of addressing threats and opportunities, determining their consequences or rewards, and applying measures to deal with their outcomes. People's view of risk is based on their perception of the topic. For example, some people think automobile racing is riskier than snow skiing (perception). Going down a steep ski run is riskier for a novice than an expert (point of view). Performing risk management activities in a methodical, consistent manner is the best approach.

Risk has many meanings to people. It is important, therefore, to understand what risk is and what it is not. The best way to do that is through an example. On construction projects, many people think "weather" is a risk. Within the financial industry, many people believe "the economy" is a risk. Unfortunately, neither one of these are (nor can they be) classified as actual risks. Risk is defined as an uncertain event or condition that, if it happens, has a positive or negative impact on project objectives. So why is "weather" not a risk? Weather is not an event, it is a category of events. A snowstorm is an event, a tornado is an event, a rainstorm is an event, and a hailstorm is an event. When thinking about risk, think about specific events that could occur.

The primary reason for looking at specific events is that the project team needs to respond to it upon occurrence. For example, how does anyone respond to a vaguely worded risk, e.g., "weather"? Do they bring suntan oil or do they bring their heavy coats? The specificity is lacking to enable any meaningful response.

However, risk is not always negative; it can be positive, too. A positive impact on an objective is an opportunity. In BC, risk can make the difference between success and failure, which means capitalizing on opportunities as well as managing threats.

The perception of risk is based on either an organization's or individual's risk attitude, influenced by the tolerance and appetite for risk. Risk appetite is the degree of risk an individual or organization is willing to assume in return for their efforts. Risk tolerance is the quantity or size of risk an organization or individual is willing to withstand. Some organizations rise and fall on the degree of risk they take; some people or organizations are willing to take huge risks, knowing huge rewards wait. Startup companies, for example, take huge risks in exchange for substantial rewards; other organizations do not assume much risk. A well-established company like Harley-Davidson, for example, does not take huge risks. The design of its product has remained the same for decades. They have no need to assume huge design risks because the product sells.

Some organizations view risk as a manageable factor, while others see it as an unwieldy beast. Risk attitude will play a key factor in determining the approach. It is possible to quantify risk attitude on a scale from 1 to 5 as illustrated in Figure 5.1.

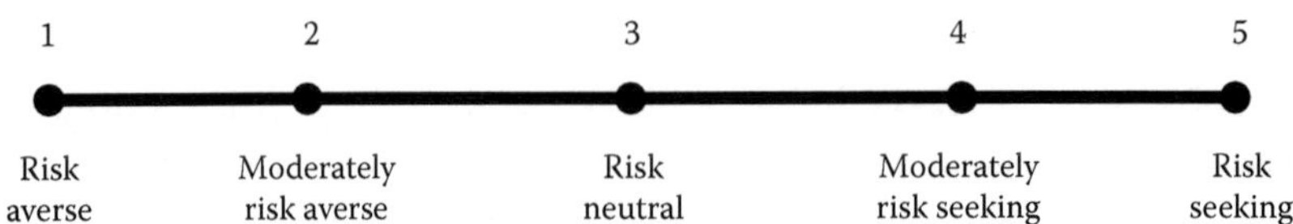

FIGURE 5.1
Risk attitude continuum.

RISK MANAGEMENT AND BUSINESS CONTINUITY

Risk management and business continuity (BC) share a number of commonalities. Both deal with uncertainty and require planning based on assumptions. Both necessitate a proactive approach. Both require a proactive systematic, consistent approach. Both are tailored to the needs of an organization and are constantly improved through updates. Perhaps one of the biggest commonalities between them, however, is that both demonstrate value to an organization. Some identified vulnerabilities will cross organizational silos because threats often have a wide operational or financial impact to an organization. Risk management and BC together should ensure that an organization, such as a company or department, operates under adverse conditions.

It is possible to reduce the probability of occurrence and the consequence of a threat. Training, for example, can reduce the probability of a worker damaging equipment. Purchasing an insurance policy can reduce the financial effect of the damaged equipment. However, purchasing an insurance policy may not cover all financial losses. Risk management cannot ensure that an organization will not be unexposed; it can only provide a reasonable assurance that if a risk occurs, an organization is at less risk. The ultimate aim is to return to normal business operations as quickly as possible.

Events can be a combination of predictable or unpredictable and controllable or uncontrollable. For example, it is possible to predict that a snowstorm might occur, but it is not controllable if it does occur. On the other hand, a severe drop in the stock market may be unpredictable but manageable with a diversified portfolio of financial assets. Integrating risk management and BC affords you the highest probability of a successful outcome like a diversified portfolio.

An integrated approach requires involving departments or other stakeholders, such as:

- BC
- Chief risk officer
- Corporate risk department
- Crisis communications
- Disaster recovery
- Emergency preparedness and response

- Environmental management
- Health and safety
- Risk management
- Security

BC areas of concern that have the highest level of interaction with risk management include:

- Backup procedures
- Critical applications
- Existing contingency plans
- Exposures to functions
- Minimum recovery requirements
- Priority of business units
- Records retention

In terms of BC, the following list includes possible threats that can be managed, depending on the complexity of an event:

- Computer virus, data loss, disruption of service
- Disputes
- Earthquakes
- Fire
- Floods
- Flu epidemic
- Hurricanes
- Interrupted communications channels (telephone, cell phone, fax, Internet, etc.)
- Interrupted power supply
- Labor strike
- Shortages
- Snowstorms
- Water damage to equipment or facilities

BENEFITS

The benefits that an organization receives from integrating risk management and BC appear infinite, but measurable. One of the largest benefits is the ability potentially to maintain operations in the event of a major risk or a catastrophe. The risk attitude of an organization plays a major role in the perception of benefits received by integrating these two common areas. More mature organizations will rate some intangibles, such as company reputation, as a highly prized commodity, and want to protect it at almost any cost. Lower maturity organizations will often wait and see before making decisions to see the impact to the bottom line.

Here are just a few specific benefits:

- Be proactive rather than reactive
- Develop better plans to account for risks
- Develop strategies for dealing with risks
- Generate more confidence among stakeholders
- Identify vulnerabilities
- Manage more efficiently and effectively
- Provide foundation for BC decisions and actions
- Serve as a guide for prioritization of activities
- Set aside appropriate levels of contingency and management reserves
- Think and perform with the present and future in mind

TERMINOLOGY

The world of risk management uses its own vocabulary; it is important to know the terminology.

- *Black Swan* is a term used to identify an extremely low probability event that has an extremely high impact.
- *Contingency plan* is a preplanned response implemented only when certain conditions exist.
- *Frequency* is how often a risk might occur.
- *Hazard assessment* involves identifying and analyzing the impact of threats on critical business functions.
- *Hazard* is a potentially harmful event that could negatively impact operations, especially critical business functions.
- *Impact* is the effect of an event or condition on the strategic and operational performance of an organization.
- *Likelihood* is a subjective determination of the potential of a risk occurring, for example, high, medium, or low.

- *Operational risk* is the potential failure of procedures and controls of a critical business function.
- *Opportunity* is a risk event that has a positive impact.
- *Probability* is the mathematical potential of a risk occurring, usually expressed as a percentage or a number between 0 and 1, for example, .45, .67, or .98.
- *Residual risk* is used to identify the part of the risk that remains after implementing a response.
- *Risk categories* are a grouping of risks into buckets of similarity to determine trends as well as provide insight on where control weaknesses will likely exist.
- *Risk controls* are measures, such as processes and procedures, to reduce the probability or likelihood and impact of risks on critical business functions.
- *Risk event* is a discrete occurrence affecting a project, initiative, or program.
- *Risk qualification* means evaluating risks and risk interactions to assess the probability and impact of each risk and its relative importance to other risks.
- *Risk quantification* means evaluating risks and risk interactions to assess a range of possible project outcomes, usually financial.
- *Risk response* means developing and defining steps for dealing with threats and opportunities.
- *Secondary risk* is a risk that arises as the direct result of implementing a response to another risk.
- *Threat* is a risk event that will have a negative impact.

IMPLEMENTATION OF, AND DELIVERABLES FROM, RISK MANAGEMENT

Risk management as it pertains to BC involves six fundamental processes.

Determine Risk Approach

Within this first process, specific actions are taken so that all concerned stakeholders are aware of the risk attitude of their organization. The risk management plan is a deliverable for this process, detailing the methodologies, tools, data sources, and specific processes for risk identification, analysis, and reporting. To determine the risk approach requires performing ongoing education and awareness of risk.

Perform Risk Identification

This requires a holistic view of the project, program, or initiative to identify specific threats and opportunities. Risk identification focuses on specific events rather than the categories of events. The more specificity about an event itself, the easier it will be to plan for it and implement an effective response. Risk identification is most easily carried out in a group setting using brainstorming techniques. The deliverable from risk identification is a list of risks recorded in a document called a risk register. Risk identification can be broken down into two sub-processes of identifying risks most likely to affect the organization and categoring those risks.

Identify Risks Most Likely to Affect the Organization

This sub-process involves using techniques like brainstorming, checklists, and interviews with key stakeholders to identify potential threats and opportunities. A risk statement has three parts:

- Causes
- Event
- Impact

Categorize Risks

Utilizing a risk breakdown structure helps to categorize and identify specific areas that are riskier than others. Ways to categorize risk besides using a risk breakdown structure include:

- Acceptable vs. unacceptable
- Internal vs. external
- Manageable vs. unmanageable
- Short term vs. long term

Risk Assessment

Risk assessment can be conducted in two ways—qualitatively and quantitatively. Qualitative risk analysis requires evaluating risk and its interactions to assess the probability and impact of a risk occurrence. This enables placing the list of risks, determined via identification, in some understandable order. Quantitative analysis involves value weighting risk and risk interactions to assess the range of possible outcomes, often expressed in financial terminology, leading to determining contingency amounts for both budget and time. Then, it becomes possible to assess the deliverable from a risk priority and outcome.

The goal of qualitative risk assessment is to capture information for each risk to determine the score to include:

- Impact
- Ownership and responsibility
- Probability

The outcome of a qualitative assessment is the relative ranking of a risk relative to other risks. Consider the following two examples. Risk "A" has been identified as a Key System Component Crashing and has been rated as a 3 on an impact scale and a 5 on a likelihood or probability scale. This risk has an overall score of 15. Risk "B" is the Loss of Critical Skills Due to Retirement and has been given a 2 on the impact scale and a 3 on the likelihood or probability scale. This risk has an overall score of 6. These values are placed on a graph called a probability and impact matrix, shown in Figure 5.2.

Quantitative risk assessment is a much more in-depth, numerical analysis of the overall effect the risk will have on the project, initiative, or program. One common way to quantitatively assess risk is through expected monetary value (EMV) analysis. To determine the EMV, calculate the probability of a risk occurring and multiply that value by the actual impact,

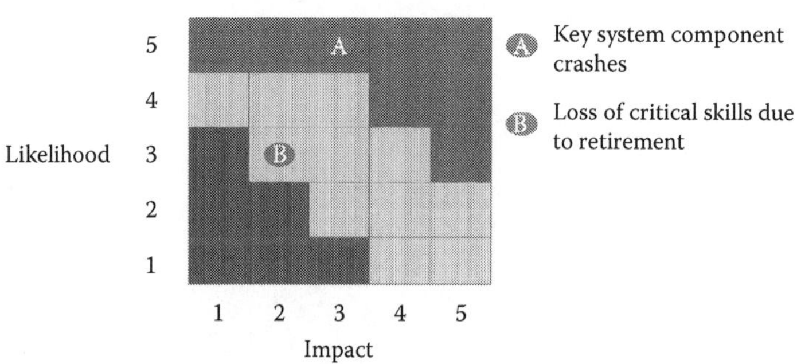

FIGURE 5.2
Probability and impact matrix.

Risk	Probability	Impact	Expected Value	Rank (1 through 5 with 1 Being the Highest)
A	0.5	$100,000	$50,000	2
B	0.7	$50,000	$35,000	3
C	0.3	$70,000	$21,000	4
D	0.8	$150,000	$120,000	1
E	0.2	$15,000	$3000	5

FIGURE 5.3
Expected monetary value table.

expressed in a currency format. Figure 5.3 is an example of how to perform quantitative assessment to determine the expected monetary value.

Response to Risk

This process requires developing strategies and actions to avoid, transfer, mitigate, or accept threats; it also includes the strategies and actions to share, exploit, enhance, or accept opportunities. Using the knowledge of the risk appetite and tolerance, a decision is made on how to handle higher impact risks (both threats and opportunities). In addition, as part of this group, it is a good idea to assign a risk owner so the risks can be tracked more easily. The deliverable from this process will be specific plans for addressing risks if they occur. This group can be broken up into specific sub-processes:

1. Determine risk owner. The risk owner may have already been identified in a previous process. If not, the risk owner will be identified here and recorded in the risk register.
2. Determine risk strategy. Risk strategies for threats can be categorized into four categories:
   a. Acceptance is doing nothing, known as passive acceptance, or setting aside a contingency in the form of time and/or money, to develop a contingency plan, known as active acceptance.
   b. Elimination or Avoidance is complete removal of the risk, or separating the impact from the objectives, or changing the objectives.
   c. Mitigation is acting to reduce the probability and/or the impact of the threat.
   d. Transfer is passing off the threat to other entities, such as in the case of buying an insurance policy.

Risk strategies for opportunities can also be grouped into four categories:

1. *Acceptance* is doing nothing, simply by taking advantage of the opportunity if and when it occurs.
2. *Enhancing* is acting to increase the probability and impact of an opportunity.
3. *Exploiting* is acting to ensure taking advantage of an opportunity.
4. *Sharing* is creating a partnership, joint venture, or teaming with another entity that has capabilities beyond your own.

Determining a strategy is only half the battle. Specific plans must fit the strategy. For example, an organization may decide to use a strategy of elimination to deal with the risk of the key system component crashing mentioned previously. During the planning of the response to that risk, the vendor assumes responsibility and bears any costs associated with the risk; the language is written into the contract. This is not elimination but transference. Elimination means complete removal of a risk. Having the vendor bear the cost does not remove the risk's probability of occurring, but rather shifts the impact of the risk to the vendor.

Control Risk

The process of controlling risk is ongoing, from the beginning of the project, program, or initiative, all the way to completion. This process includes monitoring for new risks, assessing the actual impact of an identified risk, assessing the effectiveness of individual risk response plans, monitoring for residual and secondary risks, and looking at the overall effectiveness of the risk approach. Additionally, recording information will be necessary to report on risk. Controlling risk consists of the following three sub-processes:

- Determine if the risk has occurred
- Determine effectiveness of risk responses
- Change risk priorities and responses as required

Determine if the Risk Has Occurred

Each risk should be assigned a risk owner, an individual responsible to watch for the possibility of a risk occurring, often preceded by a trigger event or symptom. In our earlier example, a symptom of our risk "B," Loss of Critical Skills Due to Retirement, could be a higher-than-average age of the workforce.

A *trigger event* is different from a symptom. A trigger event could be an actual risk or an event. For example, an earthquake is a risk event; it is also a trigger event for a tsunami, which, of course, is also a risk event. A rainstorm in Kansas during the month of May is not necessarily a risk, but it is a trigger event that may spawn a tornado, which is, in turn, a risk event.

The risk owner should be aware of a planned impact of the risk event and record its actual impact in the risk register. Recording the actual impact of a risk and comparing it to the planned one will assist an organization to assess future risks.

Determine Effectiveness of Risk Responses

This process is only used during the implementation of a risk response, after the occurrence of a risk. It is important to determine the degree of effectiveness. Each risk response, based upon the identified strategy, can have various levels of effectiveness. The risk owner should be aware of the planned impact the response will have on a risk. If the planned response does not effectively eliminate, transfer, or mitigate the impact, then it may require additional actions. Risk owners must monitor for residual and secondary risks.

Change Risk Priorities and Responses as Required

Once the degree of effectiveness of a plan has been determined inadequate, additional planning must be undertaken, consistent with the priority of a risk, to develop follow-up actions. These actions must be consistent with the policies and procedures of the organization and the specific area of the risk, for example, information technology (IT) responses used within the IT department, and the shipping responses used within the shipping department. Upon developing new plans, they are reported via the risk register.

Report Risk

This process involves communicating the risk management activities, such as the effectiveness of risk responses, to stakeholders. Depending upon the risk attitude of an organization, a risk report can be simple or complicated. One simple way to update the risk register is by providing detailed information about each risk. A more complicated way is to issue a formal written report describing in detail the risk, the implementation details of the response plan and its effectiveness, information about residual risk and secondary risk, and any variance information about the planned vs. actual impact. The major deliverable is the risk report, consisting of two additional sub-processes.

Determine Audience for Risk Report

This has been or should have been determined during the planning of risk management and could include key stakeholders such as:

- Board of directors (BoD)
- BC project managers and specialists
- Consultants
- Customers
- Investors and lenders
- Operational management
- Senior management
- Staff members from various disciplines, for example, IT, security
- Suppliers
- Vendors

Determine Content, Format, and Frequency of the Risk Report

Again, this sub-process should have occurred earlier during risk planning. However, keep in mind that, given the differing levels and interests of key stakeholders above, this requires varying and adapting content, format, and frequency. Be sure to place a copy of all risk reports in a central document repository for future reference.

ACTIONS TO TAKE

Senior Management

To begin integrating risk management with BC, here are some specific actions to take at the senior management level prior to performing actual identification, analysis, response planning, and controlling of risks. Remember the acronym DIP^2 or "DIP Squared." Some of these actions may already exist or may have been taken within your organization; however, we recommend acknowledging each of the following:

Decide

The decision to perform ERM must come from the highest levels of an organization. Senior level support will preclude wasting time and money.

Deciding means having all of the high-level key players on board with a firm, unequivocal, and unified voice stating this is good for our organization and we will reap many benefits from doing this. Of course, this statement means leadership from the top and down to the lowest levels. Trying to do most anything from the bottom-up is, at best, futile. The organizational culture will play a major role on how long this action takes and its success.

Develop

After making a decision, the next step is developing an ERM approach, a methodology and philosophy for establishing risk management while considering several tangibles and intangibles, but mostly related to an organization itself. Some factors include the following:

- Strategic plan, such as how an organization sees itself in five or ten years
- Size of the organization, which will be a factor in determining who will handle the different responsibilities
- Real or perceived risk an organization is or will be facing in the future
- Relative position of a company in the marketplace, such as a company of 100,000 people doing the same thing and having .01% market share
- Strength and will of the senior managers, which directly relates to their leadership capabilities

Developing an approach will serve an organization well, especially when risks occur and the approach is employed. So what does this involve? Basically, senior management, with input from the lower level managers and perhaps the front-line workers, develop tools used in ERM, such as an impact rating table, probability and impact matrices, operational definitions of probability and impact, risk definition parameters, a risk categorization matrix (also referred to as a risk breakdown structure) and policies on calculating risk reserves. Personnel involved in ERM can use these tools. After their development, the data collected by these tools should be recorded or written down in an accessible format for use and improved when implemented.

Inform

This is the easiest one to explain, it being self-explanatory; however, it can cause the most problems if done incorrectly. Informing requires senior management to clearly communicate the vision, mission, and philosophy of the need for ERM. This action goes beyond a memo distributed by mid-level managers. It means the senior management team must leave their offices, go to the place of action, talk with subordinates, and gain buy-in for initiatives. Again, leadership must be employed here.

Include

To include means senior managers must consider all aspects of a business. They must look beyond silos, pursue cross-functional work, and instill teamwork. ERM cannot be limited to the finance department, customer service, design, manufacturing, or sales. These departments or divisions can no longer think of themselves as independent of others. They must consider the impact of their work and their effect on other departments or divisions.

Senior management must work with each other, demonstrating and transmitting that need to the lower levels of an organization. That means dropping politics at the door and become a team player, gaining knowledge on what the impacts have on others when something occurs unplanned. It may mean a department has to relinquish something to help an organization gain a strategic advantage. Aristotle said, "He who cannot be a good follower cannot be a good leader." Sometimes a good leader follows others.

Plan

Plan the methodologies and philosophies of ERM into the organization's standard operating procedures. Conduct planning sessions, inviting the closest stakeholders to the actual outcomes, such as front-line workers. Plan to have many scenarios even if seeming somewhat far-fetched. One of the reasons why the U.S. was caught off-guard on 9/11 was the bureaucratic nature of the government; the various organizations did not communicate well between each other. The biggest reason for this was no one, in any of the intelligence agencies, had ever dreamed of someone hijacking and flying a plane into a building as a possible act of terror. It was unheard of as a possibility, and certainly not four plane. Since it had not been thought of, no one planned for how to respond when it did happen. Take action to plan as many different scenarios as possible.

Progress

This final step helps senior management enhance and sustain progress toward greater levels of performance with each iteration, by improving the systems, policies, and tools, and taking a serious introspective review about how an event or scenario was handled. "Lessons learned" is an excellent tool for attaining continuous improvement. Hold postmortems on projects, initiatives, and especially when organizations perform simulated drills.

A project postmortem or a lessons-learned meeting can help determine how well or poorly a scenario exercise or real event went. Progress may mean discarding or rewriting policies and procedures that cause a hindrance or that have little or no value. Clinging to policies simply because "that's the way it always has been done" does not work and impedes progress unless otherwise demonstrated. Improvements require being bold.

Two final thoughts on the actions mentioned above. Senior managers should know their organization well and the stakeholders involved in processes. Nonsenior management team members need to learn how to affect change in an organization in the hope of being effective.

Mid-Level and Project Managers

Actions at this level of management are dictated by several factors; however, they are mainly on what senior management decides, the current policies within the organization, and the size, importance, and type of initiative or project. Here are some actions that almost every organization can implement.

Understand the Goal

Before undertaking an initiative, project, or program, understanding the goal is paramount. Without a solid knowledge of "why" or "what" is occurring, it is impossible to plan for risks that could happen or the opportunities that may arise without knowing what the goal is. This can result in overlooking an opportunity or a threat appearing without any indication.

Use a Defined Approach

Be methodical and record everything relevant in writing. The use of preplanned, predefined definitions, tools, processes, and techniques can enhance the benefit the organization receives from performing enterprise-wide risk management (ERM). Individuals and organizations involved in identifying, analyzing, responding to, and controlling risks should be well aware of the processes and tools at their disposal.

Be Proactive

Being proactive means acting before a problem arises. The opposite is reactive, meaning behavior is directed by something else. Being proactive involves tuning in to the surroundings, anticipating problems, and reducing the possibility of, or eliminating, any threats. Sometimes the most proactive thing that can be done is taking a break. By staying so focused on a project, initiative or program, you can lose the peripheral vision, which is used in being proactive. Taking a break will allows reflection on what's being done and how you're going about it.

Clearly Assign Responsibilities

Ensuring that everyone knows what is expected of him or her and his or her area of responsibility will reduce conflict, the greatest benefit of this action. The job of the manager is to manage, not "do." Therefore, as part of leadership, a manager should delegate. Use the tools necessary to display, disseminate, and communicate responsibility. An organizational chart, a responsibility assignment matrix, or an internal web site containing everyone's title, role, and job description can go a long way in this regard.

CHALLENGES

While many challenges exist with enterprise risk management, listed below are some common ones. Reducing the effects of or eliminating these challenges will greatly enhance an organization's ability to effectively implement enterprise-wide risk management:

- A desire to operate "under the radar"
- Demonstrating value
- Distorting or "massaging" information to higher management
- Fear
- Inadequate link to organization's strategies and objectives
- Inadequate representation of risk management function at board level
- Inconsistent approach
- Insufficient time
- Intolerance to different perspectives
- Lack of adequate business data and information
- Lack of education and awareness
- Lack of management support
- Lack of relevant risk data
- Organizational structure
- Political inhibitors to good risk management, such as an imbalance of power relationships and flawed decision-making processes due to these relationships
- Predominance of convergent thinking/narrow focus
- Prejudices, such as arrogance, selective perceptions
- Silo thinking
- Tendency to act first and think later, for example, ready, shoot, aim
- Unavailability of skills and knowledge

FINAL THOUGHTS

PM and ERM are the two building blocks for instituting a reliable BC program with meaningful BP plans. Both enable focusing on what is meaningful to all stakeholders. Both also provide the discipline to ensure that resiliency is sustained. In the forthcoming chapters, a structured approach is presented using the elements of these two building blocks that will increase the resiliency of an organization if and when a major event strikes it. Failing to prepare is preparing to fail. The application of these two building blocks provides the foundation for preparing for meaningful resiliency.

6

Establish Governance

One of the first actions to take is to establish a governance program for business continuity (BC). Project management (PM) provides the focus to establish an infrastructure with the right degree of breadth and depth of governance.

WHAT IS GOVERNANCE?

Governance is establishing an infrastructure that entails setting policies and creating procedures, determining goals and strategies, and monitoring performance to achieve desired results as identified by a governing body, such as a steering committee.

From a BC perspective, governance involves two major activities: (1) establishing a program or project that supports developing and executing efficient and effective business preparedness (BP) processes, tools, and techniques; and (2) developing and deploying an education and awareness effort that communicates knowledge about BC.

Figure 6.1 shows the relationship between the two. Establish a Common Infrastructure and Build Education and Awareness work together to enhance the opportunity to develop, deploy, and sustain a supportive, successful governance infrastructure.

GOALS

Establishing BC governance structure principally has two goals.

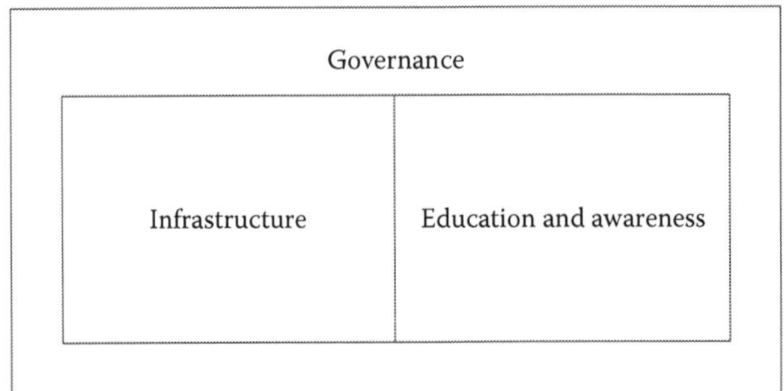

FIGURE 6.1
Two components of BC governance.

Establish Overall Strategic Direction

The BC governance structure leads the way for building, testing, and maintaining plans to achieve its overall mission. If any supporting project fails to support the overall strategic direction and does not comply with oversight, BC governance will likely prove ineffective and will be deemed by some key stakeholders as unnecessary. The governance structure must have the authority to invoke its power to ensure discipline.

Ensure Effective Execution of BC

This goal requires that all the subordinate projects, such as the ones for building plans, comply with the overall strategic direction provided by the governance infrastructure. This requires reporting on whether each project achieves its cost, schedule, and quality goals and, if necessary, takes corrective action. It also needs to perform ongoing reporting on performance.

TERMINOLOGY

Governance involves some BC terminology that necessitates a definition upfront.

BC planning involves developing, deploying, and maintaining strategies and procedures to ensure critical business processes continue or are restored. Establishing a vision for the overall project, setting policy, and determining critical business processes are just some of the activities constituting BC planning.

The *BC planning cycle* is a continuous process to develop, maintain, and test plans to enhance resiliency. The activities subsumed under the planning cycle involve determining a schedule to build, test, and maintain BP plans; establishing a development and maintenance schedule; allocating resources; and ensuring buy-in from key stakeholders regarding plans.

A *BC program* is an organization to lead and manage the development and deployment of a comprehensive set of processes, procedures, and disciplines to enhance the resiliency of a company before, during, and after the occurrence of a disruptive event. Governance is the backbone of the program. Establishing and maintaining a BC program requires setting up and deploying good program and PM practices, providing the groundwork for effective and efficient governance.

BC strategies are for restoring and recovering an organization before, during, and after a disruptive event at a high level and applicable to just about any event. These strategies, of course, should align with the ones established by the parent organization. Governance strategies should also provide reasonable assurance of recovery of a critical business process or function.

A *standard operating procedure* is a document providing direction on implementing BC strategies. For example, a procedure might cover how to build or maintain plans; it may also cover the operations of the BC program itself. A procedure can take many formats, for example, a play script, and may be supplemented with diagrams, for example, flowcharts.

KEY CONCEPTS

When establishing a governance program for BC, keep the following concepts in mind.

Obtain Buy-In from Key Stakeholders at the Executive Level

Adopting BC within a company requires a shift in mindset, particularly for people in operations. As mentioned earlier, BC is like life insurance; it is hard for someone to appreciate it until the need arises, if it ever does. Key executive involvement will help in overcoming most resistance to change when the rank and file see that it is a priority. Another way to achieve buy-in is to engage and involve key stakeholders to establish and provide ongoing guidance in governance.

Establish a Performance Measurement Baseline for the Governance Project

Metrics and their supporting measures should provide reliable facts and data on the progress of BC activities toward achieving targets. These metrics should not only cover, cost, schedule, and scope, but also provide visibility on the effectiveness of the project, such as a burn down of the critical business processes, completed BP plans, the type of information captured in the plans, common shortfalls appearing in the plans, integration or "touch points" among critical business processes, and the number and extent of suppliers and contractors supporting critical business processes.

Communicate Vertically and Laterally

BC is a high communication endeavor. Failure to communicate not only creates poor plans, but also results in poor recovery. Effective communications should occur both vertically, such as up and down the chain of command, and horizontally, such as among peers. It requires establishing a hierarchy of meetings, such as steering committees and working groups, to exchange data and information among stakeholders.

Focus on the Vision and Report Regularly to the Key Stakeholders about Program or Project Successes

All key stakeholders should have a good understanding and knowledge about the purpose of BC and BC governance. Standard PM deliverables will help. However, a high-level mission statement and goals coupled with a governing policy can go a long way to establish a vision everyone accepts.

Identify the Roles and Responsibilities for BC Governance

Roles and responsibilities include executive leadership and senior managers, such as those on the BC steering committee, as well as stakeholders building and providing input to the plans.

Document the Processes

You should not only document policies but also do the same for methods, tools, techniques, and reports when building BP plans. This documentation not only serves as a training vehicle for people joining a BC project; it also helps to ensure consistency in developing, testing, and maintaining plans. Incidentally, the larger the company, the greater the need exists for such procedures to provide greater consistency in performance.

Provide the Necessary Tools to Develop and Maintain Plans

Tools provide consistency; however, they need to support the people who build the plans. Too often, a tool is adopted without much foresight and then considerable effort is expended to adapt procedures and workflows to the peculiarities of a tool. Not only should the tool aid in building and maintaining plans, but also it should help to create a repository of data to generate project information. Too often, tools are used to collect a mass of data in a repository not lending itself to generating information to make managerial and strategic decisions.

Make Sure the Vision for the Project Aligns with the One for the Parent Organization

Misalignment of the BC vision with the parent organization can cause complications when implementing BC. Through alignment, the fate of key stakeholders, especially if an organization uses management by objectives, is closely intertwined with those of the project.

Hire a Competent Support Staff at the Project Level

It is at this level that project managers with an expertise in BC will manage the projects to develop, test, and maintain plans for the critical business processes. Additionally, project managers should have good oral and written communication skills, a solid knowledge of business practices, and they should be at ease working with different levels within an organization. An enterprise-wide perspective is also an important tool to have because BC and BP often deal with cross-functional and interorganizational issues.

Provide Ongoing Training to the Support Staff

The support staff, naturally, should have superior knowledge of the concepts, methodology, tools, and techniques of BC. This training should include certifications and ongoing seminars and workshops to enhance skills and knowledge. Attending conferences and other local BC events allows for exposure to best practices shared by trip reports and cascade training, and providing training to peers after receiving training for oneself.

BENEFITS

The achievement of the two goals outlined above provides several benefits.

Efficient and Effective Oversight of the BC Project

As mentioned earlier, many people view BC as a necessary evil, at best, and a contributor to overhead costs. Until something happens, if it does, BC is hard pressed to demonstrate value to the bottom line. Ways exist, of course, to demonstrate value but are often indirect, such as using plans to lower business insurance costs and examples demonstrating the use of plans in the recovery of critical business processes.

Encouraging Implementation of BC throughout an Organization

Providing visibility of metrics, such as the number of critical business processes and their BP plans completed, as compared to those failing to achieve progress, will encourage the adoption of BC. Naturally, metrics should reflect progress in achieving the overall strategic direction of an organization, as well as meeting cost and schedule targets.

Defining Roles and Responsibilities

Stakeholders must know their roles and responsibilities regarding BC. If the roles and responsibilities are unclear, regardless of one's position in the hierarchy, people will find BC confusing, demoralizing, and frustrating. The BC program at the strategic level should articulate stakeholder responsibilities when executing specific actions. Procedures often describe these roles and responsibilities.

Providing Common Guidelines, Standards, Tools, and Methodology

Clear plans for recovery necessitate commonality. A lack of commonality results in confusion. The governance infrastructure should take the lead in this responsibility to integrate critical business processes and plans. In addition, it provides common guidelines, standards, tools, and methodologies for critical business processes to work efficiently and effectively.

Enhancing Communication among Stakeholders

The governance infrastructure provides the necessary support for effective communications. For example, it not only provides a standard set of tools and techniques, but also provides a hierarchy of meetings ensuring that communication occurs not only up, down, and across the chain of command, but also among a variety of other stakeholders. These meetings should not only share information but also best practices.

Providing Change Management

The business environment is often dynamic, creating a need to control significant changes. For a BC project, the change can be an organizational change, such as selling off a business unit, which requires some type of impact assessment to the overall strategic direction of the BC program and the affected plans.

Addressing Corporate Issues, Concerns, etc.

A major advantage of a BC governance infrastructure is providing an opportunity for stakeholders to discuss and assess the impact of major internal and external events affecting a company. Changing market conditions or key leaders can affect critical business processes. The BC governance infrastructure enables clearly understanding and assessing impacts, for instance, to determine if its overall strategic direction also needs to change.

Providing Guidelines on Risk Management and Prioritization

A BC governance infrastructure plays a key role by encouraging both risk management and prioritization to occur. Risk management plays an integral part by identifying risks threatening the resiliency of a company; it also provides responses and controls dealing with risks. Discussing BC will always lead to a dialogue over priorities of a company. Risk management and prioritization are tightly interwoven at the strategic or operational levels.

Providing a Cross-Functional Perspective

Governance transcends narrow disciplines by requiring a broader, strategic perspective; that is, looking at the "big picture" to ensure achieving the strategic goals and objectives. It also requires all supporting functions, for example, information systems and financial, to work together to achieve strategic goals and objectives.

Overseeing the Application of Policies, Processes, Procedures, and Methodologies

Being at the high level, a governance infrastructure has oversight of the activities under its purview. It applies policy, processes, procedures, and methodologies effectively and efficiently. Its purpose, once again, is to ensure focus on achieving the strategic goals and objectives. In addition, it helps resolve problems, beyond a single critical process, for example.

Reviewing and Evaluating Recommendations for Improvement

Often, many ideas rest within the bowels of an organization, many of them smothering and dying due to a lack of consideration support. After all, organizations exist to satisfy an existing need, giving preference to maintaining the status quo. New ideas upset the status quo. With a governance infrastructure, opportunities exist for key stakeholders of a critical business process to share ideas for improvement.

Identifying and Adopting Guidelines and Standards as Well as Complying Uniformly with Laws, Regulations, Rulings, etc.

It provides uniformity throughout a cross-functional environment, the same kind that involves BC. Uniformity, contrary to popular belief, does not always mean regimentation but rather adaptability while simultaneously having people follow a common framework. For example, all BP plans have a common look and feel while still accommodating the specific requirements of a critical business process.

Clarifying Expectations about BC and BP

Key stakeholders often hold varying interpretations of BC and BP, a situation prevalent in large organizations. Governance, through its policy making responsibilities, helps to clarify those interpretations by setting and managing expectations, thereby allowing for better communications and progressing in a more focused, common direction.

Taking a Proactive Approach toward Implementing and Sustaining BC throughout a Company

Rather than react to circumstances, a proactive response enables key decision makers to prepare for the future by applying risk management and the building of BP plans to deal with risks should they occur. Most organizations often have little time or other resources to devote to BC due to operational requirements. Governance has the authority and position to take the initiative before something happens by engaging key stakeholders through ownership. Governance will not work or be effective unless key stakeholders freely engage and once engaged, the political muscle exists to take proactive action toward resiliency.

CHALLENGES

Despite all the benefits of governance, challenges do exist that require attention.

Keeping All Stakeholders, and Not Just the Important Ones, Engaged

Unless a threat is imminent, BC is just not on the forefront of people's minds. They focus on the here and now. As time goes by without any scenario exercises and continual reminders about building and updating their BP plans, stakeholder interest wanes. A governance infrastructure needs to be proactive, therefore, taking the initiative to engage stakeholders and to increase their awareness about BC.

Making Timely Decisions

A governance infrastructure is great to share ideas and information; however, it must do more. It must make timely critical decisions, to include identifying risks and ways to respond to them; determining the critical business processes to document; and setting a schedule to develop plans. Unfortunately, too often many meetings at the governance level are avenues for discussion resulting in nothing.

Ensuring Availability of Sufficient Time and Funds

Unlimited funds are rarely available for just about any project; usually it is just the opposite. Obtaining sufficient funds is necessary for a governance infrastructure to accomplish its goals and objectives. The tendency in organizations is to keep overhead to a minimum. BC is considered overhead in most places, increasing the likelihood of being short-changed and axed during less prosperous times.

Resolving Conflict

A governance infrastructure faces a host of typical organizational conflicts. These conflicts include competing for resources with other organizations, setting schedule priorities and domains among critical business processes, allocating expertise to support different critical business processes, and establishing policy. If governance fails to resolve these and other conflicts, not only do the conflicts become more intense, but also they can question the value of BC. If key stakeholders cannot resolve their differences, for example, members of a steering committee, strategic direction and guidance related to BC, the governance infrastructure will likely be ineffective.

MAKING GOVERNANCE INFRASTRUCTURE HAPPEN

Establishing a solid governance structure for BC involves the following actions, which are shown in Figure 6.2.

ID	Task Name	Predecessors
41	1.1.2 Establish governance infrastructure	
42	1.1.2.1 Manage project for governance	
43	1.1.2.1.1 Apply project management	40
44	1.1.2.2 Determine requirements for governance infrastructure	
45	1.1.2.2.1 Identify key stakeholders	43
46	1.1.2.2.2 Prepare business case for business continuity and preparedness	45
47	1.1.2.2.3 Establish an organizational structure	45,46
48	1.1.2.2.4 Identify roles, responsibilities, and authorities	45,46
49	1.1.2.2.5 Identify critical business processes	45,46
50	1.1.2.2.6 Develop business preparedness strategies	45,46
51	1.1.2.2.7 Communicate strategies and decisions	45,46
52	1.1.2.2.8 Develop policies, processes, and procedures	45,46
53	1.1.2.2.9 Adopt a business continuity methodology and supporting standards	45,46
54	1.1.2.2.10 Select tools	45,46
55	1.1.2.2.11 Develop and manage portfolio of projects	45,46,47,48,49, 50,51,52,53,54
56	1.1.2.3 Deploy governance infrastructure	
57	1.1.2.3.1 Implement governance infrastructure	45,46,47,48,49,50, 51,52,53,54,55
58	1.1.2.4 Apply project management (closing)	
59	1.1.2.4.1 Perform closing tasks for governance infrastructure	57

FIGURE 6.2
WBS for establishing BC governance infrastructure.

Manage Project for Governance

This task involves applying all of the PM concepts, tools, and techniques to enhance project performance. For example, it includes preparing a charter, developing a work breakdown structure (WBS), making time and cost estimates, building a schedule, and tracking and monitoring performance.

Determine Requirements for Governance Infrastructure

Identify Key Stakeholders

One of the most important activities to start a BC program is to identify key stakeholders. As mentioned earlier, a key stakeholder is an individual

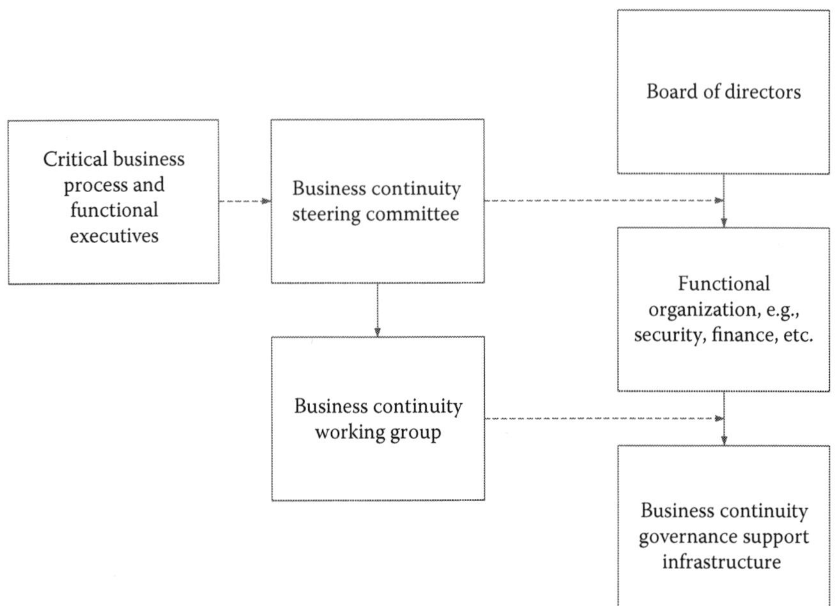

FIGURE 6.3
Typical BC governance organizational structure.

or organization having an interest, directly or indirectly, in the outcome of a project. These key stakeholders are often representatives from the executive leadership across a company. They will have ultimate responsibility for the resiliency of the critical business processes of the company. Failure to exercise due diligence in demonstrating resiliency can have legal consequences. The board of directors (BoD), its chairperson, chief executive officer, or the audit committee provides the initial guidance on who are the stakeholders. Once identified, the stakeholders begin establishing a governance program for BC. Figure 6.3 provides an example of a typical BC governance organizational structure.

Establish an Organizational Structure

The organizational structure can become quite complex for large organizations. The complexity is often a product of the company's size, whether a stovepipe or matrix in architecture, or one that is geographically spread. Regardless, the governance structure should have a BC steering committee consisting of executives and senior managers from both the operational (e.g., operations) and the functional (e.g., finance) sides of the company. It should also include individuals having unique knowledge or skills. The steering committee provides the overall guidance and direction, provides general oversight on progress, and is the final arbiter of issues unresolvable at lower levels. The steering committee often meets monthly or quarterly.

In addition, a governance infrastructure often has a BC working group of key stakeholders, but senior managers, often representatives of the operational and functional sides of an organization, handle the management of the governance program. It is here that decisions and guidance of the governance infrastructure align with the overall strategies and guidance of the BC steering committee. This working group meets more frequently than the steering committee, such as every two weeks, and assumes more of an operational oversight role for the BC program implementing the governance infrastructure for BC.

Finally, a governance structure has a program staff providing support not just to the steering committee and the working group, but also to the people in critical business processes who will build the BP plans. These staff members have the expertise and knowledge to build, test, and maintain BP plans. They are often experts on security, risk management, information technology, and other business disciplines.

Prepare the Business Case for BC and BP

This activity is the most important one for a BC governance infrastructure. It needs to demonstrate its value to key stakeholders. BC consumes time and other resources, is often absorbed through overhead, and, frankly, not at the top of the radar for many people. A business case serves as a powerful way to justify BC and its accompany governance infrastructure. A business case should not only demonstrate how it will pay financial returns to the company, but also from a nonfinancial perspective, such as provide support to achieve the long-range plans of the company. The business case should involve input from all key stakeholders and experts throughout the company. If the business case lacks credibility and buy-in, then a governance infrastructure to support the implementation and maintenance of a BC program will confront many challenges for critical business processes. A business plan should also be revisited periodically to ascertain whether the benefits have been realized.

Identify Roles, Responsibilities, and Authorities (RAA)

This activity stresses the importance of all positions and organizations having a knowledge and understanding of their contributions toward making a company more resilient. Knowing their RAAs allows for people and organizations to know the expectations to meet. It also enables better communications. The BC governance infrastructure should describe the RAAs for the steering committee and working group, process owners, recovery team members, BC specialists, authors of BP plans, and any other people or organizations involved with BC. Naturally, the governance infrastructure should communicate all RAAs.

Identify Critical Business Processes

The governance infrastructure identifies the critical business processes to realize a company's vision, mission, and values. The critical business processes support the successful execution of a company's overall strategies. Ideally, the BoD and the audit committee have this information, reflected in a strategic plan. If so, the governance infrastructure, usually done by the steering committee, uses this information to identify its own strategies. Some company strategies to which the steering committee is privy may be so sensitive that the committee must use its judgment on what, and what not, to share with certain members of the BC governance infrastructure.

Develop Business Preparedness Strategies

The governance organization formulates its strategies to enhance the resiliency of the critical business processes. All strategies should support the vision, mission, and values of the parent organization. BC strategies focus on resiliency in a manner enabling more efficient and effective downstream application of BP activities. BC strategies from an integrated perspective, vertically and horizontally, enhance resiliency by reducing complexity and waste.

Communicate Strategies and Decisions

Formulating strategies and making decisions are critical for an effective BC governance program. However, they are virtually useless if strategies and decisions are never communicated to the people responsible to turn them into reality when building, testing, and maintaining plans for critical business processes. Too often, a steering committee, whether or not related to BC, fails to communicate its strategies and decisions. As a result, people in the field, such as the operational areas, perform or fail to perform in ways supporting the strategies and decisions of the steering committee, akin to a two-layered cake whereby the top is askew from the bottom one. Communication is a key element for a successful BC governance infrastructure.

Develop Policies, Applicable Processes, and Procedures

The BC governance infrastructure should set policy for the BC of a company, define the processes, and create the procedures for applying BC. A policy states the purpose and high-level goals for BC and serves as guidelines to develop supporting processes to realize the content of the policy. These processes might include performing a risk assessment, conducting a business impact analysis (BIA), developing, testing, and maintaining plans, and using specific tools. Procedures are written, in turn, to execute the processes in normal and atypical circumstances.

Adopt a Business Continuity Methodology and Supporting Standards

A methodology is a detailed manifestation of a framework to institute and maintain BC within an organization. A framework, supported by a methodology, guides determining the essential processes and procedures to build and maintain their content but also to assess the effectiveness of the governance program to ensure the resiliency of a company which, in turn, indicates how effective the BC governance program is. Some frameworks offer maturity levels. A framework should reflect the culture of an organization. It should support all activities to institute and maintain a BC governance program. Additionally, it should support any adopted standards embraced by professional organizations, such as the International Standards Organization (ISO).

Select Tools

The governance program should provide standard tools to deploy and maintain BC. Tools should be supportive of the program, not the other way around. Tools should enable flexibility as well as all activities described earlier to further governance strategies and decisions and execute processes and procedures. Besides being relatively easy to use, they should provide useful data to generate information to ascertain the efficiency and effectiveness of major efforts to increase the resiliency of critical business processes.

Develop and Manage Portfolio of Projects

After establishing the governance infrastructure, develop a portfolio of projects that ensure greater resiliency for a company. Developing, testing, and maintaining the BP plans for each critical business process is a project itself and should be managed as such. Depending on the scale of a critical business process, employing robust concepts, tools, and techniques may be necessary or minimally required. For example, one critical business process may be small enough to warrant building one BP plan, thereby requiring a light version of PM; however, another process may be so large that a greater number of plans are necessary to document, thereby requiring extensive PM tools and techniques. Scalability plays a role in determining the degree of PM to employ.

Deploy Governance Infrastructure

This task requires making the governance infrastructure a reality in the business environment. Until deployed, governance infrastructure simply exists on paper. If all the previous tasks have been completed successfully, deployment should proceed relatively smoothly. Of course, challenges, risks, and issues will likely pop up, but with the participation of key stakeholders and the necessary deliverables in place, deployment should become smoother than if project tasks were performed in a haphazard, unplanned manner.

Apply Project Management (Closing)

This task involves ensuring that validation of the performance measurement baseline occurs prior to officially closing the project. It also involves ensuring that all administrative, financial, and contractual concerns or issues are addressed to preclude, for instance, legal problems from occurring.

Deliverables

The major deliverables for building a BC governance infrastructure are

- BC methodology
- Business case
- BP strategies
- Critical business process identification
- Organizational structure
- Policies, processes, and procedures
- Portfolio of projects
- Roles, responsibilities, and authorities
- Tool selection

These deliverables tend to be strategic in nature, meaning that they require taking a holistic, high-level perspective, rather than simply subscribing to a functional, operational, or single BP perspective.

Stakeholders

The primary responsibility for determining the requirements for the BC governance infrastructure rests with the senior executives of a company or organization. The reason is that the infrastructure will operate at the strategic level and its decisions and activities will impact the entire company or organization. Most of the other stakeholders are ancillary roles, such as consulting or simply needing to keep abreast of any decisions and activities that might affect them.

Implementation, however, is different. A project or program manager is assigned primary responsibility to fulfill the requirements and deploy them throughout the company or organization. The BC project or program manager for that matter will likely have to work closely with the BC working group to obtain additional support and help in ensuring that the infrastructure is deployed as efficiently and effectively as possible. At the same time, the BC project or program manager keeps the steering committee and other senior executives apprised of progress and may need to submit requests for help, such as political sponsorship. These responsibilities are reflected in a responsible, accountable, consult, inform (RACI) chart as shown in Figure 6.4.

Role	Board of Directors	BC Steering Committee	Business Continuity Working Group	BC Project Manager/ Program Manager	BC Specialists/ Staff Support	Business Process Owner/ Senior Management	Recovery Team Leader (Operational)	Recovery Team Members (Operational)	Audit	Customers	Suppliers/Vendors	Shareholders
Tasks												
Establish governance infrastructure												
Determine requirements for governance infrastructure	R	A	A	C	C	I			I			I
Deploy governance infrastructure		I	C,I	R	A	I			I			I
Close for instituting governance infrastructure	I	I	C,I	R	A				I			I

Legend
R = Responsible
A = Accountable
C = Consult
I = Inform

FIGURE 6.4
RACI chart for establishing governance infrastructure.

Integration of the Activities

None of the above activities occurs independently of one another. They must all work together to establish an effective governance infrastructure. The participation of key stakeholders is necessary to ensure ownership and buy-in for the BC program. The key stakeholders participate in performing the business case to ascertain whether the company should establish a BC program in the first place. Assuming that the business case supports the idea, key stakeholders then define and guide the identification and implementation of a governance infrastructure, which sets strategies and provides execution oversight to ensure that critical business processes become more resilient. The BC infrastructure identifies the roles, responsibilities, and authorities; adopts a BC methodology; develops policy, applicable processes, and procedures; determines BC strategy; selects tools; and develops and manages a portfolio of projects.

MAKING EDUCATION AND AWARENESS HAPPEN

Along with establishing BC governance infrastructure comes the need to educate and enhance awareness about BC. Without education and awareness, the efficiency and effectiveness of the governance infrastructure will fail.

Here are the activities to implement education and building awareness for a BC, as shown in Figure 6.5.

Manage Project for Building Education and Awareness

This task involves applying all the PM concepts, tools, and techniques to enhance project performance.

Determine Requirements to Build Education and Awareness Materials

Determine Affected Stakeholders

While a failure in resiliency impacts everyone in a workforce, not everyone is a direct stakeholder when developing and maintaining BP plans. It is important to identify those stakeholders who have a direct interest.

ID	Task Name	Predecessors
60	1.1.2.5 Build education and awareness	
61	1.1.2.5.1 Manage project for building education and awareness	
62	1.1.2.5.1.1 Apply project management	57
63	1.1.2.5.2 Determine requirements to build education and awareness	
64	1.1.2.5.2.1 Determine affected stakeholders	62
65	1.1.2.5.2.2 Determine strategies, goals, and objectives	64
66	1.1.2.5.2.3 Determine topics	64
67	1.1.2.5.2.4 Determine level of effort	64
68	1.1.2.5.3 Build education and awareness materials	
69	1.1.2.5.3.1 Tailor material for specific stakeholders	65,66,67
70	1.1.2.5.3.2 Prepare lesson plans	65,66,67
71	1.1.2.5.3.3 Create material	65,66,67
72	1.1.2.5.3.4 Determine media	65,66,67
73	1.1.2.5.3.5 Build delivery schedule	65,66,67
74	1.1.2.6 Deliver education and awareness materials	
75	1.1.2.6.1 Deliver education and awareness materials	69,70,71,72,73
76	1.1.2.7 Apply project management (closing)	
77	1.1.2.7.1 Perform closing tasks for building education and awareness	75

FIGURE 6.5
WBS for building education and awareness.

The original list of stakeholders identified when implementing a governance infrastructure is a good start; these stakeholders can help identify the additional stakeholders for each critical business process. These people and organizations are the ones responsible for a critical business process as well as the recovery team leaders being responsible for each plan. These stakeholders will continually need education and awareness about BC and their responsibilities for building, testing, and maintaining BP plans.

Determine Strategies, Goals, and Objectives

BC requires knowing the strategies, goals, and objectives to develop, deploy, and maintain the education and awareness of what stakeholders need to understand and know. The strategies, goals, and objectives should seek to help people understand what BC and BP are about and their role in the resiliency of the company. All strategies, goals, and objectives for education and awareness should support the overall strategic goals and objectives of the BC governance program.

Determine Topics

Education and awareness of BC will likely cover a number of topics, ranging from emergency response to restoration of critical business processes. The topics should be relevant to the audience and should enable people to have a good understanding of the topic and how to apply it. Any BC-related presentation, such as one for building, testing, and maintaining a plan, should serve as an opportunity to increase general knowledge and awareness of BC discipline. Education and awareness should seize the opportunity to augment people's understanding and knowledge of BC.

Determine Level of Effort

Building education and awareness material and delivering it takes considerable time and effort; that translates into money. By determining the level of effort, the appropriate number of resources can be assigned as well as enable preparing a realistic schedule for developing and delivering material to applicable stakeholders. Factors to consider when determining the level of effort include breadth, depth, and complexity of material for each education and awareness module and the number of people available and their degree of background with the material. If people lack the time or expertise, determine alternative means to develop and deliver presentations, such as outsourcing or borrowing people with the requisite knowledge and expertise to provide the necessary services.

Build Education and Awareness Materials

Tailor Material for Specific Stakeholders

Depending on a person's or an organization's role, responsibility, and authority as defined by the BC governance infrastructure, all BC education and awareness must adapt accordingly. For example, the higher a stakeholder is in a hierarchy, the less in-depth knowledge of BC tools and techniques is in a presentation and the subject is treated strategically. The people having to build plans or participating as a recovery team member, however, will require education and awareness of detail relevant to their specific circumstances.

Prepare Lesson Plans

After determining the stakeholders and topics, the next activity is to identify content. These are lesson plans for each training topic. Not only do these lesson plans describe the purpose, goals, and objectives of the training, but also they identify the content. You can then tailor the lesson plans to the needs of the applicable stakeholders to reflect the necessary breadth and depth. For example, an executive will receive a different level of education and awareness as opposed to someone in the operational trenches.

Create Material

The content for each education and awareness presentation is developed during this process. The material should provide an overview of the content and then burrow down into the applicable level of details, depending on the audience. As with all presentation material, it should be clear, concise, accurate, useful, and flow logically. It should also contain content applicable to the stakeholders' work environment. Often, these general topics are covered to one degree or another in an integrated fashion: BC, emergency response, and BP. Any additional applicable material may be added. In addition, you should ensure that all presentations are available to all key stakeholders for future reference.

Determine Media

The delivery methods depend on the complexity of the material, geographical dispersion of the stakeholders, availability of compatible technology, and time for delivery. In today's environment, education and awareness presentation can be delivered in a classroom, in a webinar, or on a DVD. The point is that the material is communicated efficiently and effectively in the right format at the right time in the right amount using the appropriate delivery method.

Build Delivery Schedule

Two sets of delivery schedules are needed. One is for building, testing, and maintaining BP plans. Another schedule is needed for training on topics like BC, emergency response, BP, supply chain resiliency, and risk management. The delivery of these presentations can occur on a regular schedule as well as be made available on an ad hoc basis. Stakeholders can receive training as a group or ad hoc, such as during sessions like lunch and learns (whereby people eat lunch and listen to speakers on topics) or staff meetings.

Deliver Education and Awareness Material

The moment of truth arrives. Seminars and workshops are delivered to key stakeholders at various levels of the organizational hierarchy of a company. Education and awareness may be delivered during the building, testing, and maintaining of BP plans. Repeat: the goal is to distribute the knowledge and message to the right people at the right time in the right amount using the right delivery method. The BC governance infrastructure should integrate its messages with the education and awareness presentations to ensure communicating consistently and maintaining credibility with all key stakeholders.

Apply Project Management (Closing)

This activity involves validating the completion of the performance measurement baseline and addressing all administrative, financial, and contractual concerns or issues prior to concluding the project.

Deliverables

The primary deliverables for building education and awareness are:

- Requirements
- Materials
- Delivery

Requirements include topics and delivery methods; materials include lesson plans, presentation slides, and checklists; and delivery includes actual presentations given to specific audiences according to a schedule.

Stakeholders

The BC project or program manager has overall responsibility to ensure that education and awareness occurs throughout a company or organization.

Role	Board of Directors	BC Steering Committee	Business Continuity Working Group	BC Project Manager/Program Manager	BC Specialists/ Staff Support	Business Process Owner/Senior Management	Recovery Team Leader (Operational)	Recovery Team Members (Operational)	Audit	Customers	Suppliers/Vendors	Shareholders
Tasks												
Build education and awareness												
Manage project for building education and awareness		I	C,I	R,A								
Determine requirements to build education and awareness		A	C,I	R	A							
Build education and awareness materials		I	C,I	R	A							
Deliver education and awareness materials				R	A	I	I	I	I	I	I	I
Apply project management (closing)	I	I	C,I	R	A				I			I

Legend
R = Responsible
A = Accountable
C = Consult
I = Inform

FIGURE 6.6
RACI chart for building education and awareness.

Because education and awareness covers many strategic topics as well as standards and guidelines for conducting a BIA as well as building, testing, and maintaining BP plans, the BC project or program manager works closely with senior executives and the BC steering committee by consulting them on the orientation and content of the presentation materials. Then, the supporting infrastructure, which helped him or her to build the materials, starts to deliver at the operational levels. In other words, "out in the field." Responsibilities for stakeholders can be described in a RACI chart, such as the one shown in Figure 6.6.

Integration of Activities

All the activities described must work together to produce and deliver an effective education and awareness for developing, deploying, and maintaining effective BC throughout an organization. Key stakeholders, such as the steering committee in the BC governance infrastructure, provide the necessary guidance and direction for education and awareness. They provide strategies, goals, and objectives that provide the basis for determining the topics. Each topic lays the groundwork to prepare the lesson plans, create the material, determine the media, and then tailor the material for specific stakeholders. During the course of all this work, the governance infrastructure determines the levels of effort and builds a delivery schedule. A proposal package, touching on all the activities at a high level, is usually presented to the steering committee for final review and approval. Assuming approval, the infrastructure can deliver the education and awareness modules.

FINAL THOUGHTS

BC requires governance. However, governance requires PM to become a reality. Without governance, BC will languish and likely fail. BC governance provides the cohesion; PM provides the glue that identifies the parts and seals them all together through integration and interdependence. The result is a BC governance program focusing on strategies, goals, and objectives making an organization resilient.

CASE STUDY

Background

Founded in 1964 and located in Tukwila, Washington, Rainier Wines for the Masses, Inc. (RWM, Inc.) specializes in blended wines for popular consumption throughout the world. Currently, its annual production of blended wines is 750,000 cases. RWM, Inc. has over 8000 employees and generates revenues of approximately $1.3 billion. RWM, Inc. is located in the southern Puget Sound region between Seattle and Tacoma, closer to the latter. It has access to major interstates: Interstate (I) 405 and I5 as well as State Routes (SR) 161, 164, and 167.

All of its wines are made from grapes procured from several appellations (official wine grape growing regions) in Washington State. In the United States, appellations are referred to as American Viticultural Areas (AVA). The vineyards from these AVAs provide a wide assortment of grapes to create a popular blend of red and white wines at very reasonable prices. RWM, Inc. procures a wide variety of grapes: Riesling, Chardonnay, Cabernet Sauvignon, Merlot, Syrah, Sauvignon Blanc, Viognier, Madeline Angevin, Muller-Thur-Grau, Siegerrebe, and Malbec. These grape varieties come from the following appellations and corresponding sub-appellations: Puget Sound, Columbia Valley (Horse Heaven Hills, Lake Chelan, Rattlesnake Hills, Red Mountain, Snipes Mountain, Wahluke Slope), Walla Walla Valley, Yakima Valley, and Columbia Gorge.

The wide variety of soils that exists among these AVAs allows for the growing and harvesting of these many different grapes. The Puget Sound AVA soil type is mainly glacial till that enables growing grapes like Madeline Angevin and Siegerrebe, whereas the Columbia Valley with its soil types of windblown loess, sand silts, and loams produces a wide spectrum of grapes from Riesling to Cabernet Sauvignon while Yakima Valley with its soils of loess, sandy silt, and loam grows Merlot and Riesling.

Unfortunately, such wonders of Mother Nature do not come without some risks. RWM, Inc. is located in the middle of a large earthquake zone as well as close to the base of Mt. Rainier, which may erupt at any time. The valley is also subject to flooding from the nearby rivers but just as threatening is the Howard Hanson Dam with its potential to burst. If an earthquake hits, international sales and distribution are also threatened because of the impact to the Ports of Tacoma and Seattle. The AVAs are also threatened by fire, drought, extreme cold, and pestilence from time to time. Other factors, such as the exercise of immigration policies, which result in deportation of seasonal workers, or illnesses threatening their health due to poor living conditions, can also potentially impact AVAs. Foreign firms may "dump" cheap blended wines of equivalent quality on the market at cheaper prices. Finally, RWM, Inc. is the envy of the wine industry, having automated computer-controlled equipment to prepare white or red blended wines. Just about all operations for its fortified, blended wines and its highly acclaimed rose wines rely on computing technology to deliver products quickly and competitively priced. Recently, the company has been the target of hackers, domestically and abroad.

These are just some natural and man-made threats looming in the background that are finally starting to keep the BoD at RWM, Inc. awake at night. Lessons learned from recent earthquake activity in Napa Valley in California have especially augmented their fears about being vulnerable. Fear of inaccessibility to resources and the collapse of the transportation infrastructure have shaken the BoD and they now believe the long practice of self-insurance for recovery is no longer relevant or adequate; more robust reliable action is necessary to ensure greater resiliency.

As a result, the BoD has decided to act by making RWM, Inc. more resilient in the face of many threats. It has decided to establish a BC program that emphasizes developing and testing of a series of BP plans. The BoD has established a steering committee and appointed a senior project manager to institute a governance infrastructure and a comprehensive education and training program.

Project Management

A project charter, a statement of work, and an organizational structure, shown in Appendices A, B, and Figure 6.7, respectively, have been approved by the key sponsor, program manager, and steering committee members.

The project manager, Linda Steinhauser, developed a PM plan for the entire project. This document articulated the overall processes, procedures, disciplines, and strategies to increase the resilience of the company. The steering committee approved the PM plan. The PM plan included an enterprise high-level bar chart and a responsibility assignment matrix (RAM), shown in Figures 6.8 and 6.9.

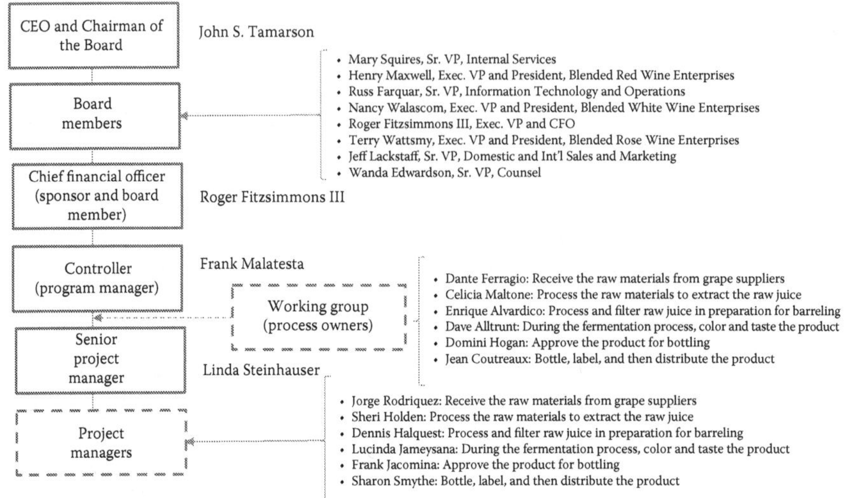

FIGURE 6.7
Organizational structure.

The steering committee provided funding for labor and nonlabor resources to make up the core team, which included six part-time project managers provided by internal services and other subject matter experts familiar with each of the six major processes for the company and their corresponding process owners:

- Process A: Receive the raw materials from grape suppliers. Process Owner: Dante Ferragio
- Process B: Process the raw materials to extract the raw juice. Process Owner: Celicia Maltone
- Process C: Process and filter raw juice in preparation for barreling. Process Owner: Dave Alltrunt
- Process D: During the fermentation process, color and taste the product. Process Owner: Domini Hogan
- Process E: Approve the product for bottling. Process Owner: Enrique Alvaridico
- Process F: Bottle, label, and then distribute the product. Process Owner: Jean Coutreaux

Steinhauser then quickly assembled her team to work with the process owners, listed above, by assigning them to each of the above processes. The processes and the corresponding process owners (senior managers

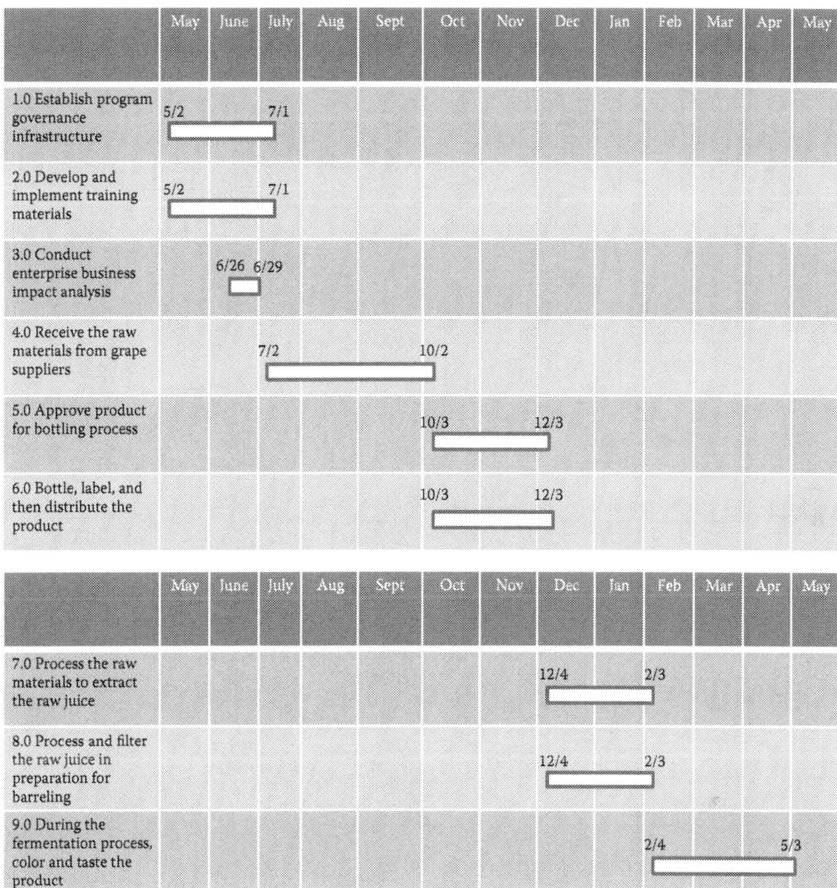

FIGURE 6.8
Enterprise high-level bar chart.

reporting to a vice president) were identified during a Lean initiative about two years ago. The process owners can designate a representative or liaison to serve on a working group. Each process owner is a senior manager.

The steering committee prioritized the processes according to the mission statement developed for RWM, Inc.

Mission Statement

Mission

To remain the premier global providers of blended and fortified wines from the Pacific Northwest.

	Malatesta	Steinhauser	Ferragio	Maltone	Alvardico	Hogan	Alltrunt	Coutreaux	Working Group	Steering Committee
1.0 Establish governance infrastructure	I	R,A	I	I	I	I	I	I	C	I
2.0 Develop and implement training	I	R,A	I	I	I	I	I	I	C	I
3.0 Conduct enterprise impact analysis	I	R,A	I	I	I	I	I	I	C	I
4.0 Receive the raw materials grape suppliers		C,I	R,A						C	I
5.0 Approve product for bottling		C,I		R,A					C	I
6.0 Bottle, label, and then distribute the product		C,I			R,A				C	I
7.0 Process raw materials to extract raw juice		C,I				R,A			C	I
8.0 Process and filter the raw juice in preparation for bottling		C,I					R,A		C	I
9.0 During the fermentation process, color and taste the product		C,I						R,A	C	I

Legend
R = Responsible
A = Accountable
C = Consult
I = Inform

FIGURE 6.9
Enterprise high-level RACI chart.

Goals

- To provide timely production and distribution of wines applying the latest information technology
- To enhance growth in global markets
- To produce and distribute fine quality wines at reasonable prices to the general public
- To sustain efficient and effective supply chain

Applying a forced choice technique, the steering committee determined the order of priority for processes to develop, test, and maintain BP plans. The order of priority precedence is (from most to least)

- Priority #1: Receive the raw materials from grape suppliers.
- Priority #2: Approve the product for bottling.
- Priority #3: Bottle, label, and then distribute the product.
- Priority #4: Process the raw materials to extract the raw juice.
- Priority #5: Process and filter the raw juice in preparation for barreling.
- Priority #6: During the fermentation process, color and taste the product.

The steering committee suggested that Priority 1 occur first and serve as a "prototype," followed by Priorities 2 and 3 occurring concurrently, followed again by Priorities 4 and 5 occurring concurrently, and concluding with Priority 6.

Steinhauser assigned project managers from internal services to be responsible for developing and testing each of their respective BP plans; she created a RACI chart (Figure 6.10).

Before beginning work on each project, Steinhauser drafted a high-level WBS for the project reflecting the input from the project managers and members of the working group. The high-level WBS reflected the following standard WBS for the project:

1.0 Establish program governance infrastructure (Tier 1)
2.0 Develop and implement training materials
3.0 Conduct enterprise business impact analysis (eBIA)
    3.1 Schedule two-hour eBIA session (Tier 2)
    3.2 Prepare for eBIA session
    3.3 Conduct eBIA session
    3.4 Review results of eBIA session

	Jorge Rodriquez	Frank Jacomina	Sharon Smythe	Sheri Holden	Dennis Halquest	Lucinda Jameysana
4.0 Receive the raw materials from grape suppliers	R,A	C	I	I	I	I
5.0 Approve the product for bottling	C,I	R,A	C	I	I	I
6.0 Bottle, label, and then distribute the product	I	C,I	R,A	C,I	I	I
7.0 Process the raw materials to extract the raw juice	I	I	I	R,A	C,I	I
8.0 Process and filter the raw juice in preparation for barreling	I	I	C,I	I	R,A	C,I
9.0 During the fermentation process, color and taste the product	I	I	I	I	C,I	R,A

Legend
R = Responsible
A = Accountable
C = Consult
I = Inform

FIGURE 6.10
RACI chart for build and test.

- 4.0 Receive the raw materials from grape suppliers' process
  - 4.1 Build BP plan
  - 4.2 Test BP plan
  - 4.3 Establish process for maintaining BP plan
- 5.0 Approve the product for bottling process
  - 5.1 Build BP plan
  - 5.2 Test BP plan
  - 5.3 Establish process for maintaining BP plan
- 6.0 Bottle, label, and then distribute the product
  - 6.1 Build BP plan
  - 6.2 Test BP plan
  - 6.3 Establish process for maintaining BP plan
- 7.0 Process the raw materials to extract the raw juice
  - 7.1 Build BP plan
  - 7.2 Test BP plan
  - 7.3 Establish process for maintaining BP plan
- 8.0 Process and filter the raw juice in preparation for barreling
  - 8.1 Build BP plan
  - 8.2 Test BP plan
  - 8.3 Establish process for maintaining BP plan

9.0 During the fermentation process, color and taste the product
  9.1 Build BP plan
  9.2 Test BP plan
  9.3 Establish process for maintaining BP plan

The team then developed a high-level schedule based on the WBS at the Tier 2 level.

Steinhauser reflected the WBS and schedule in a build and test bar chart, shown in Figure 6.11.

Each project manager was responsible to create a PM plan for their respective projects, ensuring that everything supported the overall PM plan. They also completed their own PM plan. The WBS for each project had the same contents for consistency in data collection and reporting. The project managers were expected to use the WBS to build a schedule to plan and track performance using a common software package.

Enterprise Business Impact Analysis

Steinhauser conducted a kick-off meeting with the project managers, members of the working group, and other interested stakeholders. This 2-hour session reviewed at a high level the entire PM plan, set expectations, and authored work to begin. Following is the agenda for the meeting:

Save Our Wine (SOW) project

Kick Off Meeting

May 2, 20xx

Agenda

Leaders: Linda Steinhauser

Location: Vino Conference Room, Bldg. 234-21

Telecom: (xxx) xxx-xxxx

I. Introductory remarks	Roger Fitzsimmons III
II. Background information	Frank Malatesta
III. Overview of charter	Linda Steinhauser

a. Purpose
b. Description
c. Major deliverables
d. Assumptions
e. Acceptance criteria
f. Milestone
g. Constraints
h. Costs
i. Risks

	July	Aug	Sept	Oct
4.1 Conduct business impact analysis for process	7/2 7/23			
4.1.1 Prepare for conducting business impact analysis	7/2 7/8			
4.1.2 Conduct business impact analysis	7/9 7/15			
4.1.3 Analyze results of business impact analysis	7/18 7/21			
4.1.4 Report on business impact analysis	7/22			
4.2 Build business preparedness plan	7/23		9/11	
4.2.1 Prepare for building business preparedness plan	7/23 8/1			

	July	Aug	Sept	Oct
4.2.2 Define requirements for building business preparedness plan	7/23 8/1			
4.2.3 Draft business preparedness plan		8/2	9/4	
4.2.4 Review business preparedness plan			9/5 9/10	
4.2.5 Distribute business preparedness plan			9/11	
4.3 Test business preparedness plan			9/12	10/2
4.3.1 Prepare for testing business preparedness plan			9/13 9/20	
4.3.2 Conduct testing			9/21	

	July	Aug	Sept	Oct
4.3.3 Report on testing results			9/22 10/2	
4.3.4 Schedule follow up on testing recommendations				10/2

FIGURE 6.11
Build and test bar chart.

IV. Overview of statement of work	Linda Steinhauser
V. Questions & answers/round robin	Linda Steinhauser
VI. Next Steps	Linda Steinhauser

Steinhauser invited the project managers reporting to her and members of the working group as well as the steering committee members to attend an eBIA session. The result was a list of potential risks, their prioritization, and their impact on the entire enterprise. The identified risks are:

- Bacterial spoilage
- Chemical spills
- Collapse of transportation infrastructure
- Dam collapse
- Disruption of information systems
- Earthquake
- Economic recession/depression
- Financial failure of supplier
- Flooding
- Foreign dumping of blended wines in the market
- Frost/cold temperatures
- Immigration restrictions
- Inability to self-insure
- Inaccessibility to resources
- Insect infestations
- Lack of social acceptance of alcohol
- Overproduction
- Poor soil fertility
- Shortage of fungicides/herbicides
- Social instability
- Unpredictable climate change

The risks were reflected in a table reflecting priority, corresponding likelihood, and impact on each process for managing the enterprise-wide risks, shown in Figure 6.12.

With the eBIA complete, the project's infrastructure in place, and the training materials built, Steinhauser then had Rodriquez start work with the process owner, Dante Ferragio, for the first process: Receive the raw material from grape suppliers.

Threat ID	Criticality	Threat	Likelihood	Impact	Risk Rating (Likelihood × Impact)	Process Impacted	Comments
1	Low	Bacterial spoilage	1	3	3	A	Procurement, Production
2	Low	Chemical spills	1	3	3	A	Procurement, Production
3	Medium	Collapse of transportation infrastructure	3	5	15	A,F	Procurement, Financial, Production, Distribution
4	Medium	Dam collapse	3	5	15	A,F	Procurement, Financial, Production, Distribution
5	High	Major earthquake	5	5	25	A,B,C,D,E,F	Procurement, Financial, Production, Distribution
6	High	Economic recession/ depression	4	5	20	A,F	Financial, Legal, Marketing & Sales
7	Medium	Financial failure of supplier	4	4	16	A,F	Procurement, Production, Distribution, Marketing & Sales
8	Medium	Flooding	3	5	15	A	Procurement, Financial, Production, Distribution
9	Medium	Foreign dumping of blended wines on market	4	5	15	F	Financial, Distribution, Sales & Marketing
10	Medium	Frost/cold temperatures	3	5	15	A	Procurement, Production
11	Medium	Immigration restrictions	2	5	10	A	Public Relations, Legal, Financial, Production, Procurement

FIGURE 6.12
Enterprise-wide risks.

(Continued)

12	Medium	Inability to self-insure	3	5	15	A,B,C,D,E,F	Legal, Financial, Production
13		Inaccessibility to resources other than grapes	3	3	9	A,B,C,F	Procurement, Production
14	Medium	Insect infestation	2	5	10	A	Procurement, Production
15	Low	Lack of social acceptance of alcohol	1	5	5	F	Public Relations, Legal, Financial, Marketing & Sales
16	Medium	Overproduction	3	5	15	A	Procurement, Production
17	Low	Poor soil fertility	1	5	5	A	Procurement, Production
18	Low	Shortage of fungicides / herbicides	1	1	1	A	Procurement, Production
19	Low	Social instability	1	1	1	F	Procurement, Financial
20	High	Unpredictable climate change	5	5	25	A	Procurement, Financial, Production
21	High	Disruption of information systems	5	5	25	A,B,C,D,E,F	Procurement, Financial, Production, Distribution

Legend

Likelihood & Impact		Process
5	High	A: Receive the raw materials from grape suppliers
4	Medium to High	B: Process the raw materials to extract the raw juice
3	Medium	C: Process and filter raw juice in preparation for barrelling
2	Low to Medium	D: During the fermentation process, color and taste the product
1	Low	E: Approve the product for bottling
		F: Bottle, label, and then distribute the product

FIGURE 6.12 (CONTINUED)
Enterprise-wide risks.

GETTING STARTED CHECKLIST

Question	Yes	No
1. When establishing a governance infrastructure, have you considered these concepts?		
Obtain buy-in from key stakeholders at the executive level		
Establish a performance measurement baseline		
Communicate vertically and laterally		
Focus on the vision		
Identify roles and responsibilities		
Document processes		
Provide the necessary tools to develop and maintain plans		
Make sure the vision for the project aligns with the one for the parent organization		
Hire competent support staff		
Provide ongoing training to the support staff		
2. When establishing a governance infrastructure, are you realizing these benefits?		
Providing efficient and effective oversight of the BC project		
Encouraging implementation of BC throughout the company		
Defining roles and responsibilities		
Providing common guidelines, standards, tools, and methodology		
Enhancing communications among stakeholders		
Providing change management		
Addressing corporate issues, concerns, etc.		
Providing guidelines on risk management and prioritization		
Providing a cross-functional perspective		
Overseeing the application of policies, processes, procedures, and methodologies		
Reviewing and evaluating recommendations for improvement		
Identifying and adopting guidelines and standards as well as complying uniformly with laws, regulations, rulings, etc.		
Clarifying expectations about BC and BP		
Taking proactive responses toward implementing and sustaining BC throughout the company		
3. When establishing a governance infrastructure, have you considered how to address these challenges?		
Keeping all stakeholders engaged and not just the important ones		
Making timely decisions		
Ensuring availability of sufficient time and resources		
Resolving conflict		

4. When establishing a governance infrastructure, have you considered these activities to perform?
   Identify key stakeholders
   Establish an organizational structure
   Identify critical business processes
   Develop BP strategies
   Communicate strategies and decisions
   Prepare the business case for BC and BP
   Identify roles, responsibilities, and authorities (RAA)
   Develop policies, applicable processes, and procedures
   Adopt a BC methodology and supporting standards
   Select tools
   Develop and manage a portfolio of projects
5. When establishing a governance infrastructure, have you considered PM deliverables to produce, including the following?
   Charter
   WBS
   Time estimates
   Cost estimates
   Network diagram
   Multi-tier schedules
   Responsibility assignment matrices
   Status collection and analysis
   Reports
   Change and configuration management procedures
6. When developing BC education and awareness, have you considered performing these activities?
   Determine affected stakeholders
   Determine strategies, goals, and objectives
   Determine topics
   Tailor material for specific audiences
   Prepare lessons learned
   Create material
   Determine media
   Build delivery schedule
   Determine level of effort
   Deliver education and awareness material

7

Conduct the Business Impact Analysis

With the governance infrastructure in place, the actual work of developing business preparedness (BP) plans can begin. The first action is to conduct what is known as the business impact analysis (BIA).

WHAT IS A BUSINESS IMPACT ANALYSIS?

The BIA is a process that requires analyzing all the operations within an organization to identify critical business processes and the impact of realized risks, or threats, upon them. The BIA can occur at two levels: strategic and within each critical business process. The BIA begins first at the strategic level, such as among the members of the steering committee. Then, each of the critical business processes conducts a BIA, leveraging the output of the BIA at the strategic level. Conducting a BIA is essentially the same at both levels, with the exception of capitalizing on the output of the BIA performed at the strategic level.

GOALS

The BIA has several goals.

Identify Critical Business Processes for the Overall Organization

The guidance and direction of the steering committee can help in this regard. The committee consists of executives with responsibilities for business processes and functions and has knowledge of strategic plans. Many members will also likely have participated in an enterprise risk management (ERM) exercise, such as those based on the use of the Committee of Sponsoring Organizations model, which provides additional information and background to which ordinary employees often lack access. Additionally, many companies have also documented their processes through Lean initiatives and maturity models, thereby providing important information. Identifying critical business processes can become easier by leveraging this information and experience, thereby serving as a guide for the enterprise BIA and the one for each critical business process.

Establish the Relationship between the Risks and the Critical Business Processes

The steering committee identifies and maps the relationships of the critical business processes and risks in the form of a two- or multidimensional matrix. The matrix consists of a forced ranking of the critical business processes among each other and the same for the risks, reflecting the priority from most to least important. This matrix guides each critical business process as it performs its own BIA, if necessary. Within each cell is a code representing the strategies to address the risk should it occur. Alternatively, it might reflect the degree of relationship between the relevant critical business process and a risk.

Assess the Impact of the Risks That Affect the Critical Business Processes

These risks can involve a wide range of topics. They can have an economic or a financial impact, such as a decline in stock price or profitability; a legal impact, such as a violation of federal procurement laws; a public relations impact, such as devastation to the environment; an operational impact, such as a delay in production; market risk, such as loss of competitive leadership; and many others. The point is that understanding the impact of risks enables a company to respond, rather than react, to a risk if and when it becomes a threat whether at the enterprise-wide or critical business process levels.

Determine the Firing Order of the Critical Business Processes to Prepare Their BP Plans

Not all processes are on an equal level; some are more critical than others are. The most critical ones should have their plans built and tested first. This decision allows concentrating resources, such as time and people, on what matters most to the resiliency of the company.

TERMINOLOGY

The BIA involves some BC terminology that necessitates a definition upfront.

The *maximum allowable downtime* (MAD) is the total time a process or dependency can be unavailable before it negatively impacts the performance of a critical business function. Once the downtime reaches that specific point in time, the critical business process feels the pain of an event; recovery actions should then commence.

A *business impact analysis* (BIA), described earlier, is a process to determine the priority of a critical business process, the relevant risks, and the corresponding qualitative or quantitative impacts of a disruption. The BIA provides guidelines to determine when to initiate recovery procedures, identified in a BP plan.

A *BP plan*, described earlier, is a document capturing the necessary information to guide recovery teams and enhance the ability of a critical business process or organization to recover from a disruptive event. The plan includes lists of the members of the recovery team and their roles and responsibilities; the resources (also referred to as dependencies) to enhance recovery and the time required for their availability; and instructions on executing a call tree.

A *critical business process* consists of activities the BC executive steering committee requires for an acceptable level of performance and, if a disruptive event occurs, necessitates faster recovery than if it is a non-critical business process. A critical business process is sometimes called a mission critical or vital business process. Critical business processes are identified at the strategic level; they may also further be sub-divided into multiple sub-processes deemed critical and BP plans are developed accordingly; a plan is then developed, tested, and maintained.

BENEFITS

There are five key benefits for conducting the BIA, whether at the strategic or operational levels.

Identifying and Prioritizing Critical Business Processes and Establishing Priority

It identifies the criticality of the critical business processes relative to one another. Not all processes are equal based upon their impact; likewise, not all functions within a critical process are equal, some are more important than others are during recovery. Keep in mind that a business process can still be important to the resiliency of a company but its impact is less in terms of recovery.

Taking a Holistic Perspective

Whether at the strategic or critical business process levels, key stakeholders must not only determine the impact of risks to their own process but also to other processes and even to the entire company. A big-picture perspective is necessary especially when involving many organizational silos.

Determining the Degree of Integration among All the Processes

The resiliency or the failure to recover requires determining all the dependent relationships that exist among all the critical business processes and within each one. The fact is most critical business processes are not independent islands.

Marrying Strategic and Operational Perspectives

The BIA helps executive leadership and senior management apply a holistic perspective for BC while the lower levels have a narrow focus at the critical business process level. The strategic BIA aligns with the critical business process and vice versa to ensure that a symmetrical relationship exists between both levels. This relationship allows resiliency to roll up to higher levels to enable alignment with the operational environment.

Communicating Better between the Strategic and Operational Levels

The strategic level sometimes operates in a vacuum and the operational or critical business processes go their separate ways. The BIA causes dialogue vertically and horizontally; the issues of risk and impact and other topics often transcend a single level or process within a company. Key stakeholders must engage in a dialogue on what risks confront the company and the impacts to their critical business processes. Additionally, it encourages communication on how best to recover from an event.

CHALLENGES

Despite the significant benefits of a BIA, several challenges confront it during its implementation and execution.

Determining the Interviewees to Participate in the BIA

At the strategic level, this challenge is necessary to determine the critical business processes for a company. Easier said than done when everyone thinks his or her process is critical. Even more difficult is identifying the executive owner of a critical business process. In many companies, not everyone has an idea of what is a critical business process, let alone those that exist in their company. Sometimes, even if they know, they do not know an owner for each critical business process. In this regard, the executive steering committee can play an important role. After assembling its members, the committee determines the critical business processes.

At the critical business process level, senior leadership conducts the BIA to determine which sub-processes require a BP plan. Output from the BIA done by the BC in this regard should provide the guidance and direction needed to conduct a BIA within a critical business process. The BIA for the critical business process can fill in the details.

Collecting the Right Data to Generate the Right Information

This challenge appears at both the strategic and operational levels. It is not as easy as one thinks. Data may reside across multiple legacy systems.

Data may be so protected by some organizations it is almost impossible to obtain, perhaps due to rivalry among organizations or being proprietary in nature. Such data may be of little relevance to the BIA.

Determining a consistent approach or methodology to conduct a BIA ensures that the results from each BIA at the critical business process level can be rolled up to the enterprise strategic level. It can also help to conduct a comparative analysis of the results of each BIA to ascertain if any significant findings, trends, or best practices exist.

Distinguishing between Assumptions and Facts

An assumption is treated as real until proven otherwise; facts are irrefutable bits of data allowing the generation of information. The difficulty, of course, is achieving a level that people feel confident distinguishing assumption from fact. This decision is not easy during a BIA because stakeholders view a fact as an assumption and another stakeholder views an assumption as fact. Project managers facilitating a BIA session should strive early to obtain consensus, and even agreement, over what is an assumption vs. a fact.

Resolving Conflict

Conflict may arise over what business processes are critical, what risks are important and their impacts, and what are assumptions vs. facts. For the BIA to succeed, whether at the strategic or critical business process levels, consensus—meaning understanding, acceptance, and support—must prevail at a minimum if BP plans can be built having complete buy-in from key stakeholders over their respective critical business process.

Overcoming Silo Thinking

In a traditional hierarchical organization reflected in functional stovepipes, for example, marketing, accounting, and information systems, taking a cross-functional perspective is difficult at best. Functional silos tend to protect their territory and view cross-functional perspectives as limiting their options and reducing their importance. Unless a company adopts Lean principles and practices, which emphasize providing value to the customer, many silos retreat into their own world. This challenge often surfaces during a BIA at the strategic level. At the critical business

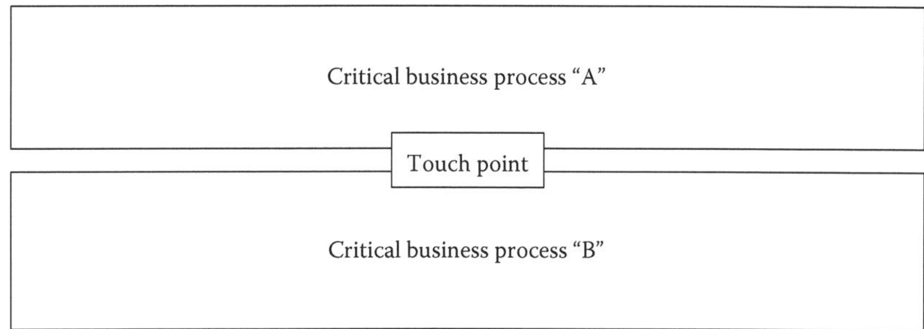

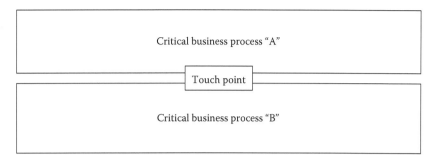

FIGURE 7.1
Touch points among critical business processes.

process level, the challenge may surface if certain functional areas supporting it have a history of not working well together. The best approach for overcoming this challenge is to have joint BC education and awareness sessions and to encourage identifying common touch points in the BP plan (refer to Figure 7.1). A common touch point occurs when two or more processes rely on one another to accomplish their goals and objectives.

KEY CONCEPTS

To effectively conduct a BIA, project managers need to understand and apply several concepts.

Identify Dependencies

A dependency is a resource needed to enhance the recovery of a critical business process. A dependency can be either internal or external to a critical business process. The list is often endless but here are a few examples:

- Equipment
- Facilities
- IT systems and applications
- People
- Records
- Supplies/materials
- Transportation
- Voice communications

For the BIA, your best approach is to identify the categories necessary for recovery. After identifying those categories, then determine the qualitative characteristics and the quantities of those resources required for recovery. Keep in mind the qualitative characteristics and quantities are not for full operational, pre-event levels. Rather, the qualitative characteristics and quantities are requirements for recovery and providing the minimum level of production or services.

Use Quantitative and Qualitative Data and Information (and Assumptions)

During the BIA, focus on facts and data to make decisions on what is needed to recover critical business processes. However, it is also important to identify and operate on assumptions just as long as they are treated as just that—assumptions. Distinguishing among data, information, and assumptions will impact decision making during a BIA. Unfortunately, avoid the tendency to treat assumptions like facts and data; it can lead to errors in judgment, such as distinguishing between processes deemed critical and ones that are not. The same idea applies to risk assessment.

Use Tables, Matrices, Graphs, and Charts

These tools are useful to sort, compile, analyze, assess, and present information. Give preference to displaying information in matrices, graphs, and charts. Usually, tables and charts are the most amenable to executive and senior managers. You should collect data and information for analysis after the BIA. You should also consider standardizing the display and use of these tools, striving for consistency, accuracy, and understandability of content.

Document Results

While self-explanatory, many BIA sessions, possibly because they were conducted superficially, lack sufficient historical information to reference later when trying to understand why a critical business process was chosen as one and any other useful information for making a decision. Ideally, two BC professionals should participate in a BIA. The project manager conducts the session while the other one takes notes but occasionally interjects insights or comments.

Use a Combination of Data Gathering, Questionnaires, and Interviewing for the BIA

Preparation is crucial for a successful BIA. Collecting as much data prior to the session will enhance the value of the results. Data gathering in advance enables developing useful questions prior to the session. For example, data gathering might cover the past performance of critical business processes, other risk assessments conducted elsewhere in the company, reviewing strategic and operational plans, and uncovering issues and concerns. The same can be said for sending questionnaires out and conducting interviews prior to the session; these tools can reveal or corroborate information. During the session, be mindful to identify any unique information that is often overlooked; such information is often found during the BIA.

Apply Risk Analysis and Assessment Information

A risk analysis and assessment is usually conducted by the BC steering committee and is predicated frequently on enterprise risk assessments conducted for the board of directors (BoD) or the audit committee; the BC steering committee uses the results to conduct risk management from a BC perspective. Within the critical business process, members of its leadership team apply the risk management output from the steering committee and then tailor it to their unique circumstances. Often the owners of the plans, subject matter experts, and other managers attend the risk session to determine what sub-processes will be impacted by the risks and, if necessary, identify appropriate responses. The output from the BIA is then used to develop the BP plans.

For Each Critical Business Process, Determine the Recovery Time Objective and, if Applicable, the Recovery Point Objective

All processes will likely experience some disruption to a certain degree from an event. However, there is a certain threshold point where the disruption can have a deteriorating effect on a process, reflecting the MAD. That threshold point could be in hours, days, weeks, or months, depending on the scale used in the plan. The risk analysis and assessment will serve as a gauge to determine what that point is, which is known as the recovery time objective (RTO). There is also a threshold point for the recovery of important systems that support a critical process, whereby a system can be down so long and then a recovery of the data becomes imperative to deliver a product or service. Again, the risk analysis and assessment will provide a gauge as to what that point is, known as the recovery point objective (RPO). Keep in mind the RTO and RPO serve as targets for recovery and are not the same as the MAD.

Restrict the Length of Time and the Number of People for the BIA Session

A BIA can generate considerable interest among stakeholders. After all, a decision will be made, especially at the strategic level, on what processes are considered critical. Many people construe being deemed noncritical as being dispensable. Not in the context of the BIA. Being critical simply means a process is required to provide minimum services to recover from an event. The larger the company, the greater the challenge exists to restrict the attendees and the length of time. At the critical business process level, a BIA will not be as unwieldy because it usually includes fewer people. Whether at the strategic or critical business process level, however, it is essential for the BC project manager and other BC professionals to come prepared to these sessions. A standard agenda should exist; tools, such as spreadsheets and forms, should be ready to capture information. Additionally, you should identify the roles and responsibilities, for example, who will facilitate the session and who will take minutes. After the session, expeditiously share the results with the key stakeholders.

Take a Multidisciplinary, Holistic Perspective during the Session

The BIA requires taking a big-picture perspective, whether at the strategic or critical business process level. The inability to take such a perspective can lead to key oversights that could imperil recovery. Critical business processes more often than not transcend a single function and involve many people at different levels inside and, in some cases today, outside the company. This level of complexity requires keeping an open mind and maintaining a broad background. Business and technical risks and issues, for example, are tightly interwoven as many Lean initiatives. Attendees at the BIA session should represent a good cross-section of an organization or critical business processes, possess a wide knowledge, and have the responsibility and authority to make decisions. Solid representation will also enable identification of important touch points among critical business processes.

Remember the Primary Goal Is to Save the Company

The focus is in the best interests of the company, not one critical business process. If the company fails, everyone fails by losing profits as well as losing livelihoods. Silo thinking sometimes overcomes people or organizations for many reasons, including lack of experience in other areas, or a desire to preserve position or gain additional influence. Left unchecked, such attitudes can have harmful effects on a company. It does not matter if the engine room on a ship is working if no one is bothering to repair the hole in the hull; everyone needs to contribute to recovery or the company sinks.

Remember Not All Processes Are Critical

This decision is a hard one to make. The risk analysis and assessment and the input from key stakeholders will demonstrate not every business process is critical to the recovery of the company. No person or organization wants to consider its contribution as not critical. The BC steering committee should define exactly what a critical process means. The variable playing a key role in the definition is time, determined by answering basic questions like: What is the overall MAD a company can experience before it feels the pain? What is the recovery time objective for a company to achieve recovery?

Time Is the Variable for Ascertaining Criticality

Time is the key determinant to decide what is and is not critical. By using something objective as time, the tension over what processes are critical is largely mollified. Time helps to determine what processes can be down before pain is felt and with that answer comes which business processes to recover to provide the minimum operational performance without impacting the survivability of a company.

Categorize Processes into Degrees of Importance for Recovery

For example, consider having a category "critical" for processes requiring faster recovery, "important" for processes that follow the recovery of the critical ones, and "nonessential" for remaining processes. Categorization helps to determine a firing order for the recovery of processes whether at the strategic or operational level. It also provides a firing order if more than one BP plan within a critical business process exists. For example, determine which plans must be developed and tested first, second, and so on.

Determine the Key Deliverables for the Session

The BIA session must produce certain deliverables for key stakeholders to feel it is of value. These deliverables prove invaluable for recovery by providing the foundation for developing, testing, and maintaining BP plans. The BIA should result in identifying critical business processes, key stakeholders in the recovery of each one, a list of critical resources (also known as dependencies) for recovery, touch points among the various processes and functions, and a list of risks affecting all of the critical business processes. The deliverables should be the same whether the BIA is conducted at the strategic or critical business process levels.

Identify Key Stakeholders to Participate in the BIA

The value of a BIA reflects who participated in it. Therefore, it behooves the project manager to have the right stakeholders participate. While too many participants can stifle a session, the wrong or missing ones can do so as well. The session should include stakeholders who are knowledgeable of the processes discussed in the BIA. At a minimum, these stakeholders should include executives and senior managers, staff members with relevant expertise, suppliers, BC specialists, and customers. Someone from other functional organizations, such as security or legal, might be involved. At the critical business process level, the leadership responsible for a specific business function should participate during all BIA sessions to verify and validate results.

Anticipate What Might Happen during the BIA Session

Initially, stakeholders participating in the session may or may not be receptive to spending an hour or so on BC. They may have more immediate concerns, feel valuable time is taken up on fictitious events, or believe the subject is too abstract to have any value. During the session, some stakeholders may have a difficult time understanding terminology like

BC, business preparedness, recovery, restoration, and MAD. You should take a few moments to prepare an introduction on the subject of BC at a high level and address any issues or concerns before starting. Then, focus on collecting the necessary information for recovery.

Preparation Is Essential

This concept is perhaps the most important one of all. Before conducting a BIA session, whether at the strategic or critical business process level, prepare for it. Preparation includes defining the goals and objectives of the session, determining the approach to take, preparing the tools, for example, spreadsheets, to capture information, identifying the key stakeholders and ascertaining their roles and responsibilities, conducting research on the critical business process in question, and preparing a list of open- and closed-ended questions to ask. This preparation will make it easier to analyze, compile, and communicate information. This preparation also includes determining what information to report to specific stakeholders, defining the level of detail tailored to them, and creating a standardized report format.

MAKING THE BIA HAPPEN

Several activities are required to conduct a successful BIA session. These activities can be grouped into one of five phases, which are described in Figure 7.2.

Manage Project for Conducting BIA

This task involves applying all the PM concepts, tools, and techniques to enhance project performance. For example, it includes preparing a charter, developing a work breakdown structure (WBS), making time and cost estimates, building a schedule, and tracking and monitoring performance.

Prepare for Conducting BIA

Identify Key Stakeholders

For a BIA session, be sure to invite the right stakeholders. Also, ensure all stakeholders understand their roles and responsibilities during the

ID	Task Name	Predecessors
78	1.2 Conduct business impact analysis	
79	1.2.1 Manage project for conducting business impact analysis	
80	1.2.1.1 Apply project management	55,77
81	1.2.2 Prepare for conducting business impact analysis	
82	1.2.2.1 Apply stakeholder guidance and direction	57,75,80
83	1.2.2.2 Identify key stakeholders	82
84	1.2.2.3 Determine and develop a systematic approach	82
85	1.2.2.4 Determine data and information requirements	82
86	1.2.2.5 Prepare tools for data and information collection	82
87	1.2.2.6 Identify organizational entities' vision, mission, goals, and objectives	82
88	1.2.2.7 Collect and review any additional information about an organizational entity	82
89	1.2.2.8 Arrange meeting with key stakeholders	82
90	1.2.3 Conduct business impact analysis	
91	1.2.3.1 Provide background on reasons for session, including its goals and objectives	82,83,84,85,86,87,88,89
92	1.2.3.2 Present high-level review on what is business continuity and associated key concepts	82,83,84,85,86,87,88,89
93	1.2.3.3 Clarify business requirements of the entities' organization	82,83,84,85,86,87,88,89
94	1.2.3.4 Determine scope of session	82,83,84,85,86,87,88,89
95	1.2.3.5 Identify critical business processes	82,83,84,85,86,87,88,89
96	1.2.3.6 Identify key dependencies for each critical business process	82,83,84,85,86,87,88,89
97	1.2.3.7 Apply risk analysis and assessment information	82,83,84,85,86,87,88,89
98	1.2.3.8 Determine maximum allowable downtime, recovery time objective, and recovery point objective for each critical business process	82,83,84,85,86,87,88,89
99	1.2.3.9 Identify touch points among critical business processes	82,83,84,85,86,87,88,89
100	1.2.4 Analyze results of business impact analysis	
101	1.2.4.1 Document results of session	91,92,93,94,95,96,97,98,99
102	1.2.4.2 Compile and analyze data and information	91,92,93,94,95,96,97,98,99

FIGURE 7.2
Work breakdown structure (WBS) for conducting business impact analysis.

(Continued)

103	1.2.4.3 Seek clarification on any data and information	91,92,93,94,95,96,97,98,99
104	1.2.5 Report on business impact analysis	
105	1.2.5.1 Prepare final report on results	101,102,103
106	1.2.5.2 Conduct presentation	101,102,103
107	1.2.6 Schedule for building business preparedness plan	
108	1.2.6.1 Determine firing order of critical business processes	105,106
109	1.2.6.2 Determine milestones for completing business preparedness plans for each critical business process	108
110	1.2.6.3 Publish schedule	109
111	1.2.6.4 Track performance	110
112	1.2.7 Apply project management (closing) for conducting business impact analysis	
113	1.2.7.1 Perform closing tasks	111

FIGURE 7.2 (CONTINUED)
Work breakdown structure (WBS) for conducting business impact analysis.

session. Answer questions like who will speak for which processes? Who will make the final decision on key issues, concerns, or risks? Who will take notes? Who will run the meeting? Who will coordinate the setup of the meeting, including setting up teleconferencing sessions, determining location, and inviting attendees?

Apply Stakeholder Guidance and Direction

The guidance received from the selected stakeholders while establishing the governance infrastructure provided information and concerns to apply during the BIA session at the strategic level. The information provided may include company business goals and objectives, enterprise risks, and strategic and operational issues and concerns. This information will influence the output of the BIA session.

Determine and Develop a Systematic Approach

A BIA should be conducted efficiently and effectively, done so by minimizing the effort required of stakeholders who have other responsibilities. The BIA should acquire only the necessary data and information. One way to achieve both efficiency and effectiveness is to copy the approach of a previous BIA, if one exists, and adapt it to the current BIA session. Another way is to develop an in-house approach to conduct every BIA. Either way, the approach should be unobtrusive by collecting only relevant, useful information consistently and enabling quick decision-making regarding the criticality of processes.

Determine Data and Information Requirements

Data is nothing more than a collection of facts; information is data generated to provide meaning to the recipient. For a BIA session, the data collected should cover topics like scope (including in and out of scope), key stakeholders, major business goals and objectives, pertinent risks and issues and their impact, MAD, RTO, and RPO, major touch points of other critical processes, and major categories of dependencies. Any data and information should be consistently collected during all BIA sessions, whether at the strategic or critical business process levels.

Prepare Tools for Data and Information Collection

With current information technology, tools for data and information collection are much easier. Applications for microcomputers and tablets enable creating forms and spreadsheets to capture and compile data and information at a BIA session. The use of these tools should be oriented toward capturing the data and information requirements at the BIA session. Other tools should include capabilities to hold instant meetings and teleconferencing sessions for participants not physically present during the BIA session.

Identify Organizational Entities' Vision, Mission, Goals, and Objectives

Whether at the strategic or critical business process levels, it is very important to understand the vision, mission, goals, and objectives of the organizations participating in the BIA session. Knowing such information in advance helps to determine a list of questions and other requests to provide before, and during, a BIA session. It also generates insights on what is critical and what are the potential touch points among processes.

Collect and Review Any Additional Information about an Organizational Entity

This data and information covers topics other than the vision, mission, goals, and objectives. It might include a listing of key stakeholders reflected in an organization chart, relevant presentations and reports, contact information, and useful content residing on an internal, or perhaps external, website. In addition, support organizations, such as security, internal audit, and information technology may also have important information, data, and insights about the organizations and processes discussed in the BIA session.

Arrange Meeting with Key Stakeholders

After previous activities, this activity is relatively simple in theory but difficult in reality. The available time to conduct a BIA session should last only one or two hours. The difficulty arises when some stakeholders reside in different geographical locations. Time zones and national holidays are two common challenges along with overcoming technological challenges, such as information systems employing different protocols. It is good practice to send an email or memorandum that provides a short background and description about the BIA session, and attach an agenda.

Conduct BIA

Provide Background on Reasons for Session, Including Its Goals and Objectives

During the BIA session, be sure that participants understand the reasons for the session. Explain the email or memo sent earlier to notify stakeholders about the reasons for the session. Do not be shy about reiterating the content. You have the opportunity to refresh people's memories as well as encourage additional questions, comments, or insights. This portion of the presentation should last only five minutes and might cite passages on the importance of business resiliency from the company's annual report, relevant policies and procedures, or senior executive presentations.

Present High-Level Review on BC and Associated Key Concepts

Some participants may lack an understanding of the rudiments of BC. Refresh their memory or increase their understanding and knowledge.

Remember to keep this short; provide only the basics. Topics might include a definition of BC, its key elements, and their interaction; how a BIA session fits within BC and leads to a more resilient company; and definitions of key terms such as resiliency, recovery, restoration, RTO, RPO, and MAD. This presentation should take no more than 10 to 15 minutes and the material should be covered at a very high level. The session is not meant to turn stakeholders into BC professionals.

Clarify Business Requirements of the Entities' Organization

This activity is simply a verification of the vision, mission, goals, and objectives of the organization or organizations attending the BIA as well as its major roles and responsibilities to deliver products and services to internal and external customers. Since the work environment changes rapidly, information can easily become outdated. Be sure to conduct the BIA using the latest available data and information.

Determine Scope of Session

Focus on what is important during the BIA session. Scoping entails determining what is in and out of scope to assess criticality, which is a challenge. Often it requires a judgment call predicated upon strategic considerations, risks, and other relevant information. The participants can then decide what is in and out of scope. A good approach is first eliminating processes deemed not critical, providing a limited set for inclusion in the scope.

Identify Critical Business Processes

With scoping complete, the difficult task is to assess the criticality of processes relative to each other. Recovery time plays an important determinant in the decision, guided by strategic and risk considerations. The most common approach is to "bucket" processes into categories according to degree of criticality, such as critical, important, and noncritical.

Identify Key Dependencies for Each Critical Business Process

A dependency is a resource, such as people, buildings, or supplies. For recovery of a critical business process, certain types of dependencies and their quantities must be available within a specific time. Without these dependencies, recovery may take longer than necessary or be impossible, jeopardizing resiliency. Several challenges arise when considering dependencies. Where do they come from? Are they shared with other processes? Which processes have priority to receive the dependencies? What if a conflict occurs and, if so, who resolves it?

Apply Risk Analysis and Assessment Information

The enterprise risk analysis serves as a basis to determine the critical business processes that will be impacted by a risk event. However, it serves only as a guide. Each BIA session, especially at the critical business level, should tailor the results to the specific scope. The risks with the greatest applicable likelihood or probability and impact should receive the highest consideration.

Determine MAD, RTO, and RPO for Each Critical Business Process

For all critical business processes, determine the MAD, RTO, and RPO. Ideally, all three of these should support one another; all three variables play an integral role on the road to full recovery, determining when recovery starts and finishes with sufficient dependencies coming onboard. At the BIA session level, these variables are at a high level. When developing BP plans, however, specificity on the needed quantities will be spread over time.

Identify Touch Points among Critical Business Processes

It is important to recognize that some critical business processes are often closely interdependent upon one another during the recovery from an event, such as a disaster. While it makes perfectly good sense initially to treat each plan as independent, it is essential to recognize that many of them do not operate exclusive of each other; rather, some require coordination with critical business processes. Not only does a sequence of critical business processes exist during recovery but also with dependencies. A BIA should try to determine such relationships whenever possible.

Analyze Results of the BIA

Document Results of Session

While software tools should help to document results from a BIA session in real time, some additional work will likely have to occur. This additional work may include interview notes, memorandums of understanding, or cleanup of charts and drawings. Once complete, it behooves you to review this documentation with key stakeholders from the BIA to ensure accuracy and completeness. It is also an excellent way to keep BC in the forefront of the participants' minds and to sustain communication and trust.

Compile and Analyze Data and Information

After the BIA, take the data gathered and format it to generate information. Often, more than enough data will be collected and must be churned into information. Be sure to compile the resulting information according to the stakeholders' communications preferences, for example, graphics.

Seek Clarification on Any Data and Information

While compiling and analyzing data, questions will likely arise or further clarification will be needed requiring contact with stakeholders. You will need to decide whether to contact one or multiple stakeholders on an individual or group basis before the final report. Clarify this decision; otherwise, any flaws appearing in the final report or presentation will create a credibility gap. It is best to compile all questions and clarifications at once rather than barrage stakeholders with an endless piecemeal list of questions.

Report on BIA

Prepare Final Report on Results

The final report is a document or presentation serving as a formal record, not only of the results from the BIA session but also to obtain buy-in to proceed to the next action—building BP plans. Regardless of format, the report should cover information like the background that led to the report; results of the BIA session and other information, such as participants, risks, issues, and concerns; a list of critical processes and functions, their dependencies, RTOs, MADs, and RPOs; and next steps.

Conduct Presentation

This activity is the last opportunity to clarify and answer questions. Additional purposes include obtaining buy-in from the key stakeholders on the results of the BIA and defining the next steps to build appropriate BP plans. It may also include a list of key milestone dates of when to start and end the building of plans for each critical business process or within each one. The presentation should last no more than 20 to 30 minutes, especially for executives and senior managers whose time is limited. You should send the presentation to everyone prior to the meeting so no surprises arise and all are prepared to ask questions or to make comments.

Schedule for BP

Determine Firing Order of Critical Business Processes

This activity occurs after the presentation about the BIA, which we hope suggests a firing order of importance. If not, you can work with the BC steering committee to determine the firing order for initial critical processes to have plans built. Usually, not all the critical processes can be done right away due to limited staff availability at the BC governance infrastructure and the critical business process levels. It is vital that the key stakeholders give their final approval on the firing order to avoid push back.

Determine Milestones for Completing Business Preparedness Plans for Each Critical Business Process

This activity occurs simultaneously with determining the firing order of critical business processes. Like the firing order, the milestones may have been already decided. If not, the BC governance infrastructure may have the authority to decide. Again, the key stakeholders give their final approval of the schedule to avoid push back.

Publish Schedule

Assuming all key stakeholders gave approvals, either at the strategic or critical business process levels, the BC governance infrastructure can publish the schedule. Publishing the schedule offers several benefits. It gives visibility to those critical business processes that contribute to the resiliency of the company and make it difficult to back out of the designation. It also demonstrates the importance that executive and senior management place on BC.

Track Performance

Once published, you need to track performance against the milestone schedule. It makes very little sense to publish a schedule and not conduct follow up. Dates will not only slide but also stakeholders will not feel the pain for not meeting commitments. Persistent and consistent follow up is essential to ensure greater resiliency. The results of the tracking should be presented periodically to the BC steering committee; members of the committee have the position and power to inquire as to why the schedule slides and offer the visibility and help they need.

Apply Project Management (Closing) for Conducting Business Impact Analysis

This task involves ensuring that validation of the performance measurement baseline occurs prior to officially closing the project. It also involves ensuring that all administrative, financial, and contractual concerns or issues are addressed to preclude legal problems from occurring.

DELIVERABLES

The BIA produces several deliverables. Some deliverables are refinements of information procured elsewhere, while other deliverables are unique to the BIA.

A *critical business process* listing is one deliverable. This deliverable reflects the guidance, input, and direction from key stakeholders, being the chairperson and chief executive officer of the company, the audit committee, and executive leadership from the various business units or functions. Critical processes can also come from strategic and operational plans. Ultimately, the BC steering committee provides the final list of critical business processes from a BC perspective.

Key stakeholders listing for each of the critical business processes is another deliverable. One or more executives or senior managers are involved in a critical business process. Often, a process owner has been assigned for each critical business process and that person is usually at the senior management or executive level. Other key stakeholders within a critical business process will likely have responsibility for executing some portion of a critical business process depending on its breadth and depth; those executives and senior managers will likely build BP plans for a critical business process.

A listing of *touch points* among the critical business processes is an important deliverable. The BC executive steering committee will determine where and when a critical business process starts and ends; it will also have to determine whether two or more of these processes are interdependent and integrated. These touch points become important during recovery. Failure to identify touch points can lead to inefficiencies and ineffectiveness in recovery, leading to confusion and hindering or delaying recovery. Often, touch points may not be identified until a draft of BP plans for critical business processes exist; then, during test and maintain exercises, these touch points are more clearly identified and captured in each plan.

Revised risk management is the final significant deliverable. The BIA at the strategic level, of course, will look at the overall picture and may incorporate input from other organizations to identify risks and assess their impacts. While an ERM may be applied at the highest levels, the audit committee or the BC steering committee is focused mainly on BC risks. However, this does not mean that it does not have to take the risk assessment results from other areas of the company and tailor the content to its unique circumstances. Usually functions like supplier management, internal audit, controller's office, and the audit committee have done their own risk management and their output may provide an excellent source of information to refine the risk assessment during the BIA. A critical business process may also determine whether it needs to refine the risk assessment from the strategic level to apply to its circumstances.

STAKEHOLDERS

The BIA, whether at the strategic or critical business process levels, involves a wide range of stakeholders to produce its deliverables as shown in Figure 7.3.

The BoD, including its audit committee, can provide strategic guidance and direction for the BIA through such documents as annual reports, strategic plans, and policy statements. Senior management, especially at the critical business process level, can make available their operations plans

Role	Board of Directors	BC Steering Committee	Business Continuity Working Group	BC Project Manager/ Program Manager	BC Specialists/ Staff Support	Business Process Owner/Senior Management	Recovery Team Leader (Operational)	Recovery Team Members (Operational)	Audit	Customers	Suppliers/ Vendors	Shareholders
Tasks												
Conduct business impact analysis												
Manage project for conducting business preparedness		C,I	C,I	R								
Prepare for conducting business impact analysis		C,I	C,I	R								
Conduct business impact analysis			A	R	A	A						
Analyze results of business impact analysis			C,I	R	A	A						
Report on business impact analysis		C,I	C,I	R,A	A	C						
Schedule for business preparedness actions		C,I	C	R	A	C						
Apply project management (closing) for conducting business impact analysis	I	I	C,I	R,A	R,A							

Legend
R = Responsible
A = Accountable
C = Consult
I = Inform

FIGURE 7.3
RACI chart for conducting business impact analysis.

and other policy statements for use when conducting a BIA. Subject matter experts can participate in a BIA, too, sharing their knowledge, insight, and experience. BC project managers and professionals usually facilitate and provide oversight when conducting the BIA, both at the strategic and operational levels. Customers, vendors, and suppliers may also participate in a BIA, especially if just-in-time principles and outsourcing play a salient role in a critical business process.

INTEGRATION OF ACTIVITIES

An effective BIA depends on the successful execution of the activities. Failure to perform an activity may have a collateral impact on subsequent activities which, in turn, negatively affects the outcome of the BIA. This situation is especially the case when the BIA is conducted at the strategic level.

After applying PM concepts, tools, and techniques, preparation becomes a key for conducting the BIA. This preparation involves determining who, what, where, when, why, and how of the BIA prior to actually performing the BIA. Then, the conduct of the BIA occurs. The approach as well as roles and responsibilities should all be defined prior to this point, so the emphasis is on data and information collection regarding risks, business processes, and recovery considerations such as MAD, RTO, and RPO.

After the conduct of the session, the next activities center on compiling and analyzing the data and information and then preparing written or oral reports on both to the stakeholders involved in the BIA. The BC project manager or program manager then presents the report. If consensus or agreement is achieved, then a firing order for critical business processes to have BP plans in place is developed along with a preliminary high-level schedule. If a BIA occurs at the operational level that is a critical business process, then the activities repeat, but only within its narrow context and scope.

FINAL THOUGHTS

The BIA is critical to the success of a BC program. It results in focusing on critical business processes. The BIA occurs at the strategic level first, which identifies at a high level the critical business processes and associated risks. The results of the strategic BIA are then applied to each of the critical business processes. Each critical business process goes through the activities listed previously until each one has a complete set of BP plans.

CASE STUDY, CONTINUED

BIA for Process and Build BP Plan

Rodriquez set up and conducted an entrance meeting with Ferragio. The purposes of the meeting were fourfold: to provide introduction and to pave the way for building and testing the plan; to review and adjust the enterprise BIA to reflect specific circumstances related to the process; to present an overview of BC and BP; and to cover, at a high level, the basic contents of what the plan would contain.

Rodriquez presented an agenda that reflected the topics described above, which also included showing a revised BIA, shown in Figure 7.4.

Rodriquez also presented an overview on BC and background information on why the topic has become a major priority for the company. Below is an outline of some of the highlights of the presentation.

Overview of Business Continuity and Business Preparedness

- I. Background information
- II. Business continuity
    - a. Definition
    - b. Purpose and goals
    - c. Deliverables
    - d. Key responsibilities
    - e. What happens if BC is not in place?
- III. Business preparedness
    - a. Definition
    - b. Purpose and goals
    - c. Deliverables
        - i. BP plan
            1. Purpose and goals
            2. What happens without a BP plan?

Threat ID	Criticality	Threat	Likelihood	Impact	Risk Rating (Likelihood × Impact)	How Impacted	Comments
1	Medium	Bacterial spoilage	2	5	10	Production	
2		Chemical spills					N/A (not applicable)
3	Low	Collapse of transportation infrastructure	1	5	5	Distribution	
4		Dam collapse					N/A
5	High	Major earthquake	5	5	25	Procurement, production, distribution	
6		Economic recession/depression					N/A
7	Medium	Financial failure of supplier	2	5	10	Production	
8	High	Flooding	4	5	20	Production, distribution	
9		Foreign dumping of blended wines on market					N/A
10	High	Frost/cold temperatures	4	5	20	Production	
11	High	Immigration restrictions	4	5	20	Procurement, production, distribution	

FIGURE 7.4
Revised business impact analysis.

(*Continued*)

12		Inability to self-insure					N/A
13	Low	Inaccessibility to resources other than grapes	2	3	6	Production	
14	Medium	Insect infestation	2	5	10	Production	
15		Lack of social acceptance of alcohol					N/A
16	Low	Overproduction	1	4	4	Production, distribution	
17	Low	Poor soil fertility	2	3	6	Production	
18	Medium	Shortage of fungicides/herbicides	2	5	10	Production	
19		Social instability					N/A
20	High	Unpredictable climate change	4	5	20	Procurement, production	
21		Disruption of information systems					N/A

Legend

Likelihood & Impact

5 High

4 Medium to high

3 Medium

2 Low to medium

1 Low

FIGURE 7.4 (CONTINUED)
Revised business impact analysis.

ii. Test
    1. Purpose and goals
    2. Content
    3. Key responsibilities

IV. Questions and answers

Finally, he presented an outline, shown below, of the typical content and structure of a business preparedness plan.

Outline for Business Preparedness Plan

I. Title

II. Key stakeholders
   a. Internal stakeholders
   b. External stakeholders

III. Maximum allowable downtime

IV. Scope
   a. In scope
   b. Out of scope

V. Call tree
   a. Instructions
   b. Recovery team members
   c. Contact information

VI. Resource (dependency) requirements
   a. Name
   b. Quality required

VII. Recovery procedures for each resource
   a. Responsibility
   b. Reason for importance
   c. Recovery actions and workarounds

VIII. Recovery time objectives

IX. Appendices

Ferragio then designated a single point of contact for Rodriquez. This single point of contact (SPOC), Don Wilson, was to assist Ferragio in identifying and assembling the key participants in the process to develop the BP plan; these very same people would also be involved in testing and maintaining the plan. Ferragio then worked with Rodriquez to develop a project plan to accommodate the schedule adopted by the Steering Committee.

GETTING STARTED CHECKLIST

Question	Yes	No
1. When conducting the BIA, are you realizing these benefits?		
Identifying and prioritizing critical business processes		
Taking a holistic perspective		
Determining the degree of integration among all the critical business processes		
Marrying strategic and operational perspectives		
Communicating better between the strategic and operational levels		
2. When conducting a BIA, have you considered how to address these challenges?		
Determining the interviewees to participate in the BIA		
Collecting the right data to generate the right information		
Distinguishing between assumptions and facts		
Resolving conflict		
Overcoming silo thinking		
3. Did you determine whether to produce these deliverables?		
Critical business listing		
Key stakeholders listing		
Touch points listing		
Revised risk management		
4. When conducting the BIA, did you consider these concepts?		
Identify dependencies		
Use quantitative and qualitative data and information (and assumptions)		
Use tables, matrices, graphs, and charts		
Document results		
Use combination of data gathering, questionnaires, and interviewing for the BIA		
Apply risk analysis and assessment information		
For each critical business process, determine the recovery time objective and, if applicable, the recovery point objective		
Restrict the length of time and the number of people for the BIA session		
Take a multidisciplinary, holistic perspective during the session		
Remember the primary goal is to save the company		
Remember that not all processes are critical		
Time is the variable for ascertaining criticality		
Categorize processes into degrees of importance for recovery		
Determine the key deliverables for the session		
Identify key stakeholders to participate in the BIA		
Anticipate what might happen during the BIA session		
Preparation is essential		

5. When preparing for and conducting a BIA, have you considered performing these activities?
    - Apply stakeholder guidance and direction
    - Determine and develop a systematic approach
    - Determine data and information requirements
    - Prepare tools for data and information collection
    - Identify key stakeholders
    - Identify organizational entities' vision, mission, goals, and objectives
    - Collect and review any additional information about an organizational entity
    - Arrange meeting with key stakeholders
    - Provide background on reasons for session, including its goals and objectives
    - Present high-level review on what is business continuity and associated key concepts
    - Clarify business requirements of the entities' organization
    - Determine scope of session
    - Identify critical business processes
    - Identify key dependencies for each critical business process
    - Apply risk analysis and assessment information
    - Determine MAD, RTO, and RPO for each critical business process
    - Identify touch points among critical business processes
    - Document results of session
    - Compile and analyze data and information
    - Seek clarification on any data and information
    - Prepare final report on results
    - Conduct presentation
    - Determine firing order of critical business processes
    - Determine milestones for completing BP plans for each critical business process
    - Publish schedule
    - Track performance

8

Build the Business Preparedness Plan

Once the business impact analysis (BIA) is complete at the strategic and critical business process levels, you can start to build the business preparedness (BP) plans. These plans are not detailed instructions; they consist of a high-level set of procedures to enhance a company's ability to recover.

WHAT IS A BUSINESS PREPAREDNESS PLAN?

A BP plan, described earlier, is a tool to identify and document high-level procedures for recovering a critical business process. Depending on the complexity, such as the breadth and depth, of the critical business process and the output of a BIA, more than one plan may be necessary.

GOALS

Building the BP plan has several goals.

Increase the Knowledge and Understanding about the Need for Business Continuity

Every session with stakeholders is an opportunity to increase understanding and learning about business continuity (BC). When building BP plans for the first time, the project manager should make every effort to share his or her knowledge and experience with BC and provide sources of information about the topic.

A plan is only as good as the content it contains. Armed with good information about recovery, people can refer to the plan to guide them through recovery although plans need to contain current information.

Get Stakeholders Engaged in Enhancing the Resiliency of Their Critical Business Process

To some people, BC seems abstract or is difficult to fathom. On recovery from an event, the project manager needs to engage them. The requirement to build a BP plan is one such vehicle for seeking engagement. Through engagement, stakeholders will have more confidence in the recovery plan.

Establish and Document a Call Tree

A call tree, mentioned earlier, is a list of people to contact when a critical business process experiences an event requiring recovery. This list should be built while developing the plan. It consists of the key stakeholders needed to start recovery.

Get Everyone to Know His or Her Responsibilities during Recovery

Stakeholders must know what to do, when to do it, under what circumstances, whom they work with, and how they fit within the entire recovery of a critical business process. By knowing their responsibilities, recovery should occur more efficiently and effectively than without that knowledge.

TERMINOLOGY

Building a BP plan involves knowing some BC terminology upfront.

A *call tree* is a listing of key individuals to contact if a disruptive event occurs. Its purpose is to establish and maintain communications and respond to a disruptive event. It is also referred to as a notification or alert list. The key is to keep the listing up to date.

Communication, as defined in the context of BP, is transmitting data and information in either soft (electronic) or hard (paper) copy form.

Communication plays an instrumental role in successful recovery; indeed, a failure to communicate will greatly jeopardize recovery.

A *dependency* is a resource important for recovering a critical business process. Failing to define or poorly describe a dependency in one or more plans hinders recovery. Including a dependency depends on the scope of a plan. If a dependency is unavailable, then alternative activities or dependencies must be identified to avoid a showstopper in recovery.

Preparedness is continuously establishing measures and controls to ensure a greater likelihood of recovery. These measures and controls include taking corrective action to provide reasonable assurance that a critical business process is resilient.

A *protocol* is a set of rules or guidelines for taking action under certain conditions. For example, the BIA provides a good set of rules and protocols to ascertain which processes are critical. The extension of the BIA results at the critical business process level also helps determine recovery requirements; this, too, is an example of protocols and guidelines. Another example is determining when to execute a BP plan and the firing order of procedures.

Recovery is implementing prioritized strategies and actions to recover from an event. The scope of the BP plan will help determine the strategies and actions to include. These strategies and actions on the dependencies, recovery time objectives (RTOs), recovery point objectives (RPOs), and many other variables over a time continuum influence recovery of business operations.

A *recovery period* is the time continuum between the occurrence of a disruptive event and the eventual return to minimum normal operations and is recorded in the BP plan. The recovery period can occur in many different formats, for example, hours, days, or weeks, depending on the magnitude and complexity of the operations. It is often graduated up to when full recovery is required.

RPO is a point in time when it becomes necessary to restore systems and data to avoid significant data loss. In today's modern world, systems and data are instrumental to the recovery of critical business processes. If a system goes down, a small point in time may exist before the critical process is impacted. A BP plan can cite that point in time but the details of the recovery should be captured in a disaster recovery plan. The focus should be on initiating the right procedures at a specific point in time to ensure recovery of a critical business process.

RTO, mentioned earlier, is a point in time when recovery must start. It is, in many respects, the point in the recovery period when a critical business process begins to feel the pain. The recovery begins by determining the quantity and quality of the dependencies needed and their accompanying procedures. Delay in achieving an RTO translates into a delay in recovery.

A *reliance statement*, as mentioned earlier, describes in a procedure the reason for a dependency and the workarounds. It also may provide a short description of a dependency and other notable information useful for certain stakeholders.

Workaround procedures are alternative ways to take action when an important critical dependency is unavailable for recovery. There are often two parts to a procedure. The first part contains a reliance statement that describes why a dependency is important as well as any additional information. The other part describes the specific actions to take if a dependency is unavailable. A procedure should exist for each category of a dependency. Ideally, a procedure should be at a high level, explaining who, what, when, where, why, and how without burdensome detail.

KEY CONCEPTS

To effectively build a BP plan, you need to understand and apply several key concepts.

The BP Plan Serves as a "Strategic" Guideline

A BP plan is a guideline, not a detailed procedure; otherwise, it becomes too cumbersome to prepare, update, and reference. It is not the typical how-to desk procedure you often see in an information technology (IT) manual. The plan should contain only the essential elements of information to enable recovery. The plan should provide the scope, list the key stakeholders, provide a call tree with accompanying contact information, list dependencies and their quantities required over a time continuum, document procedures for recovery, and offer any other pertinent information. Remember, the plan should not be a tome.

Prefer Graphics and Illustrations to Narrative Text

The best way to present information in a BP plan is to compact the contents as much as possible. Compacting means presenting information in a way that stakeholders can reference easily. For example, a matrix showing the quantity of all dependencies over a time continuum can go a long way to reduce the number of pages in a plan. A matrix shows the relationship of responsibilities with procedures. The idea is to present the information compactly and clearly for ease of reference during an event. A good tool to use is a technique called information mapping, a technical writing technique emphasizing the use of white space and simple language.

Keep the Narrative Text Clean

This concept ties closely to the last point but has more to do with understanding the content. Content should avoid jargon, acronyms, poor spelling, and inaccuracies. Failure to eliminate such defects can lead to confusion and delay recovery. A good heuristic is having someone who did not participate or draft the plan in any way review it; then, seek feedback. The key point here is that anyone should be able to pick up the plan, if necessary, and execute the contents with little or no previous experience or require very little, if any, oversight.

Seek Stakeholder Participation during the BP Plan Development

Stakeholders should not develop a plan in a void. To do so will only engender resistance and produce an incomplete document. Participation, when developing a plan, is a way to gain the necessary support for using it during an event. It also helps to ensure the readability of the plan, determine the usefulness of the contents, encourage greater widespread usage in an event, and further visibility of BC. This participation should include developing and reviewing the content of their responsibilities and, ultimately, providing their overall formal approval of the plan. Figure 8.1 shows the relationships among the different stakeholders that have either a strategic or an operational interest in the building of a plan.

Remember That Building a BP Plan Is Not Necessarily an Efficient Exercise in the Short Run

That is, of course, if an event does not occur. Getting all the key stakeholders together takes time and effort on everyone's part and, despite the intangible benefits, the plan itself does not demonstrate any hard savings. In fact, unless it can offset business insurance costs, many stakeholders

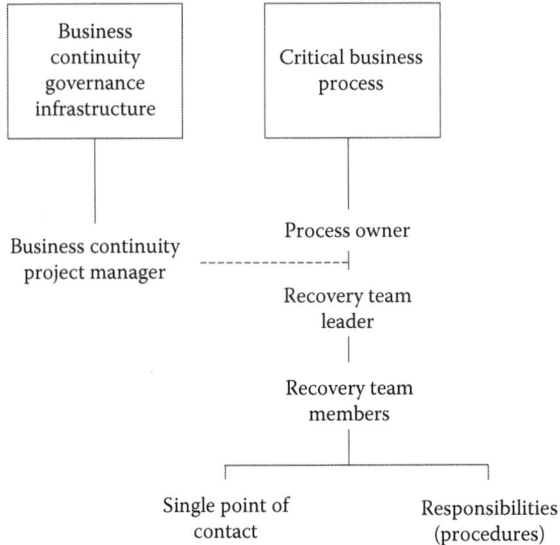

FIGURE 8.1
Typical BC organizational structure within a critical business process.

will likely construe the effort as simply an administrative burden. Of course, the best way to demonstrate a plan's efficiency and effectiveness is to use it during an event. A BP plan is much like insurance; until something happens, if it does its value is hard to prove.

Scope Definition Is Essential

What is included and, just as importantly not included, in a BP plan determines its coverage. An ill-defined scope simply provides an opportunity to create a voluminous plan. It becomes like a high school term paper about the Civil War described in 12 pages rather than focusing on one battle, such as Vicksburg. Through scoping, a more meaningful, concise, and focused plan is possible to enable quicker, more effective recovery.

The People Who Perform a Procedure Develop and Review Its Contents

The people who do the work know how to do it best under normal operations and during an event. They know what must be done when and how, and the priorities. They also know the right level of detail and can anticipate any challenges or threats that might arise and offer guidance on how to deal with them. A quick way to shatter confidence in a BP plan is for the people who are responsible for executing the work described in a procedure to express lack of buy-in or challenge the validity of the content.

Keep in Mind the Purpose of the BP Plan Is to Enhance the Survivability of the Company

The plan is not to serve as a training plan or a desk procedure covering every conceivable topic. Rather, it is a document that should focus and enhance the likelihood of a successful recovery of a critical business process. It provides only the essential elements of information to get a critical business process up to speed quickly and effectively. The important word is *minimal* in terms of time and effort.

Criticality Is Determined by Time at the Plan Level

Time to restore a critical business process determines criticality. The question at this level is by what point in time, known as the RTO, must a critical business process make recovery happen before an event degrades the ability of a process to meet its obligations? Time is of the essence at this level and a primary determinant of what is, and what is not, critical. Otherwise, everything becomes critical, making recovery impossible.

Strive for Threat Independence

This concept is harder to fathom than one would think. Most people tend to think in terms of extremes that happen in their particular milieu. For example, many people think in terms of earthquakes on the West Coast of the United States and hurricanes on the East Coast. While these events will likely have the greatest impact, they also have the lowest probability of occurrence vis-à-vis other threats, such as a disgruntled employee putting a bomb in a manufacturing facility or delivering a package containing a pathogen to the office. A meaningful BP plan should provide what is required for normal recovery, regardless of the threat. The recovery team can then decide what dependencies and procedures to apply. If necessary, a plan can contain an addendum of procedures to perform when a specific threat, having a low likelihood of occurrence, occurs.

Exercise Risk Management

Understandably, at first this may seem contradictory to the last point. However, risk management can help to determine the likely risks and the corresponding strategies and procedures to address. It can also help to determine the types of dependencies and their potential quantities needed for recovery. The idea is to provide adequate coverage for any contingency without becoming focused on simply one event, such as a fire or terrorist attack.

All Relevant Information Is Documented in the BP Plan

Nothing should be left out that is deemed essential for recovery based on the assumption that everybody knows the information. Such assumptions lead to serious oversights in the plan. A good practice is to list all relevant, significant assumptions in the plan. Taking anything for granted can lead to a delay in recovery of a critical business process. The concern is that if someone unfamiliar with its execution has to exercise a procedure, he or she will not know what to do.

Distribute the BP Plan Only to Relevant Stakeholders

The content of a plan often contains invaluable information. Blanket sharing of a plan can compromise information, especially if it contains proprietary, competitive, or personal information. Just from a reputational and legal perspective, the impacts can be immense. You should ensure stakeholders restrict access to a plan while at the same time ensure people who need it have access. This access control is a challenge if copies are stored outside the work area.

A BP Plan Is a Snapshot in Time

A plan reflects only what is known at a specific point and a product of the best available information. Unfortunately, it quickly loses its value due to changing circumstances. People change roles and responsibilities. Organizations restructure. The competitive market requires changes in processes. Whatever the reasons, change impacts the best of plans. For that very reason, a plan needs regular updating to preclude it from becoming irrelevant or misleading. Keeping a plan up to date requires overhead support.

Incorporate the Tangible and Intangible Dependencies of a BP Plan

Tangible dependencies include physical resources, such as buildings, telephones, etc. Intangible dependencies include soft resources, such as data and applications. Other intangible considerations, often overlooked, are ongoing communications among key stakeholders and maintaining awareness about the plan and its contents.

Conduct Formal Walkthroughs with Key Stakeholders

The draft of a BP plan usually involves a group of stakeholders selected because of their background, knowledge, expertise, and experience with one or more areas of a critical business process. The initial draft may not have the input of all these stakeholders due to scheduling problems. It is usually best to select a group of people to draft a plan and then present it to other stakeholders for feedback. After updating the plan, consider holding a walkthrough with the entire group not only to capture insights for specific areas, but also to raise questions about its content as well as identifying areas, such as procedures requiring closer coordination among stakeholders of other plans and critical business processes. Use the formality of a walkthrough to include assigning a facilitator and a scribe to capture notes.

Identify Opportunities for Greater Integration and Communication in the BP Plan

A plan consists of many elements of information. While developing a plan, opportunities arise to identify or improve integration and communication among the different stakeholders and their respective procedures. A benefit of building a BP plan is that it reveals the potential for synergy; that is, being more than the sum of its parts. Issues, concerns, ideas, and techniques are shared among stakeholders. This synergy becomes even more appreciated if people systemically view a critical business and the plans supporting it, if applicable. Stakeholders begin to realize how their actions impact others and vice versa while focusing on recovery. This appreciation for integration and communication can also arise on a grander scale as stakeholders begin to see how their actions affect other plans and critical business processes. In other words, they will likely identify touch point opportunities requiring greater communication and integration during recovery.

Seek Consistency among BP Plans

Within some critical business processes, multiple plans may be required. The plans should be similar in structure and layout. With consistency, it becomes easier to identify touch points among the plans. It also means that stakeholders who support related plans can read and understand the content and flow of other plans much more quickly and effectively. Updating of the plans also becomes easier because stakeholders can go directly to each plan and make the necessary changes.

BENEFITS

There are several key benefits for building one or more BP plans for critical processes and functions.

Providing Documented Guidelines for Recovery

Notice the term "documented guidelines." By documenting the plan in soft or hard copy form, recovery crystallizes within the stakeholders' minds. The mere act of putting a plan down on paper forces people to seriously think about it. The other point about the phrase is guidelines. The plan does not drill down into minutia; rather, the content is at a level sufficient for reference during recovery. A plan that is too voluminous is of little value during the recovery. The idea is to keep the plan simple, but not so simple that it provides little value.

Determining Roles and Responsibilities Upfront

The recovery of a critical business process no longer has to occur as an unruly mob. After an event occurs, people specifically know their roles and responsibilities during recovery. Under normal conditions, people go through a routine; their roles and responsibilities are set. When an event occurs and things go awry, however, confusion often results. Building a BP plan enables stakeholders to avoid the thousand-yard stare after an event occurs. They know what to expect and are ready to act.

Encouraging Communication and Coordination

The mere act of building a BP plan forces key stakeholders to talk with each other during its construction and review. It also encourages discussions among stakeholders to coordinate with each other during recovery. These benefits are also realized in other areas not even related to BP. In many cases, issues and concerns are raised during the building of BP plans that are never discussed during normal operations. These discussions of communication and coordination lead to opportunities for improvement in daily operations. This situation is especially the case in large companies where silo thinking is the rule.

Providing a Systematic Approach When Building a BP Plan

A systematic approach enhances the ability to determine who, what, when, where, why, and how elements of a plan. Collecting and documenting such information requires being systematic, such as following a logical sequence. A plan should not be simply a "rat's nest" of data; the contents must be relevant and focused. Building a plan with a defined scope can help realize this benefit.

Providing a Means to Train New Employees about Recovery

Every organization experiences turnover. As the state of the economy improves and demographics create a labor shortage, turnover becomes acute. A well-documented, relevant plan can serve as a means of getting people up to speed quickly, not just on recovery procedures but also on their roles and responsibilities.

Encouraging Proactive and Responsive Behavior

Many stakeholders get into the routine of doing business. An anomaly then throws everything in disarray; no one had even thought what to do about recovery. The result is everyone, from the top levels of the organization to the person working on the floor or cubicle, so to speak, then reacts to the situation. Quick fixes become the solution, often leading to greater problems and issues later. With building a BP plan based upon solid risk assessment, an organization can respond effectively and efficiently to an event. It can help to reduce the number of false starts by identifying opportunities to act in advance.

Reducing the Financial Impact of an Event

Instead of stakeholders standing around figuring out what to do next or going in different directions, the BP plan provides them with a sense of direction and enables focusing on recovering from an event, effectively and efficiently. One argument against building BP plans is the time, costs, and effort for handling an event do occur; however, the time, cost, and effort will exceed that of building a plan. One side benefit is encouraging stakeholders to think about priorities during recovery. Another is that it reduces insurance premiums, demonstrating an ability and capacity to recover from an event.

Encouraging Greater Awareness of BC

Focusing on BC is difficult due to competing priorities in the workplace. Building BP plans provides an opportunity for stakeholders to gain a greater appreciation of what BC can do for the company and themselves. You should stress during sessions that building a plan helps to offset the failure to respond efficiently and effectively to an event; that is, avoiding not only loss of profitability for a company but also threats to their livelihoods. To some stakeholders it may seem like an exaggeration; however, statistics do not support their feelings. The majority of businesses that experience a serious event fail to survive the next five years.

Identifying "Showstoppers" and Encouraging Stakeholders to Think "Outside the Box"

An enterprise risk assessment can go a long way to identify risks at a high level. The building of a BC plan, however, encourages thinking about how those risks will directly impact their process. During this review, stakeholders may discover risks that no one thought about and how those risks could affect the resiliency of their critical business process. Key stakeholders can determine what additional procedures are necessary.

Enhancing the Competitive Position of the Company

A company that can demonstrate its resiliency has a decided advantage over its competitors who cannot prove it. One of the best ways to demonstrate commitment to being resilient is to document BP plans, being an expression of due diligence. This evidence becomes even more important as a company becomes engaged in global operations where the intricacies of the supply chain can become quite complex. Developing BP plans is just one of several steps.

Building a BP Plan Demonstrates Confidence in Handling an Event

BP plans demonstrate a resolve to continue a company's commitment to its customers, minimize disruptions to cash flow, and lessen the impact of disruptions to customers, investors, and key stakeholders so that a company does not behave like a ship listing at sea, showing them that it is making a concerted effort to upright itself and continue onward to port.

CHALLENGES

Despite the significant benefits of building BP plans, there are a number of challenges to overcome.

Making the Time, Labor, Tools, and Information Available to Build the BP Plan

For most organizations, only so much time and resources are available to handle even a small number of priorities. Tradeoff decisions among priorities require sub-optimizing priorities. Unfortunately, BC is one of the victims of this prioritization. If a company fails to or does not decide on such matters, then its leadership might consider alternatives such as having corporate headquarters or a supporting business unit provide BC services. Leadership could also outsource the responsibility for building BP plans.

Lacking an Understanding and Knowledge of BC

To many stakeholders, the subject is often new or they have some minimal exposure to the topic. Armed with even minimal information, stakeholders can participate sufficiently when building a BP plan. Prior to developing a plan, therefore, you should give an overview presentation on the basics of BC. The presentation should cover the basics, and not attempt to transform the participants into experts on the subject. Another way to help in furthering understanding and knowledge about the topic is to have a website containing videos and presentations.

Obtaining Buy-In for the BP Plan

This challenge often exists, especially in an organization having many stakeholders, making it very difficult to achieve consensus or agreement over strategies, actions, procedures, RTO, and RPO. The more stakeholders are involved, the greater the difficulty to reconcile different perspectives and to gain acceptance of a plan, especially when some stakeholders have irreconcilable differences and an impasse occurs. Under some circumstances, achieving consensus results in a "watered down" plan, which means it lacks sufficient specificity to guide recovery. Another common circumstance is overlooking a stakeholder who then comes forth during the final review and approval of a plan, says he was overlooked, and requests the opportunity to conduct a review and make changes, if necessary. Therefore, it is imperative before you build any BP plan that you make every effort to identify the key stakeholders and to engage them from the beginning.

Scoping the BP Plan

Ideally, the stakeholders developing the plan have a good idea of the beginning of a critical business process and its ending, thereby making it easier to define the scope of the plan. In theory, they should find it an easy decision to make. Key questions need answering to scope a BP plan: At what point does the scope of the plan begin? At what point does the scope of the plan end? Does it include procedures that require coordination with other plans and, if so, where should they be referenced in the plan? Who makes the decision on the scope? Having the key stakeholders answering the questions identified early can help to provide the focus. What happens quite often is that stakeholders determine that some stakeholders need to participate while others do not. Another way to clarify scope is to determine what is not in scope, thereby using a process of elimination to determine the scope.

Determining When the BP Plan Is Complete

This challenge centers on determining at what point refining is no longer a value-added approach. To make that decision, it requires asking and applying questions like: Is the plan too high level, lacking any value to the people who must execute its contents? Is the plan so detailed that it is riddled with minutia, making it cumbersome to use during recovery? The reality is that people have different perspectives of what is too much or too little. The best approach is to have the key stakeholders who participated in developing the plan buy-off on the document. The real determination of a plan is when it is tested using a scenario.

Sharing of Data and Information

Knowledge is power in many organizations; sharing it with too many stakeholders diminishes power. Building a BP plan also may require admitting that shortfalls in the performance of responsibilities exist, translating into a failure to perform responsibilities at a satisfactory level. Trust becomes extremely important, therefore, among key stakeholders as they collaborate to build a plan. If trust is the norm rather than the exception, the quality of the plan will likely not suffer; if not, the opposite will occur. The best approach is to have the key stakeholders participate in the sessions for building the plan and to eventually sign off on it. Engaging stakeholders when building and buying off on a plan enhances opportunities for commitment and ownership in a plan and encourages sharing of information.

Protecting Data and Information

The contents of a BP plan may be very valuable to the wrong people or competitors. It can also cause legal complications if it contains personally identifiable information. The challenge arises not just while developing the plan per se, but also when it is distributed to key stakeholders. If such data and information goes unrestricted, especially in an environment relying on IT, a plan can circulate to places never intended, such as competitors.

Hard copies can also, intentionally or inadvertently, fall in the wrong hands. While it is next to impossible to prevent such behaviors or actions from occurring, using good IT security and controlled numbering of a BP plan can create an audit trail that tracks who has received a copy.

Distinguishing Assumptions from Facts

This challenge is present throughout the lifecycle of a BC initiative and is never easy to surmount. Any assumptions should be listed in the beginning of the BP plan so everyone can base their contributions on knowing the difference between what is fact and what is assumption. Assumptions are assumed to be facts until proven otherwise; relying on them is not a problem. Not recognizing them for what they are, however, can lead to extensive rework. You should revisit assumptions throughout the development of a plan to ensure the reliability of the content. Otherwise, the plan could quickly become irrelevant due to being based on incorrect assumptions.

Identifying the Interfaces with Other BP Plans

In an environment of global supply chains, for example, this can become extremely difficult. A complex process may require looking at a plan to ascertain just when a plan has touch points with one or more other plans. It also requires having access to other BP plans to determine exactly those connections. Addressing this challenge can consume time and effort in the short run because they may find themselves competing for resources due to similar or conflicting priorities. Naturally, if unaddressed, such circumstances can hinder recovery of critical business processes by prolonging their recovery. A way to address this problem is to hold a meeting with all recovery team leaders for each BP plan and determine their relationships with one another, vis-à-vis recovery priority and resource sharing, and capture it in a matrix or table indicating under what circumstances touch points occur.

Keeping the Call Tree Current

Each BP plan should have a call tree, a listing of individuals to contact if recovery must occur. The call tree includes members of the recovery team, such as key decision makers and people who exercise specific procedures in a plan. This becomes difficult if people are constantly in transit, for example, moving around within a company or departing due to layoffs or retirements. The owner of a BP plan should periodically revisit the call tree notification list to verify the accuracy of the contents. The review should ascertain whether all the necessary people are listed and that their contact information is accurate. A good heuristic is to conduct a dry run that involves executing the call tree and then review the response.

Keeping the BP Plan Current

A large effort goes into building a BP plan. Unfortunately, like many plans, the BP plan rests on a shelf or in a desk drawer for an extended time before anyone decides to revisit it. As time passes, the content of the plan becomes dated or irrelevant for a host of reasons, including internal reorganizations and changes in mission statements. The owner of a BP plan should make every effort to keep it current so that stakeholders know specifically what to execute and under what circumstances. The owner of the BP plan should make it a point to conduct periodic reviews of the plan with recovery team members.

Ensuring the Right People Participate in Building the BP Plan

A host of factors depends on who should participate. Perhaps the most important point of participation is the scoping of the process identified during the BIA. The results can help identify the overall scope and the relevance of the plan. The plan owner can invite potential recovery team members who, after analysis, may elect to reduce or enlarge the scope and the corresponding stakeholders for building the plan.

Focusing Too Much on IT

BP plans are based upon recovery of critical business processes, not technology. While important, IT is one of many enablers for recovering a business. IT may develop an accompanying disaster recovery plan, supporting one or more BP plans. The BP plans should identify RPOs for applications, hardware, and other IT services; they can also cite any relevant IT procedures, plans, etc. Remember, IT recovery facilitates critical business process recovery, not the other way around.

Developing a BP Plan Dealing with a Broad Range of Events, Not Some Specific Event

It is impossible to determine specific events that necessitate plan activation. If you plan too specific an event, it becomes irrelevant if something unanticipated occurs. Remember, BP plans serve as guidelines for recovery; they are not meant to function as a desk procedure describing every conceivable step. Otherwise, it will make the plans too cumbersome to reference during an event and make their maintenance difficult. Ideally, BP plans should be broad categories of threats having a good likelihood of occurrence. Stakeholders will have to decide what those categories are.

Communicating the BP Plan

Once complete, a BP plan may not have had all recovery teams participating. If that is the case, the recovery team may find it necessary to communicate the plan before, during, and after its distribution. You can communicate about the plan at staff meetings or special training sessions, emphasizing procedures of the plan relevant to members of the audience. Distributing the BP plan without follow up with people who will execute specific procedures increases the likelihood of ignorance about its contents, never being read, or resting on a shelf or in a file cabinet.

CHARACTERISTICS OF A "GOOD" PLAN

During the review of the BP plan, the author of the plan should ensure that the document has certain characteristics to give it a professional look and feel.

The content should be clear, concise, accurate, and useful. It should have only the information that stakeholders need. This information should be current and have been vetted by key stakeholders. Additionally, the plan should contain no misspellings or poor grammar.

The layout of the BP plan should minimize eye strain, meaning surrounding the narrative text with white space and using blocked text when possible. Nothing can be more confusing and frustrating than opening a document to reference during recovery and having to search for the applicable information. Unless the content is clearly indexed, give preference to the use of white space to display information by using techniques like information mapping.

The general structure of the BP plan should also flow logically. For instance, first comes the cover page, then the approval signature page, the table of contents, the detailed content for recovery, and appendices. The logical flow should be consistent among several plans within a critical business process, if applicable, making it easier to identify touch points, as well as finding any information of interest.

MAKING BUILDING THE BP PLAN A REALITY

A number of activities are required to produce a useful BP plan. These activities can be grouped into one of four phases, which are described in Figure 8.2.

Manage Project for Building BP Plan

This task involves applying all the PM concepts, tools, and techniques to enhance project performance. For example, it includes preparing a charter, developing a WBS, making time and cost estimates, building a schedule, and tracking and monitoring performance.

Prepare for Building BP Plan

Review the Results of the BIA

It is inefficient and ineffective to reinvent the wheel in BC. The best approach is to leverage on previous work. There are three principal reasons for following this advice. One, it capitalizes on the work done previously, thereby reducing cycle time and effort to build a BP plan. Two, it provides for consistency of approach and content among plans. Three, it allows for faster completion of a BP plan.

What is the value of the BIA being reviewed or considered when preparing the BP plan? The risk assessment can provide information on the threats facing a specific critical business process. The stakeholders can adapt this information to the needs of a particular plan. The RTO for an overall process serves as a guide to determining the RTO for a BP plan. In addition, any issues or assumptions at the BIA provide a basis to determine dependencies.

ID	Task Name	Predecessors
114	1.3 Build business preparedness plan	
115	1.3.1 Manage project for building business preparedness plan	
116	1.3.1.1 Apply project management	113
117	1.3.2 Prepare for building business preparedness plan	
118	1.3.2.1 Review the results of the BIA	111,116
119	1.3.2.2 Compile preliminary information about the critical business process	118
120	1.3.2.3 Identify key stakeholders	119
121	1.3.2.4 Schedule the session	120
122	1.3.2.5 Identify the format of the business preparedness plan	121
123	1.3.3 Define requirements for building business preparedness plan	
124	1.3.3.1 Identify recovery team membership	118–122
125	1.3.3.2 Determine scope	118–122
126	1.3.3.3 Perform risk management	118–122
127	1.3.3.4 Determine overall description of the business preparedness plan	118–122
128	1.3.3.5 Distinguish between assumptions and facts	118–122
129	1.3.3.6 Determine call tree media and contacts	118–122
130	1.3.3.7 Determine the overall recovery time objective	118–122
131	1.3.3.8 Identify key dependencies and quantities required over time	118–122
132	1.3.3.9 Determine procedures for dependencies	118–122
133	1.3.3.10 Determine recovery point objective for applications, data, servers, and other technology (if applicable)	118–122
134	1.3.3.11 Identify content for each procedure	118–122
135	1.3.3.12 Assign responsibilities for each procedure	118–122
136	1.3.4 Draft business preparedness plan	

FIGURE 8.2
WBS for building a BP plan.

(*Continued*)

137	1.3.4.1 Compile and analyze data from working session	124–135
138	1.3.4.2 Draft business preparedness plan	137
139	1.3.4.3 Check to ensure the business preparedness plan contains only essential elements of information	138
140	1.3.4.4 Proofread the plan	138
141	1.3.5 Review business preparedness plan	
142	1.3.5.1 Determine approach for review	140
143	1.3.5.2 Prepare copies for review	142
144	1.3.5.3 Conduct first review and update the business preparedness plan	143
145	1.3.5.4 Conduct second review	144
146	1.3.5.5 Conduct test of call tree	145
147	1.3.6 Distribute business preparedness plan	
148	1.3.6.1 Conduct final walkthrough	146
149	1.3.6.2 Revise the business preparedness plan	148
150	1.3.6.3 Place the business preparedness plan under configuration management	149
151	1.3.6.4 Determine method of distribution	150
152	1.3.7 Apply project management (closing) for building business preparedness plan	
153	1.3.7.1 Perform closing tasks	151

FIGURE 8.2 (CONTINUED)
WBS for building a BP plan.

Finally, the listing of other BP plans to develop a critical business process can smooth efforts to identify potential touch points among them.

Compile Preliminary Information about the Critical Business Process

For each critical business process that requires one or more BP plans, the stakeholders should take time to collect as much information in advance about the critical business process. This information should include the mission, goals, and objectives of the critical business process; organizational components supporting it; key decision makers and other important stakeholders; common challenges or risks and issues facing them; location of operations; and any other pertinent information from interviews, reports, minutes from meetings, and other documentation.

Identify Key Stakeholders

Using the compiled information, stakeholders can identify who will participate in the BP plan's development and publication. The material collected should provide formal roles and responsibilities to enhance the search for participants in the working sessions to build the plans. If names, roles, and responsibilities are not readily available, consider developing a list of potential stakeholders and then, through interviews and discussions with known stakeholders, add or delete names on the list.

Schedule the Session

Scheduling the working sessions may seem like a routine exercise. In reality, it may be more difficult than one may originally envision, especially for complex critical business processes. A complex process may be one that spans across multiple time zones or involves several disciplines. As is often the case for such critical business processes, some people can attend physically while others will have to attend electronically. The facilitation, performed by the project manager, should work to ensure everyone has an opportunity to attend the sessions and participate, if for no other reason than to capture input and achieve buy-in.

Identify the Format of the BP Plan

All plans should follow a standard format. This standard format should include a listing of all elements, their logical flow, the layout of each element, and the tools to create the plan. This advance decision offers several advantages, including ease of populating the plan, assigning responsibilities for completing certain elements, identifying potential touch points, and providing better communications among the stakeholders of a plan and other ones. A future side benefit, of course, is allowing for easier maintenance.

Define Requirements for Building BP Plan

Identify Recovery Team Membership

The recovery team consists of individuals to contact via a call tree arrangement to determine the impact of an event affecting a critical business process within the area of responsibility covered under their plan.

The members of the recovery team are definitely listed on the call tree; their responsibility is to set policy and direction when executing the plan, as well as participate to activate all or some of the procedures contained within it. The recovery team often includes other people who have no direct responsibility to exercise anything in a plan but can provide insights based on their knowledge, experience, and connections.

Determine Scope

With the recovery team members identified and hopefully participating in the working sessions to build the BP plan, work can begin on building a plan. The work begins with determining and agreeing on the scope of the plan. Scoping enables precise focus on efforts to develop a relevant plan.

Perform Risk Management

Risk management, at this point, should capitalize on the one originating from the BIA. The attendees at the working session, now knowing the scope of their plan, are ready to identify what risks relate to their plan. They may also determine what other risks may apply that the BIA did not consider. The risk assessment at this point may require adopting a different or revised RTO, and even RPO, later on while building the BP plan.

Determine Overall Description of the BP Plan

The attendees should, based upon the scope, write a short paragraph about what the plan is concerning its goals and objectives and the major components, for example, sub-processes, that comprise it. It may also include a list of other relevant BP plans.

Distinguish between Assumptions and Facts

While developing the BP plan, confusion may arise over fact vs. assumption. Confusion over the two exists simply because stakeholders hold different perceptions. During the working session, it is important for the facilitator, likely the project manager, to help the participants distinguish between the two and, if no agreement or consensus exists, then to table the fact or assumption in question and revisit it later.

Determine Call Tree Media and Contacts

The call tree is the alert line for the team. It requires having one or more methods to communicate with people concerning the occurrence of an event. It is important that the call tree listing is current with all the relevant contact information. While the recovery team leader is the one who will likely activate the call tree, everyone should be familiar with the process for activating, too. A good way to ensure that this occurs is to incorporate in the plan instructions to activate the call tree.

Determine the Overall RTO

The RTO will likely be based upon the overall one determined in the BIA. However, during the working session, the stakeholders may determine that the RTO is different due to unique circumstances. The RTO, in fact, may vary from BP plan to BP plan, which will require some effort by all recovery teams to reconcile the differences, which may, in turn, require reevaluating the RTO for the overall critical business process. If the RTO is different, then this fact must be communicated to the BC steering committee to determine the collateral impact to other critical business processes and their plans.

Identify Key Dependencies and Quantities Required over Time

The working team should determine an agreed on time continuum that can be applied across the board for all dependencies. This time continuum should allow identifying a common RTO, meaning the team must start bringing dependencies on board by a specific time, to ensure greater likelihood of recovery within a given time frame. Identifying dependencies and their quantities over time is invaluable to ensure timely recovery. The working team makes that determination based upon input and feedback from all the relevant stakeholders.

Determine Procedures for Dependencies

Every dependency should have workarounds. A workaround is a step taken to ensure that all alternatives have been explored to obtain a dependency if it cannot be procured the "typical" way. The procedure should also contain a reliance statement explaining why the dependency is important, as well as any additional information. A frequent approach to prepare a procedure is to have the person who has been assigned responsibility prepare it and then have the working session attendees review it.

Determine RPO for Applications, Data, Servers, and Other Technology (if Applicable)

A constant theme of this book is that IT supports the recovery of a business, not the other way around. Nonetheless, the two are tightly integrated and must support each other. Generally, a failed RPO should not mean recovery is dead. Workarounds can be identified if the applications, servers, repositories, etc. are down.

Identify Content for Each Procedure

The person assigned responsibility for a procedure should be the one preparing it, and then members of the working session should review the content for accuracy and completeness. The format of the procedure should include a reliance statement, steps to take if the dependency is unavailable, and any other pertinent information, such as phone numbers and websites to access.

Assign Responsibilities for Procedures

Each procedure should have a person assigned to it. This person prepares the content but also ensures that it is current. Consider assigning a backup for any person who is considered primary for executing a procedure, in case he or she is unavailable during an event.

Draft a BP Plan

Compile and Analyze Data from Working Session

After completing at least one working session, the project manager assigned to coordinate the effort should compile and analyze the information. This action may require verifying content like contact information, correct spelling of names, listing of stakeholders, and up to date content in the procedures and appendix.

Prepare Draft of a BP Plan

The draft of the BP plan is similar to preparing any business document. Give attention to the content's layout and logical flow. When drafting, ensure that it complies with standard grammatical criteria, such as spelling, active voice, etc.

Check to Ensure the BP Plan Contains Only Essential Elements of Information

When developing a draft, a tendency exists to include just about everything compiled from the working sessions. Doing so only adds confusion over recovery and makes a BP plan unwieldy. A plan should include only what is pertinent based upon the scope of the plan. People should not have to wade through minutia to obtain what they need. In addition, maintenance of the plan could consume significant time and effort. Whenever possible, cite supporting material located in different documents and give their location, for example, company library, website, or servers.

Proofread the Plan

While seeming like common sense, this activity is often overlooked. From an appearances perspective, the BP plan should be proofed to ensure correct grammar and accuracy of content. Note and highlight any questions or concerns about the content.

Review BP Plan

Determine Approach for Review

Once the draft is somewhat complete, the review with stakeholders occurs. You can take one of several approaches.

One approach is to circulate sequentially the draft among stakeholders to review the content via hard copy. The disadvantage is clear, however. It can be quite time consuming and take considerable effort to track down the document and compile the revisions when a large number of stakeholders are involved.

A derivative of the sequential approach is to send an electronic copy to all stakeholders and have them enter their feedback and electronically pass it on from one person to the next. This approach, too, can be time consuming but less so than the other approach; it still requires compiling the changes.

Rather than send the draft out sequentially, another approach is to assemble the stakeholders together in one location or over an electronic meeting and then review the draft. Before the meeting, send out a copy for their review. At the meeting, capture revisions until a consensus is reached. The challenges are getting everyone together at the same time and assuming that they will review the draft prior to the meeting.

Prepare Copies for Review

Regardless of the approach, a draft copy should appear in final form, at least as much as possible. Stakeholders should receive a copy in either hard or soft copy or both. They should also receive it in advance of the review to make any notes and formulate feedback.

Conduct First Review and Update the BP Plan

The first review is to collect additional input from the stakeholders, if any. Reviewers should look at the overall flow of the content, for example, logical layout, as well as the applicability of the content. They should also be prepared to ask questions of each other to further understanding of each other's roles and responsibilities. The plan is then updated accordingly.

Conduct a Second Review

If necessary, a second review is conducted. Stakeholders review the revisions and take one last look at the BP plan for accuracy and usefulness. In theory, you should receive minimal feedback and the session is shorter.

Conduct Test of the Call Tree

The call tree should be tested. This test should consist of contacting all members listed through various media identified in the plan. Feedback should include who responded, how they were contacted, and how long they took to respond. If the results are unsatisfactory, the call tree should be updated and retested accordingly.

Distribute BP Plan

Conduct Final Walkthrough

The purpose of the final walkthrough is to conduct one final check of the content and achieve buy-in to the BP plan. Again, this meeting should be short. The plan should be distributed prior to the meeting to allow sufficient time for review. Ideally, if consensus over the plan has been achieved, it is "golden."

Revise the BP Plan

This action occurs only if the final walkthrough uncovers anything significant. If it does, then another walkthrough may be necessary with either all the stakeholders or only those impacted by the change.

Place the BP Plan under Configuration Management

When the BP plan is complete and has received the appropriate approvals, place the document under configuration management. Any significant changes require review and approval by key stakeholders, such as those responsible for the relevant critical business process.

Determine Method of Distribution

The method of distribution usually takes one or both forms, hard and soft copy. The advantage of hard copy is that the plan is tangible to stakeholders. The disadvantages are that it is cumbersome to use, easy to misplace or lose, and people might be referencing an outdated copy. The advantages of an electronic copy are it is less bulky than paper, people will likely have the most recent version, and they will likely operate from the same version. The disadvantages are people needing common IT to communicate with each other and devices needing enough power to last if an event knocks out all power for a significant time. The best approach is to employ a combination of both methods. A hard copy as well as a soft copy is readily accessible to everyone.

Apply PM (Closing) for a BP Plan

This task involves ensuring that validation of the performance measurement baseline occurs prior to officially closing the project. It also involves ensuring that all administrative, financial, and contractual concerns or issues are addressed to preclude legal problems, for instance, from occurring.

DELIVERABLES

Two tightly integrated deliverables are produced.

The call tree is the first deliverable. The call tree consists of the media to use and a list of people to contact immediately when an event affects a critical business process. The media include landlines, pagers, personal computers, cell phones, and other media to alert people to convene. Upon response, they meet electronically or at a designated location to determine the impact and what elements of the plan to execute.

The BP plan is the other deliverable. It consists of several elements of information. The plan should provide a high-level overview of the process. The overview, just as it implies, is high level. It might describe the overall goals and objectives of the critical business process and any time or cost constraints confronting it. If the plan is one of several BP plans built to support recovery of a critical business process, the overview should list them with the title and a short description. The plan should also include a scope statement, describing the overall boundaries or parameters of the scope. It might cite the major sub-processes and their respective deliverables included in the process, as well as the organizations involved with the plan. Just as importantly, however, it might describe what the plan excludes. Dependencies, or resources, are identified in the plan. These dependencies might include people, for example, technicians or manual laborers; facilities, for example, laboratory or office buildings; IT, for example, applications, data repositories, or servers; communications, for example, landlines or satellite; records, for example, financial, certification, or compliance. The quantities of each dependency and their distribution over a time continuum are also identified. The distribution reflects a cumulative count until a certain threshold is reached, enabling full recovery.

The RTO is determined for the overall process. The RTO may have originally been determined in the BIA. As more information becomes available during plan development, the RTO may be modified closer or further along a time continuum. Key stakeholders must make a decision whether the RTO remains the same or must change. This determination is based on risks and issues related to profitability, cost, legal compliance, competiveness, reputation, etc.

In addition to the RTO, an RPO may also be determined for software applications and data. The RPO often aligns with the RTO, but does not necessarily have to. Obviously, applications and data deemed more critical than others require recovery sooner. The procedures for detailing the RPO do not appear in the BP plan but in a disaster recovery plan.

A BP plan should also include procedures consisting of alternative actions, known as workarounds, for an unavailable dependency. The procedure provides a reliance statement that describes why the dependency is important for recovery and any additional useful information. It then lists steps, often in descending priority order, to obtain alternatives to the dependency. Each step consists of an action verb and object along with other useful information, such as contact names and numbers or websites. If any alternative is not practical, instructions on how and where to elevate requests should be provided.

Also included in the BP plan is a listing of the recovery team members and the people responsible for executing each procedure. Recovery team members and the people responsible for executing the procedures may or may not be the same because the recovery team may include additional people with knowledge, interest, expertise, and experience deemed valuable for the successful recovery. Generally, the recovery team provides oversight for executing the plan and the "doers" are the people responsible for applying the procedures. The plan should also include the person responsible for the overall process as well as the signature approvals of the plan.

The BP plan may also include an appendix, consisting of checklists, glossary of terms, maps, diagrams, matrices, and other useful information. A caveat, however, is warranted. Avoid the temptation to inundate the plan with superfluous data and information. It will only confuse readers and make the document cumbersome to find information. Consider citing sources and then readers can go to those sources for information.

STAKEHOLDERS

Having the right stakeholders engaged in developing a BP plan is so essential that the very quality of a plan depends upon it. The right stakeholders involved means having a plan that instills confidence in and increases

Role	Board of Directors	BC Steering Committee	Business Continuity Working Group	BC Project Manager/ Program Manager	BC Specialists/ Staff Support	Business Process Owner/Senior Management	Recovery Team Leader (Operational)	Recovery Team Members (Operational)	Audit	Customers	Suppliers/ Vendors	Shareholders
Tasks												
Build business preparedness plan												
Manage project for building business preparedness plan		C,I	C,I	R	C	I	A					
Prepare for building business preparedness plan				R,A	C	I	I					
Define requirements for building business preparedness plan				R	C	I	I	I				

FIGURE 8.3
RACI chart for building a BP plan.

(Continued)

Draft business preparedness plan				A,C	C	I	R	A	I	C	C	
Review business preparedness plan		I	I	A	C	I	R	A				
Distribute business preparedness plan		I	I	A	C	I	R	A	I	I	I	
Apply project management (closing) for building business preparedness plan	I	I	C,I	R,A	R,A	A	A					

Legend
R = Responsible
A = Accountable
C = Consult
I = Inform

FIGURE 8.3 (CONTINUED)
RACI chart for building a BP plan.

the likelihood of use during recovery; their responsibilities are shown in Figure 8.3. The plan will likely reflect realism. Stakeholders in a BP plan are people representing key dependencies and have to execute the contents of a plan. Other key stakeholders include the BC specialist or project manager who facilitates the working sessions to develop the plan and to conduct walkthroughs; a scribe to compile input for, and feedback on, the plan; the author of the plan who has responsibility to prepare the drafts and incorporate changes; call tree members consisting of recovery team members and people responsible to execute parts of the plan; and senior managers and executives who must ultimately review and approve the plan. Occasionally, stakeholders who are subject matter experts and are from other critical business processes may attend working and review sessions to provide valuable insights. Vendors and consultants may also be involved; however, unless some form of nondisclosure or intellectual property agreement is signed, caution is warranted to avoid disclosing sensitive information.

Care must be taken, of course, not to involve so many stakeholders that the sessions become unmanageable or participants cannot come to an agreement or consensus of the plan. A core team of people, not to exceed 10 in number, can usually speak on behalf of several stakeholders. These stakeholders either act as delegates or are responsible for obtaining further input and consensus from others.

INTEGRATION OF ACTIVITIES

The successful building of an initial BP plan requires a coordinated set of tasks. These tasks ultimately result in one or more BP plans for a critical BP plan.

Initially, the tasks require collecting as much background data and information about the critical business process as possible. Using that information, the BC project manager assigned to that critical business process and who has responsibility for ensuring the BP plan is built schedules a meeting with senior management responsible for executing the critical business process. This meeting is often a formality that serves as a segue for meeting with the recovery team.

While working with the recovery team, the BC project manager provides knowledge and expertise, as well as leadership, in collecting data and information for completing a BP plan. Depending on the circumstances, the BC project manager may complete the draft of the plan. Under other circumstances, someone on the recovery team might complete it.

Regardless, the draft of the BP plan must be reviewed by the recovery team and bought into, especially by the recovery team leader and senior management. Additionally, the call tree, incorporated in the plan, is tested for accuracy and reliability. Assuming the review results in minor revisions and is approved by key stakeholders, the recovery team leader distributes the plan to recovery team members as well as to any other stakeholders having an interest in the document.

FINAL THOUGHTS

The advantage of building a BP plan outweighs not having a plan. Building a plan causes key stakeholders to collaborate and communicate when producing the document. People become more aware of their responsibilities and the impact of their failure to perform during an event if it occurs. In a sense, the act of planning is just as important, if not more so, than the plan itself.

CASE STUDY, CONTINUED

After meeting with Ferragio and having the okay to proceed, Rodriquez met with Wilson to discuss the overall approach to building the BP plan, a topic that was also discussed with Ferragio. He also presented the same training on BC and the reason for the project. However, he also discussed the role of the single point of contact (SPOC); responsibilities included supporting Rodriquez as project assistant by taking notes, setting up meetings, and serving as a knowledge resource about the process. They also developed a WBS, Responsible, Accountable, Consult, and Inform (RACI) chart, shown in Figure 8.4, and a high-level schedule, appearing in Figure 8.5, that was ultimately approved by Ferragio and other stakeholders in the critical process.

Rodriquez, with the help of Wilson, decided to set up a meeting to discuss the BP plan and approach to develop a plan for all the key stakeholders participating in the process. He needed stakeholders who have a good understanding of the overall process and their particular role in executing

	Jorge Rodriquez	Dante Ferragio	Recovery Team Members	Linda Steinhauser	Steering Committee
4.1.1 Prepare for conducting BIA for process	R,A	C			
4.1.2 Conduct BIA	R	A,C	A,C		
4.1.3 Analyze results for BIA	R,A	A,C	A,C	I	I
4.2.1 Prepare for building business preparedness plan	R,A	I			
4.2.2 Define requirements for building business preparedness plan	R,A	C	C		
4.2.3 Draft business preparedness plan	R,A	A,C	C	I	
4.2.4 Review business preparedness plan	R	A	C		
4.2.5 Distribute business preparedness plan	R	A		I	I
4.3.1 Prepare for testing business preparedness plan	R,A	A			
4.3.2 Conduct business preparedness plan	R,A	A	A,C		
4.3.3 Report on testing results	R,A	I		I	I
4.3.4 Schedule follow up of testing results	R,A	A		I	I

Legend

R = Responsible
A = Accountable
C = Consult
I = Inform

FIGURE 8.4
WBS and RACI chart for building the BP plan.

	July	Aug	Sept	Oct
4.2 Build business preparedness plan	7/23		9/11	
4.2.1 Prepare for building business preparedness plan	7/23	8/1		
4.2.2 Define requirements for building business preparedness plan	7/23	8/1		
4.2.3 Draft business preparedness plan		8/2	9/4	
4.2.4 Review business preparedness plan			9/5 9/10	
4.2.5 Distribute business preparedness plan			9/11	

FIGURE 8.5
Schedule for building BP plan.

it. In an earlier meeting with Ferragio, these stakeholders were identified. At this meeting, which was really a kickoff meeting for this project, Rodriquez also presented training on BC, how BP plays a key role, and general responsibilities of stakeholders to build the BP plan. Following is an outline for the kickoff meeting.

Kick Off Meeting

Leaders: Dante Ferragio (Process Owner)
Jorge Rodriquez (Project Manager)

Telecom Number: (xxx) xxx-xxxx

I. Introductory remarks	Ferragio
II. Background information	Rodriquez
III. BC and BP overview	Rodriquez
IV. Description	Ferragio
a. Goals	
b. Deliverables	
c. Schedule	
d. Responsibilities	
e. Challenges/risks	
V. Questions and answers, round robin	Rodriquez
VI. Next steps	Rodriquez

After addressing all the concerns of the stakeholders, Rodriquez scheduled sessions, with the help and attendance of Wilson, to inquire and capture information pertinent to the BP plan. A list of questions was prepared to capture the necessary information, as well as any additional information that might prove useful for preparing the plan. Following is a list of some of the questions.

Questions to Answers When Building a BP Plan

- What is the purpose of the BP plan?
- What is in and out of scope?
- What other critical processes will the BP plan affect?
- Who are the members of the recovery team?
- What is their contact information?
- What areas, sub-processes, or functions are they responsible for?
- What is the maximum allowable downtime (MAD)?
- What are the major resources and dependencies for this process and the needed quantities over a specific time continuum?
- What are the assumptions made for building the BP plan?
- Is there a call tree and is the contact information current?
- What is the RPO for each resource?
- What is the workaround content for each procedure?
- What are the major risks affecting the content of the BP plan?
- What additional content can be cited or appended to the BP plan?

After collecting all the necessary information, Rodriquez, with the help of the BC staff, prepared a draft of the BP plan according to the guidance provided by the governance infrastructure for the project. Rodriquez then scheduled a meeting with Ferragio to discuss the contents and to obtain additional guidance to clarify content. After the session, Rodriquez updated the plan and then decided no additional work was necessary; as far as he was concerned, the first draft was ready for review by the stakeholders for the process. He then asked Wilson, the SPOC, to schedule the 2-hour session as well as send out copies of the draft in advance asking the stakeholders to review the plan; refer to Appendix C for a copy of the draft plan.

Rodriquez then conducted the first review session. He conducted the meeting strictly following an outline, while Wilson served as the scribe. After reviewing the plan with everyone, he then encouraged discussions among the stakeholders. Wilson captured feedback and then mentioned that a final review session would be held and the plan would reflect the updates.

Wilson compiled the notes captured during the session, and he and Rodriquez reviewed them. A few questions arose but, for the most part, the feedback captured was incorporated into the BP plan. For those areas needing additional information, Rodriquez or Wilson contacted the relevant stakeholder to acquire the necessary answers or clarify contents.

The BP plan was updated one last time and then a final review session was held with the team of stakeholders to capture any last minute changes or oversights. Everyone had received a copy of the plan prior to this session. Rodriquez asked the stakeholders if they had their consensus. He also conducted a "lessons learned" to make improvements. Following is the outline of the lessons learned document.

Final Review and Lessons Learned Outline

- I. Plan review
  - a. Is the content
    - i. Current?
    - ii. Complete?
    - iii. Accurate?
    - iv. Clear?
  - b. Is there consensus over the plan?
    - i. If not, what needs to change?
- II. Lessons learned
  - a. What went well?
  - b. What are some opportunities for improvement?
  - c. Recommendations?
- III. Next steps

Having achieved consensus, Rodriquez met with Ferragio to review the BP plan and to close out activities in the schedule. Both Ferragio and Rodriquez believed the schedule was complete and both parties signed the document. Ferragio sent a copy of the document electronically to each of the stakeholders, as well as ensured that soft and hard copies were stored in a place that was readily accessible in case a disastrous event hits.

Throughout the project lifecycle up to this point in time, Rodriquez planned and executed the project using good PM practices. He developed a reliable schedule that involved the participation of key stakeholders. The plan reflected estimates of the work to be done and assigned responsibilities for completing it. During the execution of the plan, he collected status and produced reports, prepared and distributed according to the communication management plan. The status collection occurred regularly, in this case weekly, and tailored reports were generated for the process owner, the key stakeholders, the working group, and, ultimately, the steering committee. He looked for variances in the schedule and determined whether to take corrective action, and, if necessary, according to the PM plan. Schedule, cost, and scope baselines were established before work commenced and were altered only if the change board, in this case the steering committee, decided it was necessary.

GETTING STARTED CHECKLIST

Question	Yes	No
1. When building the BP plan, are you realizing these benefits?		
Providing documented guidelines for recovery		
Encouraging communication and coordination		
Providing a systematic approach when building a plan		
Providing a means to train new employees about recovery		
Encouraging proactive and responsive behavior		
Reducing the financial impact of an event		
Encouraging greater awareness of BC		
Identifying showstoppers and encouraging stakeholders to think outside the box		
Enhancing the competitive position of the company		
Building a BP plan demonstrating confidence in handling an event		
2. When building the BP plan, have you considered how to address these challenges?		
Making the time, labor, tools, and information available to build the BP plan		
Lacking an understanding and knowledge of BC		
Obtaining buy-in for the BP plan		
Scoping the BP plan		
Determining when the BP plan is complete		

Sharing of data and information
Protecting data and information
Distinguishing assumptions from facts
Identifying the interfaces with other plans
Keeping the call tree current
Keeping the BP plan current
Ensuring the right people participate in building the BP plan
Focusing on too much IT
Developing a BP plan dealing with a broad range of events
Communicating the BP plan

3. Did you determine whether to produce these deliverables?
Call tree
BP plan

4. When building the BP plan, did you consider these concepts?
The BP plan serves as a strategic guideline
Prefer graphics and illustrations to narrative text
Keep the narrative text clean
Seek stakeholder participation during BP plan development
Remember that building a BP plan is not necessarily an efficient exercise in the short run
Scope definition is essential
The people who perform a procedure develop and review its contents
Keep in mind the purpose of the BP plan is to enhance the survivability of the company
Criticality is determined by time at the plan level
Strive for threat independence
Exercise risk management
All relevant information is documented in the BP plan
Distribute the BP plan only to relevant stakeholders
A BP plan is a snapshot in time
Incorporate the tangible and intangible dependencies of the BP plan
Conduct formal walkthroughs with key stakeholders
Identify opportunities for greater integration and communication in the BP plan
Seek consistency among BP plans

5. Is your plan:
Clear?
Concise?
Accurate?
Useful?
Flow logically?
Free of grammatical errors?

6. When building the BP plan, have you considered performing these activities?
   - Review the results of the BIA
   - Compile preliminary information about the critical business process
   - Identify key stakeholders
   - Schedule the session
   - Identify the format of the BP plan
   - Identify recovery team membership
   - Determine scope
   - Perform risk management
   - Determine overall description of the BP plan
   - Distinguish between assumptions and facts
   - Determine call tree media and contacts
   - Determine the overall RTO
   - Identify key dependencies and quantities required over time
   - Determine the procedures for dependencies
   - Determine RPO for applications, data servers, and other technology, if applicable
   - Identify the content for each procedure
   - Assign responsibilities for procedures
   - Compile and analyze data from a working session
   - Draft a BP plan
   - Check to ensure BP plan contains only essential elements of information
   - Proofread the plan
   - Determine approach for review
   - Prepare copies for review
   - Conduct first review and update the BP plan
   - Conduct second review
   - Conduct test of call tree
   - Conduct final walkthrough
   - Revise the BP plan
   - Place the BP plan under configuration management
   - Determine the method of distribution

9

Test the Business Preparedness Plan

Once the business preparedness (BP) plan has been built and approved, you need to test it periodically to ensure its applicability to the critical business process. Testing reinforces the plan's contents in the minds of stakeholders and increases their readiness to respond to an event.

WHAT IS TESTING?

Testing is a systematic approach to verify and validate the effectiveness of an organization's ability to respond to, and recover from, an event. A BP plan is instrumental in guiding them.

The key words here are systematic, verify, and validate. Being systematic means taking a logical, organized, disciplined approach toward testing. The techniques and tools provide that systematic approach. Verify is providing a level of quality to ensure a plan and its implementation meet certain standards. Validate means that the testing meets the needs of the stakeholders to enhance recovery.

GOALS

Testing from a BP perspective achieves several goals.

Increase the Accuracy of the Plan

All too often BP plans are developed, sit on a shelf, and become outdated. Testing forces stakeholders to review and update their plans and apply them on a scenario.

Enhance the Knowledge and Understanding of Business Continuity

A scenario presented during testing requires stakeholders to receive an overview of business continuity (BC) and then delve into the contents of their BP plan.

Keep the Call Tree Current

A call tree must always remain up to date because a failure in communication results in a failure to recover. Testing a BP plan should include executing a call tree to include the people listed and their corresponding contact information.

Identify Opportunities for the Recovery Team to Respond to an Event

Through testing, team members can learn to communicate, collaborate, and coordinate during recovery. Chances are that a recovery team never had the opportunity to work together when confronting and recovering from an event. Testing, using the hypothetical scenario, gives them the opportunity to avoid the severe consequences of actual failure. The team then receives feedback on what went well, where opportunities for improvement exist, and any best practices to share with the current recovery team.

Provide an Opportunity to Improve the Contents of a BP Plan

During testing, team members must use the BP plan. In doing so, testing will uncover any inaccuracies and irrelevancies as the result of a review and the plan should be revised accordingly.

Determine the Effectiveness of a BP Plan

Through testing, the recovery team may discover that certain procedures or people added to the call tree do not add value to recovery. Consequently, anything not adding value should be removed or revised to ensure greater accuracy and relevancy of the content to recovery team members.

TERMINOLOGY

Testing a BP plan involves some BC terminology that necessitates a definition upfront.

Activation is deploying part, or all, of a BP plan in response to an event. It should include exercising the call tree and a significant portion of the plan itself during a realistic scenario, whether in the form of tabletop or drill.

Corrective actions are the shortcomings identified during the testing exercise. These are actions necessary to fix defects or enhance opportunities for improvement, usually identified in a lessons learned session after an exercise.

An *integrated exercise* is a cross-functional, multiprocess, interorganizational test to develop, maintain, and enhance BP. It involves applying a scenario affecting multiple BP plans to evaluate their ability to communicate, coordinate, and collaborate during an event.

An *exercise* is an event planned and executed to develop, maintain, and enhance BP for a critical business process. It can be developed and deployed either by the BC governance infrastructure or by a critical business process. It can take the form of a tabletop or drill or simulation exercise.

A *scenario* is a realistic, yet fictitious, event presenting a set of conditions and impacts challenging a recovery team when identifying, analyzing, and applying the content of their BP plan or plans. The scenario should consist of an event that occurs, plus a minor but related incident that adds an unexpected challenge. The scenario should also progress to various degrees of intensity over time to test the ability of a critical business process to attain and sustain resiliency.

A *simulation exercise* is having recovery team members actually apply the specific content of their BP plans against a scenario. Also known as a drill, it entails acquiring resources and exercising the content of procedures, thereby emphasizing less discussion and more action. The simulation exercise takes more time and effort than a tabletop exercise.

Stand down is simply a response to an event no longer necessary—whether for an exercise or real life event. Additional action is unnecessary by the recovery team.

A *tabletop exercise* is applying the contents of a BP plan to a scenario using discussion and not taking action, such as during a drill or simulation exercise. The general approach is for the key stakeholders to be presented with a scenario and, using the BP plan, discuss how they would go about responding to, and recovering from, an event. The tabletop takes less time and is less invasive than a drill.

KEY CONCEPTS

To effectively test a BP plan, it is important to understand and apply a number of key concepts.

A Scenario Should Be Realistic

It makes little sense to have a scenario that may never occur or has a very low probability of occurrence, such as a tornado in a desert. Nor does it have to be the worst-case situation; rather, it should have a good probability of occurrence and a measurable impact to the critical business process. It is best to avoid extremes of events. A scenario should also include all key stakeholders, such as customers, suppliers, contractors, and business partners. The scenario should test for the capacity of a process to work with constraints, such as an event stressing the importance of a "hard" recovery time objective (RTO). It should also occur over a time continuum that necessitates using procedures for recovery and changes to the circumstances presented. In some cases, and this is highly recommended, it incorporates a wild card situation that shakes up the team and forces them to rethink their strategies for dealing with the scenario. Avoid any discussion of the probability of an event occurring; the topic is irrelevant because everything is predicated on an event having already occurred.

A Scenario Should Test Tangible and Intangible Areas

Tangible areas are objective, physical aspects of a recovery. These areas include damage assessment and disruption impact, dependencies and procedures executed, exercise of the call tree, systems operability, and compliance with RTO and recovery point objective (RPO) requirements. Tangible areas lend themselves to an objective assessment because the evidence of their occurring is visible. Intangible areas are subjective, often nonphysical, are hard to detect their occurrence, and require some judgment based upon anecdotal evidence identified during a test. Intangible areas include communication, collaboration, coordination, leadership, decision-making, conflict management, and teaming. These tend to involve important soft skills, which are difficult to measure.

Focus on Common Issues That Are Likely To Surface during an Event

Some common problems tend to resurface from one critical business process to another. These are often referred to as common points of failure and include the following: some members of the call tree are not contacted or do not respond; manual and automated procedures are not applied or are done so inadequately; requested reviews and approvals are not exercised; lack of performance to internal standards, such as policies and procedures; not referring to the BP plan; not identifying touch points with other processes; recovery team members not participating in discussions; people responsible for exercising procedures fail to do so; having content in the BP plan that is inaccurate or incomplete; no workspace or assembly area identified for the recovery team and other stakeholders if the situation requires assembling someplace; failure or inability to access the plan during the test; and not considering RTO or RPO requirements.

Identify Common Dependencies to Test

There are many areas of a BP plan to test during a scenario. It is best to focus on testing common dependencies appearing in all plans, including data and information; location and facilities; procedures; information systems, including data, servers, and applications; security; labor; equipment; supplies; documentation and recordkeeping; and communications or telecommunications.

Consider a Wide Range of Scenarios before Agreeing on a Specific One for a Test

Scenarios can be divided into natural and human events. Natural events include a flood, tornado, hurricane, fire, earthquake, typhoon, cyclone, drought, landslide, and pandemic. Natural events often affect areas such as financial and operational performance, accessibility to physical locations, damage to facilities, injury to people, communication with key stakeholders, such as people and other organizations, and transportation. Human events include arson, sabotage, vandalism, hacking, virus, denial of service attacks, contamination, hazardous material spills, power outages, and violence in the workplace. The human events typically affect areas like product safety, public perception, market changes, financial performance, industrial relations, communications, technology performance, and property. The key is to pick an event having a good likelihood or probability of happening, while at the same time having a meaningful impact on the ability of a critical business process to recover.

Failure in Testing Is Good, Not Bad

Contrary to popular belief, testing should rarely go without finding some opportunity for improvement. If the testing goes too well, meaning no shortcomings, it could indicate that the test was incomplete, the test objectives were unclear, or the testing was more to justify the current state of whatever is being tested. Testing must be thorough, looking for opportunities to disprove as much as confirm. The larger and more complex a critical business process being tested is, the greater is the number of opportunities for improvement. It is also far better to uncover problems during testing than to do so when recovering from a real event; often at that point failures become costly in terms of time and money and will likely delay recovery.

Testing Is an Educational Opportunity

Testing is not just an effort to determine the resiliency of a process. It is also an opportunity to enhance understanding and knowledge of BC. During testing, people not only receive a high-level review of the subject, but also they receive valuable experience. Recovery team members become more intimately involved through discussion and simply by the act of participation. To a certain degree, testing has a multiplier effect when it comes to education, due to a combination of telling, showing, and doing.

Lesson Learned Should Follow the Test as Soon as Possible

Once an exercise is complete, the project manager should engage the participants in a "lessons learned" session. The idea is to capture what went well, what are some areas for improvement, and whether any best practices have been identified to share with other critical business processes. A lessons learned session has an additional benefit: to provide an opportunity to conduct a meaningful dialogue among all the participants, which will increase synergy among them. The output of a lessons learned also provides input to the report covering the results of a test.

A Test BP Plan Is Necessary before a Test

As mentioned earlier, this document details information like the purpose, goals, and objectives of the test; the expected results and criteria for evaluation; the type of test and how it is conducted, for example, tabletop or drill; the major participants; where it will occur; when will it occur and for how long; support needed; and any other pertinent information. Selected key stakeholders should participate in developing the test plan and it should have their approval. The scenario may also be described in the test plan; however, use discretion to avoid revealing too much prior to the test.

A Formal Report on Test Results Is Necessary

After the conducting of the test, the project manager issues a documented report to the leadership of the critical business process tested. The document should provide background about the test, the assessment criteria for evaluation, the strengths and weaknesses revealed during the test, and an overall assessment regarding the resiliency of critical business process. It is often a good practice to prepare a straw horse of the report with selected members of the recovery team to preclude any pushback or surprises. With buy-in, the report delivered to senior leadership of the critical business process becomes a formality. Ideally, the leadership agrees to a high-level schedule to address any weaknesses and for follow up.

Follow up on the Weaknesses Identified in the Report

It serves very little value to identify weaknesses, receive a schedule, and then never follow up after issuing a report. A follow up review, either in the form of another test or an interview session with key stakeholders, several months later should suffice to determine whether leadership has seriously corrected any weaknesses. Unfortunately, a tendency exists for stakeholders to turn their attention toward other concerns.

BENEFITS

Several key benefits exist for testing BP plans for processes.

Determining the Effectiveness of a BP Plan before a Real Event Occurs

Testing enables determining the parts of a plan that allow resiliency and the ones requiring improvement. Determining whether a BP plan is effective during an actual event is too late; testing is necessary before an event to ensure that shortcomings, such as inaccuracies and gaps, are fixed.

Determining the Ability of the Recovery Team to Communicate, Collaborate, and Coordinate before an Event Occurs

Testing brings out any difficulties in these areas in advance and provides an opportunity to improve upon weaknesses. It also provides an opportunity to leverage strengths and incorporate any best practices that enhance communication, collaboration, and coordination.

Identifying Shortcomings in the Content of the BP Plan

Before any testing occurs, the recovery team and other stakeholders should conduct a walkthrough of the plan. This walkthrough not only increases people's familiarity with the BP plan, but also identifies areas for improvement, ranging from grammatical correction to unrealistic workarounds in procedures. Any shortcomings are then addressed prior to the exercise, likely revealing additional shortcomings requiring attention.

Updating the Call Tree

The recovery team should review the listing of individuals and their contact information for accuracy. Any updates are made prior to an exercise. A call tree may or may not be part of the BP plan. However, they should always be exercised together.

Sustaining and Augmenting Awareness and Knowledge about BC

This subject is often not on the forefront of people's minds until something actually happens. Before and during testing, the project manager gives a short overview to orient people about the subject. The presentation should be brief and at a high level and serve only to enhance the quality of the walkthrough and participation during the exercise. The intent is not to make anyone an expert.

Validating Whether the BP Plan Meets Standards and Expectations of the Key Stakeholders

A plan should address standards set by the BC governance infrastructure as well as meet the expected needs of the people using the BP plan. Testing is a way to ensure standards and expectations are met.

CHALLENGES

Despite the benefits of testing BP plans, a number of challenges exist that project managers must overcome.

Having All the Right Stakeholders Participate in Testing

This challenge can be the result of a host of factors, including turnover of stakeholders, competing priorities, and lack of interest. Regardless of the reason, inadequate participation can hinder testing. When preparing for testing, the project manager should seek to engage as many key stakeholders as possible. Participation will offset much of this challenge because it encourages ownership. The downside of participation, of course, is that it eliminates the element of surprise. Consider restricting the number of participants when preparing the test.

Having the Time and Resources to Prepare a Meaningful, Realistic Scenario

Developing a testing scenario requires knowledge of BC, understanding of the process being tested, and having a creative imagination. Few people in an organization have people with such a combination of qualities. In addition, it requires time and effort to build the scenario. Typically, the BC governance infrastructure, often the assigned project manager, will develop the scenario with the assistance of a limited number of stakeholders. However, in some circumstances, stakeholders may develop their own scenario and conduct the test themselves; that is, of course, if they have the requisite resources and expertise to perform the test. In some cases, the governance infrastructure or the stakeholders can reuse previous scenarios to overcome this challenge. They can also modify an existing scenario for their unique circumstances.

Preventing a Few People or One Organization from Dominating a Testing Event

Twenty percent of people often produce 80% of the results; this statistical principle applies in just about every environment, except when involving testing. Recovery requires all people working together and communicating during a test and an actual event; everyone depends upon others to perform their responsibilities. Whether conducted by the project manager assigned by the BC governance infrastructure or by a recovery team itself, everyone participates, not just a few. One way to overcome this challenge is to track responses to the call tree exercise and to have recovery team members exercise their relevant responsibilities. Then, assess the results of the test, highlighting successes and shortcomings.

Lacking Knowledge or Awareness about the BP Plan

As mentioned several times before, BC and BP are often not in the forefront of everyone's minds. After building a BP plan, stakeholders often go on to other business. Over time, some or all of the content is forgotten; in fact, some people may even have forgotten a BP plan exists. Therefore, it is important to conduct a walkthrough of the plan before any testing occurs. This walkthrough will refresh people's minds about the plan and identify any necessary updates. Even if stakeholders do not participate in a test, the walkthrough will help them become more aware and knowledgeable about the contents of the plan.

Taking the Time to Prepare a Test Plan and Receiving Buy-In from the Key Stakeholders

Testing is not always planned out, at least to the depth proving value-added to the participants. A way to overcome this challenge is to develop a test plan led by the project manager. This planning should include the test's goals, objectives, and expected results; when the test will occur; why it is occurring; how it will be conducted; who will participate; and where it will occur. The test plan should never occur in a void; that is, it should involve a select group of key stakeholders. The only exception to this point is the actual details of the scenario should not be shared widely, if for no other reason than to test the recovery team's performance under uncertainty.

Determining the Best Time to Conduct a Test and Whether to Give Advance Warning

The critical business process being tested will likely have operational priorities conflicting with an exercise. The more complex the critical business process, the more difficult it is to test over a meaningful period of time. The loss of operational time means a loss of money vis-à-vis conducting a BC test that may never happen. It may also mean people have to work overtime to compensate for the disruption in productivity. The timing of the test, therefore, is critical. The best approach is to let key stakeholders determine when to conduct the test for a specific period of time. This approach should reduce resistance and further encourage ownership of the test.

Ensuring Follow up of the Test Results Identifying Improvements

Any testing creates anxiety and testing for a critical business process is no different. Most of the time a sense of relief follows a test even after identifying opportunities for improvement. Avoid allowing this sense of relief to slow momentum. The project manager should press for dates to rectify shortcomings and when follow up can occur, to ascertain if recommendations have been implemented. Otherwise, key stakeholders of a business process or function will shift priorities and improvements may not occur without any follow up.

MAKING TESTING HAPPEN

A number of activities are required to conduct a successful exercise. These activities can be grouped into one of four phases described next and shown in Figure 9.1.

ID	Task Name	Predecessors
154	1.4 Test preparedness plan	
155	1.4.1 Manage project for testing business preparedness plan	
156	1.4.1.1 Apply project management	152
157	1.4.2 Prepare for testing business preparedness plan	
158	1.4.2.1 Review the results of the BIA and the building of the business preparedness plan	151,156
159	1.4.2.2 Compile the latest information on the process since building the last business preparedness plan	151
160	1.4.2.3 Identify key stakeholders	158,159
161	1.4.2.4 Determine the type of exercise	158,159
162	1.4.2.5 Develop the test plan	161
163	1.4.2.6 Schedule and conduct meeting or meetings with critical business process leadership	162
164	1.4.2.7 Update test plan	163
165	1.4.3 Conduct testing	
166	1.4.3.1 Schedule and conduct meeting or meetings with recovery team members	164
167	1.4.3.2 Conduct walkthrough of the business preparedness plan	166
168	1.4.3.3 Revise and distribute the business preparedness plan	167
169	1.4.3.4 Schedule and construct exercise	168
170	1.4.4 Report on testing results	
171	1.4.4.1 Prepare report	169
172	1.4.4.2 Update the business preparedness plan	169
173	1.4.4.3 Schedule and conduct meeting with recovery team	171,172
174	1.4.4.4 Schedule and conduct meeting with critical business process leadership	173
175	1.4.4.5 Update and distribute the critical business plan	174
176	1.4.5 Follow up on testing recommendations	
177	1.4.5.1 Conduct follow up on recommendations	175
178	1.4.6 Apply project management (closing) for testing business preparedness plan	
179	1.4.6.1 Perform closing tasks	177

FIGURE 9.1
WBS for testing a BP plan.

Manage Project for Testing a BP Plan

This task involves applying all the PM concepts, tools, and techniques to enhance project performance. For example, it includes preparing a charter, developing a WBS, making time and cost estimates, building a schedule, and tracking and monitoring performance.

Prepare for Testing a BP Plan

Review the Results of the BIA and the Building of the BP Plan

Use research and material compiled previously, which offers two advantages: It provides leverage to perform a test faster and more efficiently, and enables linkage between what was done earlier and what will be done in the future.

Compile the Latest Information on the Process since Building the Last BP Plan

This activity ties in closely with the last one because the context may have changed, for example, organizational strategies and reorganizations. However, it is imperative to reevaluate what was done previously for applicability to current circumstances. This activity requires conducting research, such as reviewing a website and interviewing people to ascertain if the context still applies.

Identify the Key Stakeholders

This activity may be easy or it may not. The difficulty is that many companies face turnover, reorganizations, promotions and demotions, retirements, and outsourcing, just to name a few. For small to medium companies, this situation will likely be relatively easy. For large companies, this activity can be quite challenging because of the complexity of the organizational structure supporting the critical business process.

Determine the Type of Exercise

Armed with sufficient information, this activity requires determining the type of exercise, such as a tabletop or a drill. The decision should not come lightly. Generally, if the test is the first one since the first build of the BP plan, a tabletop exercise is the best approach. This exercise allows people to become more familiar with the plan and to understand and explore issues related to its implementation, and it allows key stakeholders to start working together. In fact, several tabletop exercises may be necessary before going to the other type of exercise, the drill. This type of exercise involves the stakeholders treating the scenario as an actual event and then exercising actual recovery of their critical business process. During a drill, the project manager takes a more facilitative role than what is required under a tabletop exercise. The decision over what type of drill to conduct rests with the key stakeholders, usually at the senior leadership level. The proposed type of exercise is included in the test plan.

Develop the Test Plan

At this point, the test plan is a proposal for the type of test, its conduct, and expected outcomes. It is a draft, until reviewed and bought into at least by the senior leadership of the critical business process. Remember, the test plan should be as complete as possible before conducting an exercise.

Schedule and Conduct Meetings with Critical Business Process Leadership

This meeting, or series of meetings, is critical to the success of an exercise. It is during this activity that overall direction of a test and buy-in to a test plan are necessary to ensure greater attendance and participation during an exercise. If stakeholder buy-in is not possible, then the project manager must determine if it is something occurring outside of his or her control or is an issue needing elevation by the BC steering committee. Naturally, it is preferable that buy-in occurs either through agreement or consensus rather than to elevate any issue. Agreement or consensus is often reflected in revising the contents of a test plan.

Update Test Plan

After the meeting with the senior leadership of a critical business process, the next activity is to revise the test plan and submit it for final approval. The test plan now becomes the roadmap to conduct the exercise.

Conduct Testing

Schedule and Conduct Meetings with Recovery Team Members

This activity entails meeting with the members of the recovery team for the critical business process. This meeting can be held on a one-on-one basis or with everyone assembled in a conference room or attending electronically. The purpose is to discuss the contents of the test BP plan, identify any minor revisions to it, and explain the need for a walkthrough of the current plan. The presentation should also include a brief overview of BC and BP.

Conduct Walkthrough of the BP Plan

This session has the same goals and objectives as reviewing the initial building of a BP plan. A light presentation is given on BC to set the context, and then an in-depth review of the plan occurs, identifying areas of improvement.

Revise and Distribute the BP Plan

After updating the BP plan, the next activity is to distribute it to the applicable stakeholders. It is advantageous to distribute a plan in a manner allowing the recipients to review the content and to prepare themselves for an exercise. The time frame should also allow sufficient time to make any last minute corrections.

Schedule and Conduct Exercise

The exercise should be scheduled sufficiently in advance to allow people time to read the plan to become familiar with the contents and to prepare for the exercise. Additionally, depending on the size of the recovery team and other members who might attend, 2 hours are usually sufficient to conduct a tabletop. For drills, exercise encompasses 4 to 8 hours, depending on the number of stakeholders and the complexity of a critical business process.

For tabletops, the project manager usually takes the lead to move the exercise forward by presenting the scenario and facilitating the recovery team through the flow of the exercise. However, the project manager does not manage or lead the response he or she only ensures the team progresses towards coming up with an appropriate response. The project manager often assigns a scribe among the attendees and how the recovery team leader manages and leads the team through the scenario. For drills, the project manager mainly observes and provides guidance on the approach to follow described in the test plan. Remember, the project manager provides a hands-off approach because the recovery team runs the drill.

Report on Testing Results

Prepare Report

This activity entails compiling the observations, lessons learned, and other information about the results achieved during an exercise. The report, along with the other documentation, for example, test plans and updates to the BP plan, provides an audit trail and presents opportunities for improvement.

Update the BP Plan

Any revisions identified in the plan during an exercise should be incorporated now. The BP plan normally accompanies the report and the project manager jointly reviews both with the leadership of the critical business process. A good practice is to send both the updated plan and the report to senior leadership prior to the meeting. However, the plan is not distributed at this point because senior leadership may have additional revisions.

Schedule and Conduct a Meeting with the Recovery Team

It is usually a good practice to present a preliminary draft of the report to the recovery team prior to presenting the final version to the leadership of the critical business process. This action will increase buy-in and lessen push back from those stakeholders being evaluated. Naturally, the report should stress facts, data, and anecdotal evidence supporting the findings and recommendations. After achieving buy-in, the project manager is ready to present the report before the senior leadership of the critical business process.

Schedule and Conduct a Meeting with the Critical Business Process Leadership

It is a good practice to send the report and the updated plan to senior leadership of the critical business process so that they have sufficient time to review both items and to collect their thoughts. The meeting should be held two to three days after the session; any shorter time may be insufficient for the leadership to review the material in their often-busy schedules; any longer time may cause them to forget what they reviewed or to overlook what they were supposed to review.

Update and Distribute the Critical Business Plan

The review with senior leadership may result in requested revisions to the BP plan. After making revisions, circulate the document for final approval. Then, assuming approval, distribute the plan.

Follow up on Testing Recommendations

The report on the exercise will likely have recommendations. Few exercises go perfectly and, if they do, that is often a bad sign. If senior leadership finds the recommendations acceptable, then the project manager should negotiate a time to assess whether the recommendations have been implemented and, if so, how effectively.

Apply PM (Closing) for Testing BP Plan

This task involves ensuring that validation of the performance measurement baseline occurs prior to officially closing the project. It also involves ensuring that all administrative, financial, and contractual concerns or issues are addressed to preclude legal problems, for instance, from occurring.

DELIVERABLES

Six major deliverables are produced, several of which are integrated.

The *walkthrough* is the first deliverable. The walkthrough is the same as the one conducted to build a test plan with one exception—the recovery team is reviewing an existing BP plan. The walkthrough has three purposes. One, it encourage people to refresh their knowledge about the purpose and contents of a plan. Two, it captures improvements to a plan, ranging anywhere from grammatical corrections to revisions to the content. Three, it provides an updated plan for use during a test.

The *test plan* is the second deliverable. The test plan, as mentioned earlier, provides information about the upcoming exercise to determine the resiliency of a critical business process. The emphasis is on describing who, what, when, where, why, and how about the test. It serves as a requirements document for the exercise.

The *exercise* is the third deliverable. The exercise can be either a drill or a tabletop. A drill is run by the recovery team of the critical business process under the guidance of the project manager from the BC governance infrastructure. The tabletop involves a project manager from the BC governance infrastructure, too, but becomes more directly involved in facilitating the exercise.

The *report* is the fourth deliverable. The report should be brief, no more than 10 pages, and is sent to senior managers and executives responsible for the performance of the critical business process. The report should contain background information about the exercise, such as a high-level description of the scenario; a description of the results, such as how well the recovery team responded to the scenario; a list of recommendations for improvement; a tentative implementation plan and follow-up review of the effectiveness of the changes; and any additional relevant information, such as next steps. Before actually delivering the BP plan to senior or executive management, review a draft report with the recovery team to obtain buy-in to preclude surprises.

An *updated BP plan* is the fifth deliverable. After the exercise, the plan should catch any final updates before redistribution. Collect the requisite signatures on the plan and have the leader of the recovery team distribute it.

Follow up is the final deliverable. The follow up is on the "bought off" recommendations listed in the report. The whole purpose is to ensure that any identifiable improvements were implemented and done so effectively. The follow up should occur in a relatively short time, such as three to six months, depending on the complexity of the critical business process. Follow up could be formal or informal, depending on the environment, and does not require, unless deemed so by senior management or the leadership of the BC governance infrastructure, another exercise. More often than not, the follow up usually involves a few interviews with key stakeholders and a review of documentation demonstrating the implementation of recommendations.

STAKEHOLDERS

Several stakeholders are involved in testing a BP plan for a critical business process, as shown in Figure 9.2.

Role	Board of Directors	BC Steering Committee	Business Continuity Working Group	BC Project Manager/ Program Manager	BC Specialists/ Staff Support	Business Process Owner/Senior Management	Recovery Team Leader (Operational)	Recovery Team Members (Operational)	Audit	Customers	Suppliers/ Vendors	Shareholders
Tasks												
Test preparedness plan												
Manage project for testing business preparedness plan		C,I	C,I	R	C	I	A					
Prepare for testing business preparedness plan			C,I	R	C	I	C					
Conduct testing		I	C,I	R		I	A	A		I	I	
Report on testing results		I	I	R,A		A	A	A	I			
Follow up on testing recommendations		I	I	R	C	A	A		I	I	I	
Apply project management (closing) for testing business preparedness plan	I	I	C,I	R,A	R,A	A	A					

Legend
R = Responsible
A = Accountable
C = Consult
I = Inform

FIGURE 9.2
RACI chart for testing a BP plan.

The project manager is one. The project manager initiates the effort and may or may not conduct the effort. At a minimum, the project manager meets with the key stakeholders to explain the exercise and shares any relevant information. The project manager is from the BC governance infrastructure.

The leadership of a critical business process is another stakeholder. They are usually involved before and after an exercise. The project manager meets with them to present the test plan, revises it accordingly, and then coordinates with the recovery team leader for the BP plan or plans. After the exercise, these stakeholders receive a report from the project manager on findings and recommendations.

The recovery team responsible for exercising the contents of the BP plan is the final category for stakeholders. These people apply the content of the plan, use their judgment, and act to respond to a scenario. They must demonstrate the ability to restore resilience to their critical business process according to the BP plan.

INTEGRATION OF ACTIVITIES

After putting in place the PM concepts, tools, and techniques, the BC project manager can start working with the recovery team of the critical business process to begin testing the BP plan.

Preparation is the key for conducting an effective test. The BC project manager and key stakeholders work together to build a test plan that describes who, what, when, where, why, and how of conducting a specific test.

Assuming consensus or agreement over a test plan, the BC project manager, his or her supporting BC specialists, and the recovery team members conduct the test. The test, depending on whether a drill or table top exercise, usually lasts a couple of hours to a full day. During the session, a BC specialist, usually not the project manager because he or she must focus on what is going on, takes notes on issues, concerns, skirmishes, observations, suggestions, insights, etc. This data and information provide the basis for what comes next.

The BC project manager then prepares a draft of the report. This draft report provides background information about the test, for example, what the scenario was about and why the topic was selected, but also findings and recommendations. A good practice to follow is to review the draft with at least the recovery team leader and his or her selected designates to avoid surprises and to minimize conflict when presenting it to the recovery team leader's management.

Ideally, consensus and agreement is reached and the next task is to present or issue the report to the recovery team leader's management. If no consensus or agreement is reached with the recovery team leader, note it in the report and still conduct the presentation or issue the report.

After an agreed on time period with senior management and the recovery team leader, the next task is to conduct a review to ensure that all agreed on recommendations have been addressed. The project is then closed accordingly.

FINAL THOUGHTS

Testing a BP plan for a critical business process is not trivial. Considerable time and energy are spent on preparing, conducting, reporting, and following up with many stakeholders. Each stakeholder has unique interests in the outcome of an exercise. Some want the company to become resilient; some want to be able to sleep better at night; some see it as an opportunity to improve current business models; and some see it as a means to communicate and come together as a team.

CASE STUDY, CONTINUED

Testing Phase

The BP plan tells what must be done to recover a critical business process. However, the real value of a plan is ensuring that people understand the content and know how to apply it to recover from an event. Rodriquez put together a test to ensure that all the key stakeholders knew their responsibilities identified in the plan as well as the pertinent resources and the quantities required for recovery. He also developed a draft of the WBS and RACI chart and a schedule, shown in Figures 9.3 and 9.4, respectively.

Rodriquez scheduled a meeting with the process owner, Ferragio, to receive input on expectations concerning the plan. He then took the

	Jorge Rodriquez	Dante Ferragio	Recovery Team Members	Linda Steinhauser	Steering Committee
4.3.1 Prepare for testing business preparedness plan	R,A	A			
4.3.2 Conduct business preparedness plan	R,A	A	A,C		
4.3.3 Report on testing results	R,A	I		I	I
4.3.4 Schedule follow up of testing results	R,A	A		I	I

Legend
R = Responsible
A = Accountable
C = Consult
I = Inform

FIGURE 9.3
WBS and RACI chart for testing.

	July	Aug	Sept	Oct
4.3 Test business preparedness plan			9/11 10/2	
4.3.1 Prepare for testing business preparedness plan			9/13 9/20	
4.3.2 Conduct testing			9/21	
4.3.3 Report on testing results			9/22 10/2	
4.3.4 Schedule follow up on testing recommendations				10/2

FIGURE 9.4
Schedule for testing.

information collected from the interview to build a test plan. After completing the test, he scheduled another meeting with Ferragio to receive feedback and seek buy-in regarding the test plan's contents. Following is an outline of the test plan.

Test Plan

I. Executive summary
II. Purpose/description
III. Goals
IV. Scope (in/out)
V. Stakeholders
VI. Test criteria
  a. Plan knowledge
  b. Performance
  c. Communication
  d. Coordination
VII. Potential scenarios
  a. Logistics
  b. Location
  c. Time
  d. Supplies
  e. Roles and responsibilities
  f. Approach
VIII. Appendices

Having received the go-ahead to proceed with a tabletop exercise, Rodriquez built a test scenario that key stakeholders must address using the contents of the BP plan associated with the process. This test scenario consisted of some background information about the reason for the test, basics of BC and BP, the results of an exercise of a call tree just prior to the test, and the application of the plan's contents to recover the process from an event.

Rodriquez coordinated closely with Wilson to prepare in advance of the meeting and to help him conduct the exercise. Before the meeting, he had Wilson set up a 2-hour session for the tabletop exercise and to distribute the most recent copy of the BP plan to the participants. He also asked Ferragio to send an email to all the participants describing the purpose, goals, time, and place for the tabletop exercise. Rodriquez knew that an email by the process owner, due to his position in the company organization, gave extra emphasis to the importance of the plan; the email also emphasized the need for everyone to be physically present unless located geographically far from the test site. Wilson selected a conference room with an overhead projector, a computer station, a telecom device, and a white board, supplies such as markers and easel paper, and sufficient seating capacity.

For several days, Rodriquez prepared the presentation for the test. He ensured the scenario was not too easy that no one would be challenged but not too difficult that the test had no chance of demonstrating the ability of the team to recover from an event. Following is an outline of the test presentation.

Test Presentation Outline
Facilitator: Rodriquez
Location: Harold Room, 24-234 Building
Time: 1 p.m.

I. Background
II. BC and BP overview
III. Test overview
  a. Description
  b. Scope
  c. Test criteria
  d. Approach
IV. Attendance for test
V. Call tree test results
VI. Scenario
  a. Initial scenario (incident)
  b. Events plus time elapse (multiple)
VII. Debriefing/lessons learned
VIII. Next steps

Rodriquez facilitated the session with the process owner, Ferragio, serving as the key decision maker to handle the event described in the upcoming scenario. He also had Wilson serve as the scribe, taking notes on comments, insights, and suggestions for improvements. Wilson also ran the laptop that used a projector to show the presentation on the screen in front of the conference room. Rodriquez facilitated the entire session, ensuring that it moved at a steady pace and that everyone had a chance to participate in the recovery exercise.

The day of the test arrived. Approximately one hour before everyone convened for the test, Rodriquez had Ferragio demonstrate the workability and completeness of the contact listings for the call tree. This call tree had to contact people via several different modes of technology. Data was collected on who was contacted and who responded using a specific mode of technology, for example, laptop, phone, or email; the results also revealed who should have been on the call tree, but was not. The results were reviewed at the test session. However, before that occurred, Rodriquez provided background information regarding the reason for the test as well as a short educational session on BC and BP so that everyone had the same understanding and knowledge; the educational session was as short as possible because most attendees had already been exposed to this information. Rodriquez answered questions.

Rodriquez then presented the scenario to the stakeholders sitting in the room. He described the situation and any significant information about the scenario. The recovery team, with the process owner running the meeting, discussed how to respond to the event using the contents of the BP plan. Over a time continuum, the event included changing circumstances altered to challenge the team's ability to recover. At the end of the test, a "lessons learned" was conducted so that people learned from the experience.

Rodriquez conducted the lessons learned section of the presentation as more than just an information collection endeavor. Rather, he treated it as a means to discuss how the stakeholders felt they operated as individuals responding to the scenario and, just as importantly, how they performed as a team. It was also a chance to share his observations, insights, and comments as well as provide others the opportunity to share their own.

He also emphasized that it is okay to experience shortcomings from the session. The shortcomings often included, but were not limited to, errors and omissions in the plan as well as failures in communicating and coordinating efficiently and effectively as a team and with other external participants, for example, other organizations within the company.

Finally, Rodriquez concluded with a round robin for all participants with an opportunity to share any additional thoughts and comments about the test or anything related to the exercise. Wilson captured anything of significance to share and Rodriquez then presented next steps, which was compiling and presenting a report to management on the overall performance of the recovery team.

Rodriquez returned to his office and prepared a draft report, either in narrative or presentation format, covering the following topics.

Test Results Report

I. Executive summary
II. Background information
III. Purpose and description
   a. Test criteria
   b. Scenario
   c. Approach
   d. Location and date
   e. Stakeholder
IV. Results
   a. Call tree execution
   b. Observations
   c. Impact assessment of scenario
   d. Knowledge and use of BP plan
   e. Communication (internal and external stakeholders)
   f. Coordination (internal and external stakeholders)
   g. Necessary revisions and corrective actions
   h. Overall performance assessment and resiliency
V. Follow up
   a. Actions
   b. Schedule
VI. Next steps

He presented the draft of the report to Ferragio for final review and, upon receiving buy-in, scheduled a joint meeting with Ferragio, his senior management, and any other people deemed important to the process.

During the testing phase of the report, Rodriquez issued weekly status reports on his project, which covered cost, schedule, risks, scope, and issues arising that may impede progress. He issued the report at the bi-weekly staff meeting held with the senior project manager, Linda Steinhauser. The information was compiled with that of the other BC and BP projects. The report was then communicated to the program manager, Frank Malatesta. Since Rodriquez's project was the first one, he shared his experience and knowledge with the other project managers who would manage future BP projects; this information would help them to prepare for potential challenges and pitfalls as well as leverage what works. Rodriquez did the same after building the BP plan for the critical business process assigned to him.

GETTING STARTED CHECKLIST

Question	Yes	No
1. When testing the BP plan, are you realizing these benefits?		
Determining the effectiveness of a BP plan before a real event occurs		
Determining the ability of the recovery team to communicate, collaborate, and coordinate before an event occurs		
Identifying shortcomings in the content of the BP plan		
Updating the call tree		
Sustaining and augmenting awareness and knowledge about BC		
Validating whether the plan meets standards and expectations of key stakeholders		
2. When testing the BP plan, have you considered how to address these challenges?		
Having all the right stakeholders participate in testing		
Having the time and resources to prepare a meaningful, realistic scenario		
Preventing few people or one organization from dominating a testing event		
Lacking knowledge or awareness about the BP plan		
Taking the time to prepare a test plan and receiving buy-in from the key stakeholders		
Determining the best time to conduct a test and whether to give advance warning		
Ensuring follow up of the test results identifying improvements		
3. Did you determine whether to produce these deliverables?		
Walkthrough		
Test plan		
Exercise		
Report		
Updated BP plan		
Follow up		
4. When testing the BP plan, did you consider these concepts?		
A scenario should be realistic		
A scenario should test tangible and intangible areas		
Focus on common issues that are likely to surface during an event		
Identify common dependencies to test		
Consider a wide range of scenarios before agreeing on a specific one for a test		
Failure in testing is good, not bad		
Testing is an educational opportunity		
Lessons learned should follow the test as soon as possible		
A test plan is necessary before a test		
A formal report on test results is necessary		

5. Is your updated BP plan:
   Clear?
   Concise?
   Accurate?
   Useful?
   Flow logically?
   Free of grammatical errors?
6. When testing the BP plan, have you considered performing these activities?
   Review the results of the BIA and the building of the BP plan
   Compile the latest information on the process since building the last BP plan
   Identify the key stakeholders
   Determine the type of exercise
   Develop the test plan
   Schedule and conduct meetings with critical business process leadership
   Update the test plan
   Schedule and conduct meetings with recovery team members
   Conduct walkthrough of the BP plan
   Revise and distribute the BP plan
   Schedule and conduct exercises
   Prepare report
   Update the BP plan
   Schedule and conduct meetings with the recovery team
   Schedule and conduct meetings with critical business process leadership
   Update and distribute the BP plan
   Conduct follow up on recommendations

10

Maintain the Business Preparedness Plan

During testing, the recovery team, under the guidance of a project manager, is responsible for maintaining the business preparedness (BP) plan. Testing, however, occurs only at intervals or when deemed necessary by the business continuity (BC) governance infrastructure. Maintenance occurs much more frequently.

WHAT IS MAINTENANCE?

Maintenance is updating one or more BP plans to ensure better resiliency of a critical business process. It can occur regularly or ad hoc. Although maintenance occurs during testing, too, the focus in this chapter is on maintaining BP plans as an ongoing responsibility of a recovery team. A project manager from the BC governance infrastructure is often assigned to provide guidance on maintaining a plan.

GOALS

Maintenance of BP plans has two goals:

1. Enhance stakeholders' understanding and knowledge about BC and specific content in a BP plan for a critical business process. Effective maintenance necessitates that all people involved with a plan have a

rudimentary concept of the BC. It also seeks to increase knowledge and understanding about the BP plan that currently exists for a critical business process so that stakeholders can contribute meaningfully to its improvement.

2. Keep the BP plan relevant to a critical business process. Many changes can occur that can impact a critical business process, such as restructuring or outsourcing. Maintenance of a BP plan occurs by ensuring all the contents answer who, what, when, where, why, and how, so if an event does occur, the relevant stakeholders referencing it have the most recent plan for recovery.

TERMINOLOGY

Maintenance of a BP plan involves some BC terminology necessitating a definition upfront.

A *gap analysis* is a review of a BP plan to ascertain any discrepancies in its content. It involves a review of the current plan to capture any changes since its last distribution. Changes in the context of a critical business process often serve as a "trigger" to identify additional ones to a plan. These changes are adds, deletes, or updates. Here is a partial list of some of the causes for modifying a BP plan:

- Call tree notification list changes
- Change in the complexity of the business
- Changes in regulatory requirements
- Changes in RTO, RPO, and MAD
- Changes in vendors, suppliers, or contractors
- Changes in recovery team members
- Dependencies, or resource, changes
- General change in business environment, for example, competitive pressures
- Organizational restructuring, for example, new partnerships
- Physical environmental changes, for example, real sales of company properties
- Process changes
- Product changes

- Promotions and demotions of recovery team members
- Risk changes
- Technology enhancements
- Transfers and terminations of recovery team members
- Workaround changes

Configuration management is setting a baseline for deliverables produced on a project. From a BC perspective, setting a baseline for the BP plan and then managing its integrity becomes important to account for which version of a document a recovery team will reference. It also provides an audit trail of the changes made to a document.

A *review cycle* is a regular, ongoing approach to ensure a deliverable is up to date. From the perspective of BC, a BP plan is reviewed, for example, quarterly or semi-annually, to ensure it contains the latest information.

A *single point of contact* (SPOC) is a person assigned in a process with a specific responsibility. From the perspective of BC, it involves assigning a specific individual with responsibility to maintain a BP plan. This person is often someone in the critical business process.

Accessibility is ensuring people have access to the product, service, information, equipment, etc. to perform their responsibilities. From the perspective of BC, it involves ensuring people have access to a BP plan. In today's environment, it might mean people having information technology (IT) operating on the same protocols to reference a copy of the plan during recovery.

KEY CONCEPTS

To effectively maintain a BP plan, a project manager needs to understand and apply a number of key concepts.

Maintain Configuration Control over an Existing BP Plan

During recovery, everyone on the team should use the same plan; otherwise, miscommunication, confusion, and frustration will arise and delay progress in recovery. Configuration management involves recording the baseline of the document, documenting any changes, and periodically ensuring everyone has the right copy.

Use a SPOC for Maintaining a BP Plan

Upon plan completion, unless someone is given the responsibility to maintain the BP plan, it often sits on a shelf and loses its value. Circumstances change and they correspondingly affect the plan. By having a SPOC, this person has responsibility to keep abreast of those changes and reflect their impacts in the plan. Additionally, the single point of contact ensures an ongoing review cycle occurs.

Provide Ongoing Accessibility to the BP Plan

People need access to their plans, especially during recovery. While this makes sense, it can become quite challenging if people rely on IT or hard copies. If relying on IT, everyone should use common hardware and software; otherwise, they will find access difficult. If relying on hard copies, everyone will need access; however, sometimes people may not have access to a hard copy. The best approach is to enable people to access a plan via both modes. That way, they have alternative means to gain access to the plan during recovery.

Remember a BP Plan Is a Reflection of Time

The environment changes constantly, especially during a period when globalization means facing competitive pressures, thereby requiring organizations to adapt through restructuring, new partnerships, etc. Upon approval and sign off, a BC plan, like plans in general, reflects what is known at the time. As time progresses, the value of the plan depends on how relevant the contents are to the people referencing it during recovery. Keeping a plan current and relevant, therefore, is essential for providing value to the recovery of a critical business process.

Changes in One BP Plan Can Affect Other BP Plans

The odds are great that a change in one BP plan will affect those of other critical business processes. As a company becomes more sophisticated in BC and its processes and functions become more interwoven, a change in one plan will likely affect touch points in other plans. This situation is especially the case for global companies whose value stream is highly integrated and transcends geographical boundaries. An update to a critical business process in New York, for example, may impact one for delivering a product or service in Tokyo.

Update BP Plans to Reflect the Latest Business Impact Analysis at the Companywide Level

Decisions at high levels may directly impact certain critical business processes. New risks, strategic goals and objectives, and priorities may arise, necessitating revisions to BP plans. These new directions often affect multiple critical business processes. Failure to account for these changes may result in a recovery failing to support the overall recovery of a company. A SPOC for a critical business process should keep abreast of what is happening at the strategic and operational levels and update the plans accordingly or at least alert key stakeholders so they can determine the necessary changes.

Use Common Terminology

Unless absolutely necessary, BC terminology used in a BP plan should be the same for all plans published throughout an organization, and this is especially the case for multiple plans being built for a critical business process. Common terminology enhances communication, collaboration, and coordination. Ideally, the BC governance infrastructure should provide a common glossary to use for plans of all critical business processes. Naturally, only jargon for a specific process is defined in a plan.

Conduct Walkthroughs When Needed

Sometimes the changes in the context of an organization dramatically impact BP plans altered to such an extent that simple updates and revisions are insufficient. In other words, the plans become useless. If this situation arises, the only recourse is to hold a walkthrough with key stakeholders and to have them comb through the plan to identify all the significant changes. If changes are significant, a rewrite may be warranted, meaning one or more new plans must be built. It would also behoove the stakeholders of a critical business process to consider coupling the rebuilding of a plan with a test to validate the ability to guide recovery and enhance knowledge about BC.

BENEFITS

Maintaining the BP plan provides several benefits.

Have a BP Plan Containing Relevant, Accurate Information for the Stakeholders to Reference during Recovery

Confusion reigns during recovery if everyone refers to a different version of a BP plan, especially one containing incorrect or outdated information, for example, contact information and procedures no longer applicable. Remember, resiliency requires recovery of business processes to occur quickly and effectively under what are atypical circumstances.

Encourage the Use of the BP Plan during the Recovery

People will refer to a BP plan if they see its value. If they do not, they will avoid using it. Maintenance enhances the desire for people wanting to reference a plan during recovery.

Further Awareness about an Existing BP Plan

After building and testing a BP plan, people often shift focus to ongoing, regular responsibilities. Since events are atypical, a plan can end up resting in a desk drawer, on a shelf, or some other place and then forgotten. Maintenance of a plan keeps its existence in the forefront of everyone's mind.

Encourage Communication among All the Stakeholders of a Critical Business Process

A process or function often transcends organizational boundaries, especially if a company is organized in silos, for example, engineering, manufacturing, information systems, marketing, and sales. Each silo often becomes wrapped up in its own mission, goals, and objectives. Revisiting a BP plan helps to break the walls, so to speak, among the silos as they discuss the content of a plan and its execution during the recovery from an event.

CHALLENGES

While maintenance of BP plans makes good sense, making it happen often involves overcoming some challenges.

Keeping the Importance of Maintaining a Current BP Plan in the Forefront of People's Minds

BC is usually not a top priority vis-à-vis ongoing operational activities for a critical business process. Until an event occurs, focus is frequently elsewhere. One way to deal with this challenge is to schedule regular, ongoing maintenance of a BP plan with key stakeholders. Another way is to assign someone in the organization with the responsibility to ensure that the plan is updated on a regular basis and when circumstances change.

Allocating the Administrative Overhead to Maintain a BP Plan

This challenge is often the most salient one because, too often, some stakeholders view maintaining a BP plan, for lack of a better term, as an administrative burden. They may not view it as a means to enhance operational efficiency, especially if organizations must operate as profit centers. One way to deal with this challenge is for a company to treat plan maintenance as overhead with costs allocated across the business units. Another way is for a company to require BC as a goal and objective in the performance reviews for executives and senior managers throughout an organization; not surprisingly, the administrative burden often goes away when BC becomes a key measure for incentive for advancement and pay increases.

Maintaining Knowledge about What Is in a BP Plan

Over time, people tend to forget the content of a BP plan. By regularly revisiting a plan, people must review it for accuracy and, in doing so, reenforce their knowledge of their responsibilities inside it.

Keeping the BP Plan Current in an Environment of Constant, Ongoing Change

In today's business environment, change is constant and its impact affects many aspects of a company. Globalization, IT, and restructuring are just a few of the dynamic forces affecting a company as it strives to perform faster, better, and cheaper. As a result, a BP plan can lose its value very quickly. A common way to deal with such a circumstance is to have regularly scheduled reviews along with assigning one or more people in an organization to evaluate the impact of such changes on a plan and update it accordingly.

MAKING MAINTENANCE HAPPEN

A number of activities are required to maintain a BP plan. These activities can be grouped into one of four phases, which are shown in the diagram in Figure 10.1 and described next.

Project Management for Maintaining a BP Plan

This task involves applying all the project management (PM) concepts, tools, and techniques to enhance project performance. For example, it includes preparing a charter, developing a work breakdown structure (WBS), making time and cost estimates, building a schedule, and tracking and monitoring performance.

Establish Disciplines for Maintaining a BP Plan

Set Up an Ongoing, Regular Update Cycle

An update cycle can be monthly, quarterly, or bi-annually. The principal benefit of this activity is instilling the necessary discipline to update a BP plan at prescribed times during the calendar year. This update cycle occurs in addition to the one with testing.

Assign a SPOC for Each BP Plan

This activity assigns one individual within an organization or supports a critical business process having responsibility to ensure BP plans are up to date. If involving multiple plans, a SPOC may be assigned to maintain them all and to engage the appropriate stakeholders for review and approval of any changes. Depending on the scale and complexity of the critical business process, it may be necessary to assign a SPOC for each plan.

ID	Task Name	Predecessors
180	1.5 Maintain business preparedness plan	
181	1.5.1 Project management for maintaining business preparedness plan	
182	1.5.1.1 Apply project management	151
183	1.5.2 Establish disciplines for maintaining business preparedness plan	
184	1.5.2.1 Set up an ongoing, regular update cycle	151, 182
185	1.5.2.2 Assign a single point of contact for each business preparedness plan	184
186	1.5.2.3 Apply configuration management over the business preparedness plan	184
187	1.5.2.4 Set up a disciplined change management process	184
188	1.5.3 Conduct review of business preparedness plan	
189	1.5.3.1 Review of the business preparedness plan	185, 186, 187
190	1.5.4 Revise business preparedness plan	
191	1.5.4.1 Determine good criteria checklist for revised or newly built business preparedness plan	189
192	1.5.4.2 Update or rebuild the business preparedness plan	191
193	1.5.4.3 Obtain approvals from key stakeholders	192
194	1.5.5 Distribute business preparedness plan	
195	1.5.5.1 Educate stakeholders about the revised or rebuilt business preparedness plan	193
196	1.5.5.2 Distribute the business preparedness plan	195
197	1.5.5.3 Ensure ongoing accessibility to the revised or rebuilt business preparedness plan	196
198	1.5.6 Apply project management (closing) for maintaining business preparedness plan	
199	1.5.6.1 Perform closing tasks	197

FIGURE 10.1
WBS for maintaining a BP plan.

Apply Configuration Control over the BP Plan

After key stakeholders review and approve a plan, it should be placed under configuration management, meaning exercising version control, controlling distribution, and documenting any changes for recording and auditing purposes. No significant changes by the project manager, the recovery team, or senior management should be made to a plan until vetted under change management.

Set up a Disciplined Change Management Process

Change management provides the discipline to ensure only permitted revisions to a plan occur. The degree of formality depends on the complexity and scope of the critical business process. A change request is submitted, reviewed, analyzed, and dispensed with accordingly. No change should occur until key stakeholders have reviewed and approved it, whether by a specific person or group, such as a change board.

Conduct Review of BP Plan

Based upon a review cycle or whether an ad hoc change has arisen, review of a plan can take many forms. A principal way to conduct a review is serial, whereby a copy is sent to one person after another for review. The main advantage of a serial review is lessening the impact of peer pressure; however, it extends the review cycle. The other way is to conduct a group review, whereby key stakeholders assemble in a central location or attend virtually and review, approve, or disapprove of any changes. The main advantage of a group review is it being faster than a serial review; however, it is subject to peer pressure. The chosen approach depends on the scale and complexity of the critical business process and the availability of the reviewers.

Revise BP Plan

Determine Good Criteria Checklist for Revised or Newly Built BP Plan

This checklist should be the same as for building a BP plan. This activity should proceed quickly unless additional criteria are added to the checklist, generating conflict.

Update or Rebuild the BP Plan

Key stakeholders for a plan must decide whether to update the existing BP plan or to write a new one. This decision depends on the degree and extent of the changes affecting a critical business process. Obviously, revisions to an existing plan will likely take less time than a complete rewrite.

Obtain Approvals from Key Stakeholders

Whether revised or completely rewritten, a BP plan will require review and approval. The degree of formality will depend on the processes set up by the BC governance infrastructure. It is best to err on the side of formality than to treat approvals casually.

Distribute BP Plan

Educate Stakeholders about the Revised or Rebuilt BP Plan

The best approach is to assemble the relevant stakeholders of a plan, often consisting of the recovery team members, in a meeting to discuss the changes and to reiterate responsibilities.

Distribute the BP Plan

The plan is sent to the applicable stakeholders, in electronic or hard copy form or both. It is important to emphasize the need to destroy the previous version or return it to the applicable people, usually the SPOC, for destruction to protect sensitive information and to lessen the chance of stakeholders referencing an outdated plan.

Ensure Ongoing Accessibility to the Revised or Rebuilt BP Plan

A revised or rebuilt BP plan in today's environment can be accessible electronically and physically. The key to success is ensuring that everyone needing a copy of the plan can obtain one with minimum or no difficulty.

Apply Project Management (Closing) for Maintaining a BP Plan

This task involves ensuring that validation of the performance measurement baseline occurs prior to officially closing the project. It also involves ensuring that all administrative, financial, and contractual concerns or issues are addressed to preclude legal problems, for instance, from occurring.

DELIVERABLES

There is only one deliverable for maintaining a plan: a new or updated BP plan. The plan should meet the requirements of any plan. It should be clear, concise, correct, relevant, and, ultimately, provide value to the stakeholders during recovery. Of course, distribute the plan to all stakeholders having an interest in its application during an event.

STAKEHOLDERS

The key stakeholders for a revised or new BP plan are the same for building and testing plans. The recovery team, support personnel who are not members of the recovery team but participate in the executing procedures, senior managers and executives for a critical business process, and other parties, such as trusted vendors or suppliers, should receive a copy. These responsibilities are shown in Figure 10.2.

INTEGRATION OF ACTIVITIES

Maintaining a BP plan is perhaps the most neglected action of all the seven ones described in this book. The simple reason is that unless the topic of BC and BP is constantly placed in the forefront of people's minds, they will soon forget about it and that includes the plan itself. Fortunately, by exercising the tasks in the work breakdown structure in this chapter, a company or organization can maintain one or more BP plans.

After putting in place PM concepts, tools, and techniques, the next task is to establish an update schedule for the BP plan, for example, monthly, quarterly, semi-annually, etc. The recovery team leader assigns a member of the team or another person on his or her staff to have the responsibility for upkeeping the plan. This person is known as an SPOC. The SPOC gathers the updates, revises the plan, and obtains approvals for the updates from the applicable stakeholders. At this time, the BC project manager serves as a guide to help facilitate and manage BP plan maintenance.

With final approvals in place, the recovery team leader distributes the BP plan to the applicable people, including the assigned BC project manager. The BC project manager then closes the project accordingly.

Role	Board of Directors	BC Steering Committee	Business Continuity Working Group	BC Project Manager/ Program Manager	BC Specialists/ Staff Support	Business Process Owner/Senior Management	Recovery Team Leader (Operational)	Recovery Team Members (Operational)	Audit	Customers	Suppliers/ Vendors	Shareholders
Tasks												
Maintain business preparedness plan												
Project management for maintaining business preparedness plan		I		C		I	R					
Establish disciplines for maintaining business preparedness plan				C		I	R	A				
Conduct review of business preparedness plan				C		I	R	A		I	I	
Revise business preparedness plan				C		I	R	A		I	I	
Distribute business preparedness plan				C		I	R	A				
Apply project management (closing) for maintaining business preparedness plan	I	I		C		I	R,A	A				

Legend
R = Responsible
A = Accountable
C = Consult
I = Inform

FIGURE 10.2
RACI chart for maintaining a BP plan.

FINAL THOUGHTS

Maintaining a BP plan should be straightforward. Project managers, recovery team members, and other stakeholders should apply the concepts and activities persistently and consistently. Any exceptions to this advice can impede recovery, having recovery members using different or outdated versions of a plan. Such situations make communication, coordination, and collaboration during recovery difficult and, in some cases, impossible.

CASE STUDY, CONTINUED

Maintenance

Maintenance of the plans occurred six months after the build and test of the BP plan. Rodriquez was the first project and the others followed the same approach. Maintenance of the plan was straightforward. He scheduled a meeting with the process owner, Ferragio, to request to work with the other stakeholders to update the plan. He received the necessary permission to proceed. He contacted Wilson and asked whether any changes to the critical process had occurred since the test. Wilson noted that some had occurred and he had captured them. However, Wilson commented that he did not have visibility of all the changes. Rodriquez decided to contact each stakeholder to submit any changes related to their responsibilities identified in the plan. He and Wilson compiled the changes and then updated the plan. Some typical changes that could occur in the plan include the following.

List of Potential Changes to Plan

1. Updates to
    a. Recovery team membership
    b. Call tree
    c. Plan content, including
        i. Responsibilities
        ii. Procedure/workaround content
        iii. Recovery time objectives

iv. Scope
v. Assumptions
vi. Resource requirements
vii. Quantity
viii. Time

2. Business impact analysis (BIA) specifically
   a. Likelihoods
   b. Impacts
   c. Threats

Rodriquez and the team built a schedule for the maintenance of his plan as well as a WBS and RACI chart, shown in Figures 10.3 and 10.4, respectively.

Before publishing the BP plan, however, Rodriquez presented the updated plan to the process owner for review. Ferragio decided to have a 1-hour session with each of the recovery team members present; he believed that some of the changes identified by one stakeholder might have a collateral impact on others. The change might also affect other critical business processes that would have plans built.

Wilson scheduled the meeting, distributing in advance the most recent copy of the BP plan to each participant. Each participant reviewed the plan prior to the meeting, noting any comments, changes, or questions. During the session, Rodriquez facilitated, Wilson took notes, and Ferragio asked questions and concerns because he had an understanding of the "big picture."

	January	February	March
1.0 Maintain business preparedness plan	1/15		3/15
1.1 Conduct review of business preparedness plan	1/15 1/31		
1.2 Revise business preparedness plan	2/1		3/14
1.3 Distribute business preparedness plan			3/15

FIGURE 10.3
High-level schedule for maintaining the BP plan.

	Malatesta	Steinhauser	Ferragio	Maltone	Alvardico	Alltrunt	Coutreaux	Working Group	Steering Committee
1.0 Establish governance infrastructure	I	R,A	I	I	I	I	I	C	I
2.0 Develop and implement training	I	R,A	I	I	I	I	I	C	I
3.0 Conduct enterprise impact analysis	I	R,A	I	I	I	I	I	C	I
4.0 Receive the raw materials grape suppliers		C,I	R,A					C	I
5.0 Approve product for bottling		C,I						C	I
6.0 Bottle, label, and then distribute the product		C,I						C	I
7.0 Process raw materials to extract raw juice		C,I						C	I
8.0 Process and filter the raw juice in preparation for bottling		C,I						C	I
9.0 During the fermentation process, color and taste the product		C,I						C	I

Legend
R = Responsible
A = Accountable
C = Consult
I = Inform

FIGURE 10.4
WBS and RACI chart for maintaining the BP plan.

Rodriquez updated the BP plan and then submitted it to Ferragio for his final approval. Ferragio approved and sent the updated BP plan to the members of the recovery team. He then updated the project schedule and submitted a final report to Steinhauser who, in turn, presented it to Mary Squires, senior vice president of Internal Services, the BC program sponsor, and other members of the steering committee. Again, Rodriquez shared his knowledge and experience with the other project managers who will be building, testing, and maintaining BP plans for other critical business processes.

GETTING STARTED CHECKLIST

Question	Yes	No
1. When maintaining the BP plan, are you realizing these benefits?		
Having a BPP containing relevant, accurate information for the stakeholders to reference during recovery		
Encouraging the use of the BP plan during the recovery		
Furthering awareness about an existing BP plan		
Encouraging communications among all the stakeholders of a critical business process		
2. When maintaining the BP plan, have you considered how to address these challenges?		
Keeping the importance of maintaining a current BP plan in the forefront of people's minds		
Allocating the administrative overhead to maintain a BP plan		
Maintaining knowledge about what is in a BP plan		
Keeping the BP plan current in an environment of constant, ongoing change		
3. Did you determine whether to produce these deliverables?		
New or updated BP plan		
4. When maintaining the BP plan, did you consider these concepts?		
Maintain configuration control over an existing BP plan		
Use a SPOC for maintaining a BP plan		
Provide ongoing accessibility to the BP plan		
Remember a BP plan is a reflection in time		
Changes in one BP plan can affect changes in other business preparedness plans		
Update BP plans to reflect the latest BIA at the companywide level		
Use common terminology		
Conduct walkthroughs when needed		

5. Is your updated BP plan:
   - Clear?
   - Concise?
   - Accurate?
   - Useful?
   - Flow logically?
   - Free of grammatical errors?
6. When maintaining the BP plan, have you considered performing these activities?
   - Set up ongoing, regular update cycle
   - Assign an SPOC for each BP plan
   - Apply configuration control over the BP plan
   - Set up a disciplined change management process
   - Conduct review of the BP plan
   - Determine a good criteria checklist for a revised or newly built BP plan
   - Update or rebuild a BP plan
   - Obtain approvals from key stakeholders
   - Educate stakeholders about the revised or rebuilt BP plan
   - Distribute the BP plan
   - Ensure ongoing accessibility to the revised or rebuilt BP plan

11

Perform Process Improvement

Occasionally, the business continuity (BC) governance infrastructure should revisit the processes, procedures, techniques, and tools to build, test, and maintain plans for critical business processes. By doing so, it enhances resiliency, effectiveness, and efficiency of a company.

WHAT IS PROCESS IMPROVEMENT?

Process improvement is analyzing, evaluating, and improving BC processes, procedures, techniques, and tools to ensure more efficient and effective application across an enterprise and within a critical business process. Process improvement can occur at two levels. One level is at the BC governance infrastructure level. The other level is at the critical business process.

GOALS

Process improvement has essentially two goals.

1. Increasing resiliency by enhancing the efficiency and effectiveness of BC processes, procedures, techniques, and tools. It accomplishes that by removing obstacles and redundancies that add more time and cost when applying BC and BP.
2. Identify opportunities to improve cycle time, reduce costs, and eliminate waste without negatively impacting an organization's

resiliency. The larger the organization, the greater these opportunities will likely exist. It is simply a matter of organizational willpower to make the time and effort to identify and implement improvements.

TERMINOLOGY

Process improvement of BC and BP involves some terminology that project managers need to understand.

Quality is focusing on meeting the requirements and expectations of a customer. Notice the word *meeting*. There is no mention about exceeding requirements and expectations in the definition because excesses add to costs and dashes schedules. BC should always be deployed to meet, not exceed, the requirements and expectations of the customer.

Kaizen, known as perfection through continuous improvement, is an effort to achieve perfection in a process. Kaizen is repetitive and requires identifying opportunities to reduce variation and other anomalies impacting quality. No process is perfect, albeit a point in time arrives when the payback in improvement is less than the costs to achieve it. BC should strive for perfection as much as possible; but, remember, the law of diminishing returns requires serious consideration where the gain from improvement decreases in terms of payback.

Muda is Japanese for waste. Thanks to Lean principles, waste has taken over from perfection as the focus of attention in quality and rightly so. Opportunities for waste abound in most organization and critical business processes, which not only impact the ability to deliver a product or service to a customer, but also add to overhead. Since the focus is often performing faster, better, and cheaper, from a BC perspective effectiveness, not efficiency, may pose a challenge to some organizations. Still, opportunities will arise whereby efficiency and effectiveness apply even to processes, procedures, techniques, and tools.

PDCA cycle, also known as the Deming cycle, involves four phases that repeat: plan, do, check, act. Plan is determining what to address; do is addressing what; check is determining progress in addressing the what; and act is making adjustments, if necessary. PDCA is instrumental in process improvement, working clearly with the application of kaizen.

A *process*, mentioned earlier, is a high-level, cross-functional view, for example, information technology (IT), human resources, finance, and manufacturing, involving multiple procedures or operations to accomplish a goal. A process might include a value stream to deliver a product or service to a customer. A process orientation is a useful tool to identify waste and other variables impacting delivery to a customer. BC requires taking a process orientation in most cases.

A *procedure*, mentioned earlier, is a detailed set of steps or operations to accomplish a narrow set of objectives within a specific function or siloed organization, for example, finance or IT. Multiple procedures make up a process. From a BP perspective, a plan consists of multiple procedures containing a reliance statement and workarounds. A critical business process can contain one or more BP plans.

Lean, mentioned earlier, is a customer-focused perspective transcending siloed or narrow functional thinking to deliver value to the customer. BC may involve one or more customers, some internal, for example, key stakeholders of a critical business process, and some external, for example, the recipient of a product or service necessitating resiliency by the deliverer of the product or service.

Value is satisfying the requirements and expectations of the internal or external customer at the right time efficiently and effectively. In the case of an event, the ultimate value of a company is being able to deliver a product or service to the customer with little or no waste.

Cycle time is the time needed to complete a process, procedure, or operation. The goal is to reduce cycle time. From a BC perspective, cycle time is reflected in the time required to bring a process back to normal operations, sometimes referred to as business as usual, as soon as possible without degradation in performance.

Value stream is a series of procedures or operations making up a process to create a product or deliver a service of value to the customer. Defining a value stream of importance is instrumental to determine a critical business process. A value stream can be a simple critical business process or a complex one consisting of several processes.

A *customer*, for example, internal or external person or organization, is the recipient of a product or service. From a BC perspective, the recipient of a BP plan for a critical process is a customer that, in turn, has a customer receiving its product or service. The failure of a critical process negatively impacts a customer; the faster and more effective the recovery of a critical business process, the greater the likelihood of providing value and satisfaction.

KEY CONCEPTS

To effectively evaluate and improve BC processes, procedures, techniques, and tools, project managers need to understand and apply several key concepts.

Keep in Mind, Improvements Occur on Two Levels

Improvements occur at the BC governance infrastructure level where processes, tools, and techniques are evaluated for their effectiveness and efficiency across an enterprise. This level of process improvement requires taking a holistic perspective by looking at common approaches to conduct a business impact analysis (BIA) and risk management; determining common approaches to build, test, and maintain plans; developing common metrics; and assessing the overall resiliency of the enterprise. Within each critical business process, process improvement takes a narrower view of applying many of the common BC processes, procedures, techniques, and tools within its own domain.

Seek Opportunities to Reduce Waste

Implementing BC the first time involves applying BC processes, procedures, techniques, and tools more efficiently and effectively than in subsequent attempts. With change often comes waste, for example, long approval processes and redundant meetings. Once the initial wave of change completes, special effort is often made to reduce variation and waste among and within processes through process improvement. Overhead costs will decrease, buy-in from stakeholders should increase, and resiliency improves. Testing a BP plan will also likely identify opportunities to reduce variation and waste.

Remember That Continuous Improvement Is Iterative

As noted earlier, the first time BC deploys variation and waste will occur. Critical business processes will likely remain resilient rather than more efficient or effective until a level of maturity is achieved. Until that point, keep metrics on the performance of critical business processes and their ability to recover from a cost and cycle time perspective. This data will provide an invaluable basis for making process improvements.

Focus on the Customer

Do not let the act of process improvement be the center of attention; the customer should remain the focus. Any opportunity for improvement should demonstrate a positive impact on the customer; otherwise, efforts at process improvement should be called into question. Making changes for the sake of change can backfire, adding to needless disruption and actually increasing costs and resulting in an dissatisfied customer.

Rely on Facts and Data and Revisit Assumptions

Process improvement requires collecting meaningful facts and data and making decisions on whether improvement is necessary. Assumptions, treated as real until proven otherwise, should be reviewed before making any improvements. Project managers should scrutinize the assumptions made behind the collection of facts and data; assumptions can influence the way facts and data are collected through the introduction of bias. Collecting facts and data provides the basis for metrics not only to help determine whether change is necessary but also to ascertain whether the improvement provides enough value to the customer. Metrics in BC are difficult to define and collect due to the abstract nature of the subject. However, some possible metrics might include the number of plans applied during the recovery of an event and how many plans are completed or tested over a specific time frame and the time to complete each one.

Minimize Relearning, Set-Up Times, and Cycle Time

All three of these areas often occur together, creating a bird's nest of problems. Constant stop and go, frequently the result of doing too much by jumping from one task to another, jumping back on the task on which a team member was working previously but never completed, and the expansion of time to complete the task and deliver the work to the recipient of the output only adds waste related to time, effort, and, ultimately, cost. So much waste exists today even in an environment of faster, better, cheaper that, ironically, it slows work, adds costs, and causes rework, especially if quality is not "built in." Building, testing, and maintaining BP plans should focus effort on recovery time, for example. While sometimes not possible to cease work to build or test a plan, it is advisable to assign someone in an organization with full-time responsibilities to oversee its completion with minimal disruption.

Seek Buy-In from Stakeholders

Unless the people making change accept that change, resistance will occur. This situation is especially the case for large organizations where identifying all stakeholders impacted by a process is difficult. Special effort should be made to identify stakeholders as early as possible and engage them. It is a cardinal rule in process improvement that the people impacted by a change participate as early as possible by obtaining and leveraging their knowledge and experience. It also helps in breaking down resistance. Implementing BC transcends many boundaries within an organization, especially concerning critical business processes, affecting many people and organizations. Identifying them is important to obtain their engagement, impact, and buy-in.

Remember the 5 Ws and H When Performing Process Improvement

The 5 Ws are who, what, where, when, and why; the H is how. This information lays the groundwork to collect facts and data about any process. If done correctly, the BIA and the BP plans provide this information, which project managers can leverage to improve processes. The synergy for process improvement comes when a critical process involves multiple plans. Chances are good that they contain shortcomings and redundancies among the plans, thereby providing opportunities for improvement in resiliency.

Graphically Document the As-Is and the To-Be

The As-Is is the current way of doing business; the To-Be is the improved way of doing business. Drawing roadmaps or flowcharts of the As-Is and noting opportunities for improvement lay the groundwork to draw the To-Be. Graphics can be used to identify the impacts of improvements before taking action. Upon implementing improvements, continuous improvement and measurements can then be used to determine the effectiveness of the changes and determine whether corrective action is necessary. The BIA and the BP plans provide a wealth of information to document the As-Is along with the processes, procedures, techniques, and tools deployed by the BC governance infrastructure.

Apply Good Listening Skills

The most important communication skill a person can have is listening. When identifying opportunities for improvement, listening is critical for success. Even if certain stakeholders do not participate in the improvement effort, listen to them (not just hear) by seriously considering their feedback. The goal is to have key stakeholders support, not necessarily embrace, improvements. As long as stakeholders feel they have some say in changes, the less the likelihood that resistance will arise and, if it does, will do so in less intensity. From a BC perspective, stakeholders at a steering committee who represent key processes should be offered the opportunity to communicate their thoughts, issues, and concerns involving recommendations for improvements. Within a critical business process, members of the recovery team for each plan should also have the opportunity to suggest or review improvements to the application of BC processes, procedures, techniques, and tools.

BENEFITS

Evaluating BC processes, procedures, techniques, and tools provides several benefits.

Increasing Effectiveness and Efficiency When Employing BC Processes, Procedures, Techniques, and Tools

It does so by applying Lean principles to eliminate waste while simultaneously delivering to the customer.

Adding Greater Relevancy to Customers

By using Lean principles and other quality tools and techniques, focus should shift from deploying all the BC processes, procedures, techniques, and tools at a broad level to concentrate on providing value that is more specific to the customer. The initial deployment of BC often has a "hit the beach" perspective; as BC matures within an organization and stabilizes in an organization or within a critical business process, its deployment has a more "take that hill" perspective. In others words, it allows for focused improvements that augment effectiveness and efficiency as well as resiliency. This new orientation then places less emphasis on more and more emphasis on less.

Increasing Ownership among the Key Stakeholders

When initially implementing BC, the emphasis is on deploying the deliverables, often resulting in waste. As more critical business processes and their organizations become more mature, knowledgeable, and receptive about BC, the next action is to improve implementation and refinement to enhance efficiency and effectiveness but just as importantly to encourage greater stakeholder engagement in process improvement. The BC governance infrastructure shifts from directing to facilitating. Each organization or critical business process begins to identify ways to "Lean out" BC processes, procedures, techniques, and tools, for example, that fail to add value.

Increasing the Relevancy of BC to Organizations

The initial implementation is often "force fed" due to requirements established by very senior executive leadership, for example, board of directors (BoD) and the BC infrastructure. Enthusiasm for the subject is tepid at best. As the processes for implementing BC improves, the greater the chances that organizations responsible for a critical business process will appreciate the value to them in attaining their own goals and objectives.

Focusing on Customer Satisfaction

To have any value other than remove variation and achieve perfection, process improvement must focus on the customer. All improvements regarding resiliency must put the customer at the center. By making the customer the focus, process improvement can more easily distinguish between what is and is not of value. If any tool, technique, or approach toward resiliency does not add value to the customer, it is considered waste.

Taking an Integrated, Holistic Perspective of BC

Process analysis begins at several levels for BC. The first level is looking at the overall strategic levels vis-à-vis enterprise risks; the second level is determining critical business processes transcending silo thinking; and the third level is identifying the key stakeholders involved in each critical business process to determine what BC processes, procedures, techniques, and tools to apply. Taking an integrated big-picture perspective of all three levels provides opportunities to identify and eliminate waste.

CHALLENGES

While process improvement makes good sense, project managers must overcome some challenges.

The Business Environment for Industries Is Dynamic

In other words, it constantly changes. Restructuring, outsourcing, etc. are ongoing events that make taking a snapshot of a process or value stream very difficult. This challenge becomes even more acute for a firm operating globally and involving alliances, partnerships, and subsidiaries that appear, disappear, and reappear over a relatively short time period. The best approach to deal with this challenge is to conduct a BIA on a scheduled regular basis to ascertain if processes are deemed critical for the resiliency and to revisit them to identify opportunities for improvement as they relate to BC processes, procedures, techniques, and tools.

Lack of Available Resources to Perform Process Improvement

In an era of faster, better, and cheaper, being top heavy in resources eats away at profitability and competitiveness. "Lean and mean" is the mantra of the day. Unfortunately and ironically, this philosophy can become a liability by hamstringing opportunities to work smarter simply by scrimping on resources. Management needs to set priorities and focus accordingly. BC should be a priority but it is often overlooked until it is too late. To overcome this challenge, project managers should seek strong executive sponsorship and other key stakeholders when building a plan as an opportunity to create a document on recovering from an event but also to identify ways to improve processes. Process improvement should occur when building, testing, and maintaining a plan whenever possible.

Lack of Stakeholder Buy-In of BC

There will always be stakeholders who find BC a waste of time. This perspective is especially the case for companies having considerable cash reserves and viewing "self-insured" as better than wasting overhead building, testing, and maintaining BP plans. This attitude assumes, of course, that no event can cripple a firm to such an extent and put it out of business. It also assumes that all events are predictable in terms of probability and scale, which is not the case with Black Swan events. Another assumption is that cash reserves will always be present or sufficient, which is not always the case in a dynamic work environment replete with currency fluctuations, commodity price rises, etc. Through process improvement, especially with customer satisfaction as the focus, it becomes easier to engage stakeholders because BC via process improvement puts the interests of the customer at the center, not simply building, testing, and maintaining a plan. No savvy stakeholder will ignore the interests of a customer. Process improvement puts the customer in the forefront, even concerning BC.

Higher Priorities

The operational environment will always focus on delivering services or products to the customer. To do otherwise would impact profitability. It becomes very difficult for certain stakeholders to shift aside temporarily their operational mindset to improve processes despite many improvements often increasing the ability to deliver services and products to customers more efficiently and effectively. The best way to deal with this challenge is to have senior executive sponsorship that values both BC and process improvement.

MAKING PROCESS IMPROVEMENT HAPPEN

Project managers of process improvement projects have a number of activities that are required to lead and manage, whether at the enterprise or critical business process level. These activities can be grouped into one of seven activities, which are described and shown in Figure 11.1.

ID	Task Name	Predecessors
200	1.6 Perform process improvement	
201	1.6.1 Project management for performing process improvement	
202	1.6.1.1 Apply project management	179,199
203	1.6.2 Prepare for performing process improvement	
204	1.6.2.1 Capture As-Is processes in flowcharts	202
205	1.6.2.2 Conduct reviews of As-Is processes flowcharts	204
206	1.6.2.3 Revise As-Is processes flowcharts	205
207	1.6.3 Analyze for performing process improvement	
208	1.6.3.1 Identify opportunities for improvement	206
209	1.6.3.2 Document To-Be processes in flowcharts	208
210	1.6.3.3 Conduct reviews of To-Be process	209
211	1.6.3.4 Revise To-Be process	210
212	1.6.4 Propose recommendations for process improvement	
213	1.6.4.1 Prepare Situation-Target-Proposal (STP)	211
214	1.6.4.2 Conduct internal review of STP	213
215	1.6.4.3 Revise STP	214
216	1.6.5 Present recommendations for process improvement	
217	1.6.5.1 Present STP to key decision makers	215
218	1.6.5.2 Revise STP and resubmit, if necessary	217
219	1.6.6 Implement recommendations for process improvement	
220	1.6.6.1 Build the project plan to implement the revised or new process	218
221	1.6.6.2 Obtain approval of the project plan	220
222	1.6.6.3 Implement the project plan	221
223	1.6.6.4 Take corrective action, if necessary	222
224	1.6.7 Apply project management (closing) for performing process improvement	
225	1.6.7.1 Perform closing tasks	223

FIGURE 11.1
WBS for performing process improvement.

Project Management for Performing Process Improvement

This task involves applying all the project management (PM) concepts, tools, and techniques to enhance project performance. For example, it includes preparing a charter, developing a WBS, making time and cost estimates, building a schedule, and tracking and monitoring performance.

Prepare for Performing Process Improvement

Capture As-Is Processes in Flowcharts

One of the most important activities to perform is to capture the current, or As-Is, way of doing business. From a BC perspective, it requires identifying who, what, where, when, why, and how of critical business process. Typically, the flow of a critical business process is captured via flowcharting, collecting information such as individuals and organizations providing and receiving inputs and outputs, that is, as the customer and vendors; the processes performing transactions and transformations of the resources; and any controls such as signals and states affecting performance; and using manual and information systems as well as tools. Understanding the existing critical business process through flowcharting is a good visual way to identify potential opportunities for improvement when developing the To-Be process. The sources for preparing the As-Is diagram include BP plans, BC procedures, and interviews with key stakeholders.

Conduct Reviews of As-Is Processes Flowcharts

Once a critical business process is captured via a map or flowchart, the next activity is to verify accuracy. A reliable diagram is one having unassailable content to preclude or counter people who may eventually protest any recommendations for improvement. The chart serves as a baseline to identify shortcomings and make recommendations. It is imperative, therefore, to review the As-Is process with key stakeholders who will eventually approve recommendations and will be responsible for implementation.

Revise As-Is Processes Flowcharts

During and after the As-Is review, it is important to revise quickly the flowcharts to ensure accuracy. For extensive revisions, consider holding additional review sessions to verify changes. For insignificant changes, make them and baseline the chart.

Analyze for Performing Process Improvement

Identify Opportunities for Improvement

The real purpose behind capturing the As-Is process is to help identify those changes that improve the resiliency of a critical business process. The best way is to assemble key stakeholders in a room to walk through the flowchart and identify opportunities for improvement. Following are some generic problems to look for when reviewing the As-Is process flowchart:

- Bottlenecks
- Complex interfaces and exchanges among activities
- Decision delays
- Defective inputs and outputs
- Excessive approvals
- Excessive queue time
- Excessive storage of materials
- Frequent and lengthy downtime
- High level of work in process
- Idle labor
- Nonvalue-added activities
- Redundant activities
- Rework of output
- Too many inspections
- Too many interruptions
- Transportation delays
- Unclear roles and responsibilities
- Unused space

Following are some common specific opportunities to improve BC with the goal of reducing waste:

- Dated contents of call tree
- Difficult or no access to plans
- Excessive reviews and approvals
- Information overload and incompleteness

- Lack of participation
- Poor or degraded communications
- Redundant activities
- RPO and RTO not synchronized
- Transportation delays
- Unclear roles and responsibilities
- Unclear scope
- Vague content in plans

The list above is not exhaustive, of course, but serves as a starting point for process improvement. These and other shortcomings only add to cycle time due to ineffectiveness and inefficiency. Translated, that means having difficulty or inability to recover from an event.

Some of the more common tools to identify the shortcomings listed above include:

- Affinity diagramming
- Brainstorming
- Check sheeting
- Fishbone diagramming
- Force field analysis
- Histograms
- Interrelationships digraphs
- Pareto charting
- Run charting
- Scatter diagramming

Document To-Be Processes in Flowcharts

After evaluating the As-Is process and collecting data about performance, the next activity is to design the To-Be process. The To-Be process diagram reflects the necessary improvements identified using the As-Is process. The To-Be process, however, does not just reflect improvements; it also provides the overall potential to lower costs, achieve strategic goals, reduce cycle, and increase customer satisfaction.

Conduct Reviews of the To-Be Process

After completing the draft of the To-Be process, now is the time to obtain buy-in from key stakeholders. This activity requires presenting and discussing the As-Is and To-Be processes, noting the differences and explaining how the company and critical business process benefit from the changes. This activity requires applying effective listening skills and speaking skills; it also requires putting aside one's ego. The project has now laid the groundwork to achieve buy-in from all stakeholders.

Revise the To-Be Process

This activity requires compiling the input from the reviews of the As-Is and To-Be processes. The project manager updates the flowcharts, supporting documentation, and data accordingly.

Propose Recommendations for Process Improvement

Prepare Situation–Target–Proposal

With the updated documentation, prepare a summary executive presentation to deliver to the senior management and executives who must give their approval for the improved process. The presentation should be short and contain no more than five to seven pages, each one containing summary information, in the form of bullet lists or diagrams or both. Typically, the STP consists of these pages: a cover page, purpose statement, background information, target description, recommendations, and next steps.

Conduct Internal Review of STP

Before presenting the STP to senior management and executives for review and approval, conduct an internal review with key stakeholders. It behooves the project manager to identify and handle objections early on, thereby generating support for the STP. The final presentation, having received buy-in, makes giving it a perfunctory exercise.

Revise STP

Most internal reviewers will likely have some revisions. Include those revisions if they make sense. If not included, have supporting information readily available to justify why a certain revision was not included in case the topic surfaces during the presentation. Having facts and data available to support the content of the STP is critical to justify a position. Project managers can keep the facts and data hidden in their "hip pocket" by having them available on a separate slide or sheet of paper.

Present Recommendations for Process Improvement

Present STP to Key Decision Makers

The best approach is to send a copy of the STP to the key decision makers prior to the meeting. By doing so, they can take time and effort to digest the content. Two to three days often suffices. It is wise for project managers to follow up with a phone call to remind them that they have a copy of the presentation. During the presentation, the project manager should have spare copies in case the stakeholders forgot their copy or unanticipated attendees appear. At the beginning of the presentation, let stakeholders know whether to hold or ask questions.

Revise STP and Resubmit, if Necessary

In some cases, revisions to the STP are necessary. Important information may have been omitted, need verification, or a key decision maker wants further research conducted to verify and validate content. A project manager must determine whether to simply send an updated STP or request another formal presentation.

Implement Recommendations for Process Improvement

Build the Project Plan to Implement the Revised or New Process

The plan should include the participation of all stakeholders who have a direct interest in the new or revised process. This is especially the case for stakeholders directly impacted by the changes. The plan should include all the major PM practices, only restricted in breadth and depth based upon the complexity and scale of the project.

Obtain Approval of the Project Plan

The implementation plan should include the review and approval of stakeholders affected by the new or revised process. If involved in developing the plan, this activity will likely be unnecessary or should occur with very few objections.

Implement the Project Plan

Again, this activity involves the application of good PM practices related to execution and control. These PM practices are only restricted in breadth and depth based upon the complexity and scale of the project.

Take Corrective Action, if Necessary

Ironically, plans frequently do not happen according to plan. Under the worst-case scenario, replanning may occur. Often, though, corrective action is the best solution. If corrective action or replanning is necessary, the best way to determine that is to deploy and monitor key metrics and then decide on the action to take. Then, apply PDCA, which is a good way to assess whether that action is effective.

Apply PM (Closing) for Performing Process Improvement

This task involves ensuring that validation of the performance measurement baseline occurs prior to officially closing the project. It also involves ensuring that all administrative, financial, and contractual concerns or issues are addressed to preclude legal problems, for instance, from occurring.

DELIVERABLES

Six major deliverables are produced, which are tightly integrated.

The *As-Is documentation* is the first major deliverable. This deliverable is straightforward. The best way to generate this deliverable is to translate an existing process into a graphic so people can visualize the flow of inputs, processes, and outputs. The flowchart can be a traditional workflow, swim lane, or SIPOC chart (Supplier, Input, Process, Output, Customer), for example.

The *As-Is analysis* is the next deliverable. This deliverable requires the participation of key stakeholders, either at the steering committee level for the entire enterprise or the recovery team level for a critical business process. The stakeholders review the As-Is flow to determine opportunities for improvement. These opportunities might include reducing the number of approvals, having joint recovery team meetings, or adopting better methods or tools to expedite or increase the effectiveness of recovery. The analysis may include collecting data and other information via measurements to generate performance metrics about the performance of the As-Is and To-Be processes to compare their performance relative to each other upon implementation of changes.

The *To-Be analysis* comes next. The To-Be uses the same approach as the As-Is to compare before and after states of a process. To-Be documentation is created, too, and reflects areas of the As-Is process requiring changes to enable reviewers to note the differences between the two flows. These differences may include reducing the number of steps, cycle time, and performance errors.

With the To-Be analysis complete, the next deliverable is the *STP*. This document enables presenting information about improvements. The *situation* presents background information concerning the existing way of doing business, for example, who requested it and why issues exist. The *target* is the end state reflecting improvements you hope to achieve, for example, cycle time reduction. The *proposal* is what is necessary to achieve the target, both from a business (cost and schedule) and technical (tools and techniques) perspective.

Assuming approval of the STP, *metrics* and their accompanying measurements are the next deliverables. With consensus or agreement over the need to change, the target to reach, and the requirement for action, this deliverable provides a way to verify progress toward achieving the target. With metrics, corrective action can occur to keep the improvements on track with expectations. Metrics often cover four topics: cost, schedule, quality, and technical performance indicators.

An *implementation plan* is the final deliverable, expanding on the proposal presented in the STP. It consists largely of PM and quality tools and techniques, such as scheduling, trend analysis charts, histograms, and matrices to implement the target.

STAKEHOLDERS

Who the key stakeholders are depends on the level in a company where process improvement occurs, as Figure 11.2 shows. At the enterprise-wide level, the board of directors, stockholders, senior management (often consisting of representatives from the critical business processes sitting on the

Role	Board of Directors	BC Steering Committee	Business Continuity Working Group	BC Project Manager/ Program Manager	BC Specialists/ Staff Support	Business Process Owner/ Senior Management	Recovery Team Leader (Operational)	Recovery Team Members (Operational)	Audit	Customers	Suppliers/ Vendors	Shareholders
Tasks												
Perform process improvement												
Project management for performing process improvement		I	C,I	R	A							
Prepare for performing process improvement			C,I	R	A							
Analyze for performing process improvement		I	A	R	A	C	C					
Propose recommendations for process improvement		A	A	R	A	C	C					
Present recommendations for process improvement	I	A	A	R	A							
Implement recommendations for process improvement		I	I	R	A	I						I
Apply project management (closing) for performing process improvement	I	I	I	R	A							I

Legend
R = Responsible
A = Accountable
C = Consult
I = Inform

FIGURE 11.2
RACI chart for performing process improvement.

BC steering committee), and customers are the key stakeholders having an interest in the outcome of enterprise-wide process improvement efforts.

At the critical business process level, executives, the recovery team members, suppliers, vendors, and customers are some of the key stakeholders. While having perhaps an indirect interest at the enterprise level, their focus is more direct and narrow regarding their critical business process. In other words, they focus on process improvement within the domain for their critical business process.

INTEGRATION OF ACTIVITIES

Although process improvement should occur continuously, occasionally it occurs as a major project. What follows is treating process improvement as a major project.

After applying PM concepts, tools, and techniques, the BC project manager, working with his or her team and other key stakeholders, needs to capture and review the As-Is process, or current way of doing business, to understand and identify opportunities for improvement.

After performing an analysis of the As-Is process, the BC project manager and his or her team note opportunities for improvement, that is, areas needing changes, and generate recommendations. In addition to preparing a To-Be process that reflects the recommendations, the BC project manager and his or her team prepare an STP.

The BC project manager presents the STP, in oral or written form, to key stakeholders, who are often members of the BC working group, and the BC steering committee for approval.

Upon receiving approval of the STP, the BC project manager, working with project team members and other stakeholders, prepares and executes a project plan to implement the recommendations.

FINAL THOUGHTS

Process improvement is vitally important to BC. The initial deployment of BC is often riddled with waste. Once implemented at the enterprise-wide and critical business process levels, improvement can occur based on greater knowledge and experience of all stakeholders who participated. At that point, the enterprise, a composite of BC governance infrastructure and the critical business processes, becomes more mature in its resiliency.

CASE STUDY, CONTINUED

Process Improvement

Now that all the BP plans for the critical processes were complete and up to date, Steinhauser was ready to tackle process improvement. She assigned a team consisting of the project managers assigned to each of the critical processes, selected members of the BC staff, and representatives from the working group.

Steinhauser assembled the team members to determine how to approach this phase of the project. The team members developed a WBS and schedule that accommodated the overall completion date for process improvement, shown in Figures 11.3 and 11.4, respectively.

	Project Managers	Process Owners	Working Group	Steinhauser (Sr. Project Manager)	Malatesta (Sponsor)	Steering Committee
1.0 Prepare for process improvement	A	C	C	R,A		
2.0 Analyze for process improvement	A	C	C	R,A		
3.0 Propose recommendations for process improvement	A	C	C	R,A	I	I
4.0 Present recommendations for process improvement	A	C	C	R	C	I

Legend
R = Responsible
A = Accountable
C = Consult
I = Inform

FIGURE 11.3
WBS and RACI chart for process improvement.

	March	April	May
1.0 Prepare for performing process improvement	3/16 – 3/25		
2.0 Analyze for performing process improvement	3/26	4/15	
3.0 Propose recommendations for process improvement		4/10	5/15
4.0 Present recommendations for process improvement			5/16

FIGURE 11.4
High-level schedule for process improvement.

As the schedule indicated, the team elected that each of the project managers for their respective critical process compile "lessons learned" as well as conduct interviews with process owners to receive any additional feedback on how to build, test, and maintain plans.

Steinhauser, with the help of the BC support staff, provided a standard format to collect and display this information. This format is shown next.

Interview Notes Sheet

Interview Date & Time	Critical Process	Interviewee	What Went Well	Areas for Improvement	Recommendations for Improvement	Comments

Once the process was complete, she set up a meeting to conduct a review of the As-Is process (the current way of doing business) to pinpoint where opportunities for improvement exist and what areas went well. She prepared an agenda for the meeting. The As-Is process was in the form of a process flowchart.

During the session that she facilitated, Steinhauser assigned a person to take notes to capture opportunities for improvement and other observations, comments, and feedback. During the same session, the team developed a To-Be process in the form of a process flowchart reflecting improvements. Both the As-Is and To-Be flowcharts make it easier to depict changes. At the conclusion, she described the next step, which was to prepare an STP that the team members were expected to review prior to the presentation to the program manager, Frank Malatesta, and the members of the steering committee for final approval.

Steinhauser prepared a straw horse of the STP. She sent it to each team member for review and feedback. She incorporated any relevant suggested revisions and held one final meeting with the team. Upon reaching consensus, she then scheduled a meeting with individuals who provided some minor suggestions for improvement. Steinhauser then set up a meeting, along with Rodriquez, in the office of Roger Fitzsimmons III, the CFO and executive sponsor for BC, for final buy-in. The meeting resulted in Fitzsimmons III's buy-in and his office administrator arranged for the STP to have final review and approval by the steering committee, which it granted. Following is an outline of the STP that received final approval by the steering committee.

Situation-Target-Proposal (STP)

- I. Situation
  - a. Challenges
  - b. Symptoms
  - c. Causes
- II. Target
  - a. Description
  - b. Benefits
  - c. Proposal
- III. Options
  - a. Recommendation
  - b. Explanation

Steinhauser set up a celebration event for all the major participants on the team and other key stakeholders who participated on the project. She also recognized certain individuals for exceptional performance as the project ended and transitioned to sustaining both maintenance and process improvement. She also conducted close out activities, such as compiling lessons learned, closing remaining activities in the schedule and any other outstanding items or issues, and archiving records.

GETTING STARTED CHECKLIST

Question	Yes	No
1. When performing process evaluation, are you realizing these benefits?		
Increasing effectiveness and efficiency when employing BC processes, procedures, techniques, and tools		
Adding greater relevancy to customers		
Increasing ownership among the key stakeholders		
Increasing the relevancy of BC to organizations		
Focusing on customer satisfaction		
Taking an integrated, holistic perspective of BC		
2. When performing process evaluation, have you considered how to address these challenges?		
The business environment for industries is dynamic		
The lack of available resources to perform process evaluation		
Lack of stakeholder buy-in of BC		
Higher priorities		
3. Did you determine whether to produce these deliverables?		
As-Is documentation		
As-Is analysis		
To-Be analysis		
To-Be documentation		
STP		
Metrics		
Implementation plan		
4. When performing process evaluation, did you consider these concepts?		
Improvements occur on two levels—strategic and operational		
Seek opportunities to reduce waste		
Remember that continuous improvement is iterative		
Rely on facts and data and revisit assumptions		
Minimize relearning, set up times, and cycle time		
Seek buy-in from stakeholders		
Remember the 5 Ws (who, what, when, where, and why) and H (how) when performing process improvement		
Graphically document the As-Is and the To-Be		
Apply good listening skills		

5. When performing process evaluation, have you considered performing these activities?
   - Capture the As-Is processes in flowcharts
   - Conduct reviews of As-Is processes in flowcharts
   - Review As-Is processes in flowcharts
   - Revise As-Is processes in flowcharts
   - Identify opportunities for improvement
   - Document To-Be processes in flowcharts
   - Conduct reviews of To-Be processes
   - Revise To-Be processes
   - Prepare STP
   - Conduct internal review of STP
   - Revise STP
   - Present STP to key decision makers
   - Revise STP and resubmit, if necessary
   - Build project plan to implement the revised or new process
   - Obtain approval of the project plan
   - Implement the project plan
   - Take corrective action, if necessary

12

Keystones for Success

Project management (PM) is the primary keystone for business continuity (BC) and business preparedness (BP). Without applying PM concepts, tools, and techniques, achieving resiliency, if it becomes a reality, will be far more costly and ineffective than with PM. If a company has money and time, and they often go hand in hand, to burn, then go ahead and conduct a BC project without PM. The odds, however, to achieve success are not in your favor simply because you have no idea of what success looks like; however, you will certainly know what failure looks like.

PROJECT MANAGEMENT, THE FIRST KEYSTONE

The reality is that PM provides the focus and discipline to execute projects that support every one of these actions necessary for BP: establish governance, conduct a business impact analysis (BIA), build, test, and maintain BP plans, and implement process improvement. Each action can be defined, designed, developed, and deployed using PM concepts, tools, and techniques.

Of course, the degree of applying PM depends on several factors. These include the scale of the project, which involves a large number of people from different disciplines; complexity, such as the difficulty of the critical business process being addressed; position within the strategic and operational levels of the company; and financial magnitude, such as the budget allocated to become resilient.

PM is, therefore, not just good practice to increase the resiliency of a company; it also helps to ensure doing so effectively and efficiently.

Therefore, PM enhances the effectiveness and efficiency. BC project and program managers should heed the other keystones as well.

KEYSTONE: BE PROACTIVE, NOT REACTIVE

One of the biggest issues concerning BC and BP is the high visibility and importance they receive after an event occurs, not before. A disaster hits and suddenly the topic receives top priority, which is, as an old saying goes, "a day late and a dollar short." A BP plan after an event is like purchasing auto insurance after an accident; it may help you in a future accident, but it does you absolutely no good after the last one. The reality is that events do not occur at a company's convenience; they arrive when it least expects it.

BC project managers and, indeed, executive leadership should take the initiative by pushing BP to be a major priority before an event occurs. They need to become true believers or advocates by raising the flag to warn people that failure to prepare is to prepare for failure. BC project managers are the only ones who can do this for the project because of their unique position: interacting with stakeholders at all levels of an organization, from the strategic to the operational.

KEYSTONE: ADOPT A FORMAL, SYSTEMATIC APPROACH

In this book, we have provided a systematic approach with PM being at the core. A tendency exists to treat BC and BP projects as something gradually being addressed until they reach some level of completeness. Small wonder that many BP plans are incomplete and, if complete, are woefully inadequate.

By adopting a formal systematic approach, a company has a greater reasonable assurance that its BIA or BP plans, for instance, have some value to help increase resiliency; a formal, systematic approach provides the necessary discipline and rigor. Using PM with the other six actions described in this book provides the discipline and focus to enhance resiliency. All stakeholders, having a direct or indirect interest in the outcome of the project, follow a common, expected way to progress toward greater resiliency for the company. Other advantages include better communications and greater definition and focus on the vision for a BC project.

KEYSTONE: PRACTICE, PRACTICE, PRACTICE

Having a BP plan is only one part of recovery. Another part is to ensure everyone knows his or her roles and responsibilities. Therefore, BC project managers need to conduct an effective, reliable test, such as a tabletop or drill, for each plan to reinforce its importance to recovery team members. Ongoing practice increases knowledge and understanding of your own and others' responsibilities, enhances communication and collaboration with greater effectiveness, and enables operating with less oversight. Practice, however, does not mean having to wait for a test to occur. Ideally, BC project managers should encourage the recovery team of a specific plan to practice periodically without a formal test so that if, and when, a real event occurs, members are ready to perform recovery procedures.

KEYSTONE: PREPARE EMPLOYEES

Having a BP plan is fine but if members of a recovery team are unavailable, the plan may be useless. A recovery team may be unable to participate because an event impacts their personal lives.

In parallel with the building of a BP plan, BC project managers working with the recovery team leaders should do whatever is necessary for recovery team members to have the tools, supplies, materials, information, etc. to enhance resiliency at home. By becoming personally more resilient, recovery team members will be better able to participate more fully in the recovery of a critical business process.

Another part of personal resiliency is to ensure that team members have the information and technological tools to communicate with other members of the recovery team, especially once the telecommunication infrastructure is restored. They should also have maps with alternate routes to return to their workplace as well as have a hard or electronic copy of the BP plan. If a company has a website or telephone number to call for information regarding the status of the workplace, it should keep that information nearby.

KEYSTONE: INCORPORATE SOCIAL MEDIA IN RECOVERY

Social media plays an instrumental role in our businesses and private lives. It is also playing an increasing role in BC. As the name implies, social media involves the exchange of information, pictures, etc. among members of an electronic or virtual community using applications and hardware. Blogs, websites, and other forms of social media allow creating and sharing content on a select or widespread scale. Due to the network, nonhierarchical nature of social media, content can be distributed and received under a multitude of circumstances.

Therefore, BC and BP should take advantage of the power of social media as a means to recover a critical business process. Its use should be addressed in the BP plan, postured mainly as a means of primary and alternative communications. People will need to have the latest hardware and application technologies to allow sharing of information, such as documents and photographs, with restrictions, for example, compliance with company procedures and laws. BP plans should provide instructions on using social media as it relates to recovery.

KEYSTONE: EMPHASIZE THE IMPORTANCE OF COMMUNICATIONS AND INFORMATION SHARING

One of the biggest challenges during an event is the failure of communications and information sharing among organizations and people. This challenge occurs whether responding to a disaster or recovering from it. People need to communicate and share information, yet it becomes difficult. The telecommunications infrastructure may be down, limiting the ability to gain access to vital information to begin recovery. Key stakeholders may be unavailable or be unable to communicate decisions and impart vital information. Without communications and information sharing among key stakeholders, to include members of a recovery team, recovery will be awkward and inefficient at best, and perhaps even ineffective.

BC project managers need to ensure BP plans place special emphasis on communications and information sharing. The workarounds identified in each procedure should identify the alternative ways to ensure communication and information sharing. During testing, BC project managers should stress the importance of communication and information sharing and should note any shortfalls in the report. Remember, communication and information sharing is the lifeblood of recovery.

KEYSTONE: STRESS ONLY THE ESSENTIAL ELEMENTS OF INFORMATION

This might seem contradictory concerning information sharing discussed in the last keystone, but it is not. The idea here is that more data and information may make matters worse, especially if it comes in large volumes and overwhelms people making decisions about recovery. Therefore, too much data and information can impede recovery; hence, more is not necessarily better.

BC project managers and recovery team leaders should view information needs based on what is necessary for recovery. Unfortunately, many people believe that the more information the better. As a result, BP plans become too thick and cumbersome to use during recovery because ironically people cannot find what they need. The reality is that during recovery most people lack the desire and time to wade through minutia to find the information they need to execute their responsibilities. BC project managers and recovery team leaders need to ensure that plans contain only the information necessary for recovery. No guideline or rules exist other than a plan needs to be reviewed carefully and BC project managers and team leaders must make a judgment on what minimal information is required for recovery. Knowing priorities during recovery can also go a long way to help determine what to include and what to omit in plans.

KEYSTONE: THINK STRATEGICALLY

BC project managers need to think from a strategic perspective. This perspective will help them determine what is and is not important for consideration when conducting the BIA as well as what to include in BP plans. Thinking strategically can help them develop BP plans that not only enhance the resiliency of their critical business processes, but also identify touch points with other processes, too.

Thinking strategically also helps in other ways. Executive sponsorship for BC and BP is essential to gain acceptance throughout a company. Having a strategic mindset enables project managers to posture BC and BP from a strategic perspective, increasing the chances of gaining the necessary support at higher levels in the company. So, what does thinking strategically entail as it relates to BC and BP? It means ensuring that the BIA and the accompanying BP plans address the enterprise-wide mission, goals, and objectives. It means considering the enterprise-wide risks, as well as the risks specific to a critical business process. It means recognizing the relationships of BP plans among one another. It means keeping the board of directors (BoD) and executives apprised of progress in enhancing the resiliency of the company. It means taking a multidisciplinary perspective by avoiding the tendency to think one discipline, for example, information technology or finance, is more important to recovery than other disciplines are. Finally, it means BC project managers think in terms of not just today but also of tomorrow, such as three to five years out. In other words, BC project managers consider the future as well as the past and present requirements for maintaining the resiliency of the company.

KEYSTONE: LOOK BEYOND THE ENTERPRISE

Recovery often goes beyond the enterprise. When a major event occurs in the external environment, it could, and often does, have a considerable impact on internal operations and can affect their ability to recover. For example, recovery, not just response, often depends on what the public sector does. For example, if power goes out throughout a region, if flooding blocks off avenues to a work location, if a pandemic spreads, or if a terrorist act occurs, the public sector will act one way or another and its decisions will impact the recovery efforts of a company, locally, nationally, and even internationally.

Unfortunately, many BIAs and BP plans seem to overlook this fact. BC project managers and recovery team leaders prepare plans as if the external environment does not matter. Yet, area-wide events can, and often do, have an impact on a company. The public sector determines the priorities for response and recovery of utilities, for example, without any consideration of a company's critical business process; a company will have to make decisions to adjust to recovery efforts accordingly.

The reality is the public sector seeks and needs the participation of the private sector for both response and recovery. Unfortunately, this interchange between the two often does not occur for many reasons. Yet, both the public and private sectors really have a symbiotic relationship that necessitates cooperation, not competition. The private sector has knowledge, expertise, and resources that, after an event occurs, can help the community to recover faster and more effectively. The public sector has an interest in helping businesses recover, too, so it can support the tax base to rebuild the community. Effective recovery, therefore, necessitates a positive working relationship between both parties. An adversarial, reclusive relationship hurts both private enterprise and the public sector.

Therefore, BC project managers should seek to engage members of the public sector, such as fire and police, during the conduct of a BIA, if applicable, and during the test of BP plans. In some cases, they may want to invite representatives from the public sector to provide insight and suggestions for BP plans. This will help avoid or alleviate the impact or surprises of actions attributed to the public sector. Again, BC project managers should encourage and enhance opportunities for greater communication and collaboration between the two sectors concerning recovery.

Whenever possible, it may also behoove BC project managers to develop and test BP plans, which at least identifies the need for, if not encourages the participation of, other businesses, especially suppliers and customers. Oftentimes, an area-wide event may make it beneficial for both parties to help each other to recover if for no other reason than self-interest. This joint participation may include sharing of resources or expertise.

The same can be said for nongovernmental organizations (NGOs). NGOs can provide services, for example, food, water, and transportation, if a business is unable to provide for itself. Businesses, too, can reciprocate. BC project managers should know that NGOs could play a crucial role in the recovery of their critical business processes.

KEYSTONE: STRESS AGILITY

BC and BP require discipline, but not in a manner hindering the adaptability to circumstances. The five actions for enhancing resiliency—establish governance, conduct BIA, and build, test, and maintain BP plans—should not create disciplines that impede the ability of a company to respond to events.

BC project managers need to keep this fact in mind. They must communicate that BP plans serve as guides to help recovery team members recover from many types of events, not just a specific one. BC project managers should ensure all plans operate at a sufficient level of abstraction without sacrificing useful content while simultaneously allowing recovery team members the independence to make decisions and take action.

To ensure agility, BC project managers should prepare BP plans that are risk-independent while at the same time identifying some risks that have a reasonable likelihood of an appreciable impact on a critical business process. For example, if an earthquake is a very likely event, then it behooves the recovery team to have some procedures in the plan contain work-arounds for recovering from such an event. However, the plan should also include general procedures that apply to all recovery efforts regardless of risk. The idea is not to become so narrowly focused in a way that makes it difficult, if not impossible, to recover from an event or even a Black Swan.

BC project managers can also ensure agility by supporting process improvements. This support can occur at the strategic and operational levels. At the strategic level, BC project managers who have led building and maintaining plans, for example, may notice that some BC and BP activities add no value or actually lessen the resiliency of a critical business process. BC project managers should document and communicate such circumstances to the BC working group or BC steering committee for possible areas of improvement. At the operational level, BC project managers should work with recovery teams of a critical business process to identify opportunities for improvement. Through continuous process improvement, BC project managers can also remove obstacles that impede the resiliency of critical business processes and become more agile without the approval of the BC steering committee, for example.

KEYSTONE: ADHERE TO A MULTIDISCIPLINARY SYSTEMS PERSPECTIVE

BC project managers should always be mindful to avoid subscribing to a linear perspective of a critical business process. BC and BP involve a multiplicity of elements that do not necessarily operate linearly, whereby a dynamic interplay of elements, including objects, people, data, signals, processes, relationships, thresholds, methods, systems, and many other variables, occurs. All of these elements interact when recovering from an event. The interaction may be different when an earthquake affects a critical business process as opposed to a disgruntled employee coming into an office and shooting everyone. The responses are different, and so is the recovery.

By subscribing to a systems perspective, BC project managers can better identify how a recovery team might go about recovery based on a given scenario vis-à-vis another scenario. Largely, a systems perspective allows BC project managers to take a high level, strategic perspective of recovery while simultaneously being able to ensure agility of a critical business process. A systems perspective also enables BC project managers to view recovery in a way that goes beyond just a single critical business process. For example, BC project managers can more easily determine whether their critical business process has touch points with other ones. It also enables BC project managers to see how their critical business process interacts with other entities in the external environment, such as the public sector and NGOs.

KEYSTONE: NEVER FORGET THE SUPPLY CHAIN

The supply chain for many companies nowadays has become critically important to the survival of a firm, thanks largely to the rise of modern international commerce. Keeping the supply chain resilient is no small chore as it becomes more complex and all its elements become more interdependent and integrated. Risks and their impacts to the supply chain are no longer restricted to a local area but beyond and, in some cases, globally. The Butterfly Effect, discussed in the beginning of this book, may cause a local event to have cascading effects in unanticipated ways a considerable distance away. The diagram in Figure 12.1 shows the impact of a failure in a supply chain, such as a second-tier supplier unable to deliver a component or service.

BC project managers need to understand the bigger picture on how their critical business process for which they are responsible contributes to the supply chain. They also need to know the impact of a failure by their critical business process on the overall supply chain for a company. This knowledge and understanding will enable developing a BP plan that not only recovers a critical process but also contributes to the overall resiliency of a company. This assessment requires having a good strategic understanding of the company as a whole, subscribing to a systems perspective,

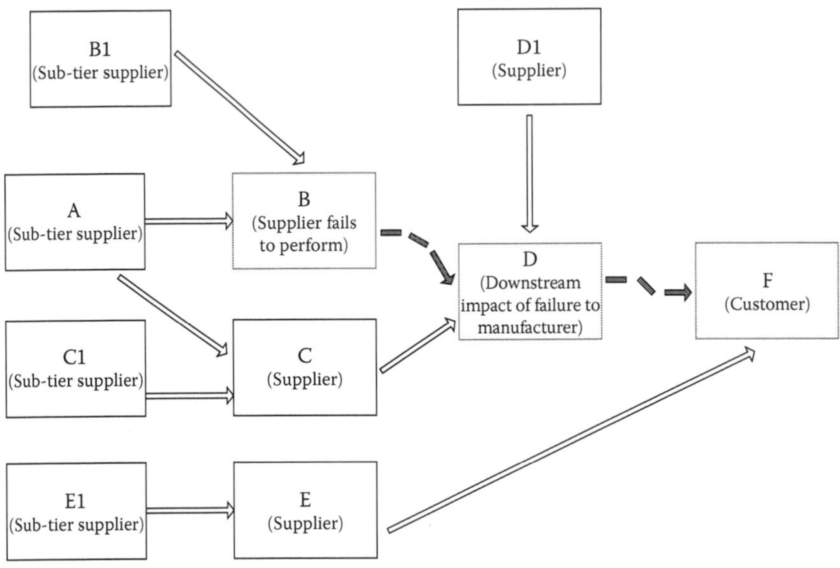

FIGURE 12.1
Downstream impact of supplier failure on the supply chain.

having a solid knowledge of ERM from a BC perspective, recognizing the major touch points with other critical business processes, and furthering communication and sharing of information with others.

THE KEYSTONE OF KEYSTONES: BACK TO NUMBER 1

BC managers can capitalize on all of the above keystones more efficiently and effectively if they use the discipline of PM, whether establishing governance, conducting a BIA, building, testing, and maintaining BP plans, or performing process improvement. The challenge is getting the support and latitude to apply PM in a manner that can help a company become more resilient. This, of course, is easier said than done. Too often, BC and BP projects start as a journey rather than a destination. The journey usually ends up nowhere anyone expects, resulting in a tremendous waste of time and money and carrying on forever with no end in sight. When all is said and done, the company is no more resilient than when it started on the journey.

By applying solid PM on BC and BP projects, BC project managers can lead as well as manage their projects to success. Their projects become a destination, not a journey—and the company becomes resilient.

Glossary

Accessibility: Ensuring people have access to the product, service, information, equipment, etc. to perform their responsibilities; from the perspective of BC, it involves ensuring people have access to a BP plan.

Act of God: An incident due to natural causes.

Activation: Deploying part or all of a BP plan in response to an event; it should include exercising the call tree and a significant portion of the plan itself during a realistic scenario.

Affinity diagramming: A graphical technique to take an assortment of items and divide them into groups based upon one or more characteristics.

Apply project management: One of seven BC actions that involve applying business disciplines to establish a program or project to deploy BC throughout an organization.

As-Is analysis: Stakeholders review the As-Is flow to determine opportunities for improvement such as reducing the number of approvals, having joint recovery team meetings, and adopting better methods or tools to expedite or increase the effectiveness of recovery.

Assumptions: Assumed to be facts until proven otherwise.

Baseline: The approved version of something in a project, that is, scope baseline, schedule baseline, cost baseline, quality baseline, etc.

Black Swan event: An unanticipated event having a significant effect that is rationalized after its occurrence.

Brainstorming: A free-flowing approach used to generate a random list of ideas, options, etc. without casting judgment.

Build BP plan: One of seven BC actions that involve developing one or more plans to guide the recovery of a critical business process.

Business continuity (BC): The discipline of developing, deploying, and maintaining strategies and procedures to ensure that critical business processes resume by increasing the likelihood of responding and recovering from an event crippling or destroying the existence of a business entity.

Business continuity (BC) governance infrastructure: A combination of a framework, organizational structure, and resources to make decisions and take actions to achieve the vision, mission, goals, and objectives of the BC program or project.

Business continuity planning: Developing, deploying, and maintaining strategies and procedures to ensure critical business processes continue or are restored.

Business continuity planning cycle: A continuous process to develop, maintain, and test plans to enhance resiliency.

Business continuity program: An organization to lead and manage the development and deployment of a comprehensive set of processes, procedures, and disciplines to enhance the resiliency of a company before, during, and after the occurrence of a disruptive event.

Business continuity steering committee: Representatives from both the strategic and operational levels of the company providing overall guidance and direction, general oversight on progress, and final arbitration of issues unresolvable at lower levels.

Business continuity strategies: High-level decisions and actions dealing with the recovery of a critical business process before, during, and after a disruptive event.

Business continuity working group: Group of key stakeholders, as well as senior managers often representative from the operational and functional sides of an organization; its focus is on ensuring the execution of the governance program complies with the decisions and guidance of the overall strategies and wishes of the BC steering committee.

Business impact analysis (BIA): A process that requires analyzing all the operations within an organization to identify critical business processes and the impact of realized risks, or threats, upon them; the BIA can occur at the strategic level and within each critical business process.

Business preparedness (BP): A subset of BC, it requires developing plans for a company to recover from an event having a significant impact on processes it deems critical to its survivability.

Business preparedness plan: A subset of BC, a document guiding the recovery and ultimate restoration from an event having a significant impact on processes deemed critical to its survivability.

Butterfly effect: Predicated on chaos theory, a small change in one location can have significant consequences elsewhere.

Buy-In: Also known as ownership, having a stake in something or an outcome.

Call tree: A listing of key individuals to contact if a disruptive event occurs; its purpose is to establish and maintain communication and to respond to a disruptive event.

Change management: Provides the discipline to ensure only permitted revisions to a plan occur.

Check sheeting: Collecting and compiling data in real time to identify trends, such as types of defects.

Committee of sponsoring organizations (COSO): A group of private organizations addressing issues of governance, from finance to ethics to risk management, and controls.

Communication: Transmitting data and information either in soft (electronic) or hard (paper) copy form.

Conduct BIA: One of seven BC actions using risk management to determine the effect of various events on a critical business process and corresponding plans to ensure recovery.

Conduct process evaluation: One of seven BC actions that involves keeping the other actions and their corresponding steps "Lean" by eliminating waste and providing value to the customer.

Configuration management: Setting a baseline for deliverables produced on a project. From a BC perspective, setting a baseline for the BP plan and then managing its integrity becomes important to account for what version of a document a recovery team will reference.

Contingency plan: A preplanned response implemented only when certain conditions exist.

Corrective action: The shortcomings identified during the testing exercise and recorded in a "lessons learned" session after an exercise.

Crisis: An event far exceeding normal expectations of disruption and necessitating recovery actions, which, if not taken, threaten the survivability of an organization.

Critical business process: A series of procedures and activities key stakeholders have identified as vital to the survival of an organization; a critical process can have one or more BP plan supporting it.

Cross-functional perspective: Adhering to a process-oriented vantage point, which transcends functional, silo-like thinking.

Customer: Internal or external person or organization that is the recipient of a product or service. From a BC perspective, the recipient of a BP plan for a critical process is a customer, which, in turn, has a customer receiving its product or service.

Cycle time: The time needed to complete a process, procedure, or operation.

Dependency: A resource needed to enhance the recovery of a critical business process; a dependency can be either internal or external to a critical business process.

Disaster: A sudden, unexpected event having severe consequences on a critical business process for a considerable time unless a recovery team takes immediate action.

Due diligence: A legal concept meaning an organization or person must take reasonable actions to protect people and property under a set of circumstances.

Emergency: An event threatening life, safety, and property, requiring immediate attention; it may not, quite yet, be a disaster but does require attention to preclude becoming a disaster or catastrophe.

Enterprise risk management: Applying risk management at a strategic level for a company by taking a holistic perspective to ascertain the risks potentially impacting it.

Event: The occurrence of an incident impacting a critical business process; an event can range in intensity and impact, such as very mild to catastrophic.

Exercise: An event planned and executed to develop, maintain, and enhance BP for a critical business process.

Export administration regulations: Department of Commerce regulatory direction on the use and types of export licenses related to commodities, software, and technology.

Fishbone diagramming: A graphical technique to determine the relationships between a problem and its causes.

Force field analysis: Identifying and analyzing the pros and cons affecting an organization's ability to achieve its objectives.

Framework: Supported by a methodology, guides determining the essential processes and procedures to build and maintain their content but also to assess the effectiveness of the governance program to ensure the resiliency of a company which, in turn, indicates how effective the BC governance program is.

Gap analysis: A review of a BP plan to ascertain any discrepancies in its content; changes in the context of a critical business process often serve as a "trigger" to identify additional gaps in a plan.

Global sourcing: Procuring resources or services in countries other than the host location of the home office.

Governance: Frameworks, processes, procedures, methods, techniques, etc. adapted by organizations to make decisions and take actions to achieve their vision, mission, goals, and objectives.

Hazard: A potentially harmful event that could negatively impact operations, especially critical business functions.

Hazard assessment: Identifying and analyzing the impact of threats on critical business functions.

Histogram: A graphical technique for displaying data distribution to ascertain frequencies of occurrence.

Impact: The effect of a risk event or condition on the strategic and operational performance of an organization.

Implementation plan: Consists largely of PM and quality tools and techniques, such as scheduling, trend analysis charts, histograms, and matrices to implement the target.

Incident: An event impacting a process; an incident impacts a process, not necessarily a critical one, and inconsequentially.

Information mapping: A method of presenting categories of meaningful content to enhance readability and content.

Institute governance: One of seven BC actions, which involves establishing an infrastructure to support developing and deploying BC throughout an organization.

Integrated exercise: A cross-functional, multiprocess, interorganizational test to develop, maintain, and enhance BP involving multiple BP plans.

Integration: The essential integration among two or more components within a process or system to function holistically.

Interdependence: The reliance upon another process, procedure, object, etc. to fulfill its own purpose.

International Traffic in Arms Regulations: Department of State direction on the export of information, material, and technologies deemed in the interests of national security and foreign policy.

Interrelationships digraph: A nonlinear graphical technique to display cause and effect relationships among objects, ideas, etc.

Just-in-Time: A manufacturing system based upon pull rather than push, thereby reducing waste, for example, excessive inventory and timely delivery of materials, supplies, etc.

Kaizen: Also known as perfection through continuous improvement, this is an effort to achieve perfection in a process.

Key stakeholder listing: One or more executives or senior managers involved in a critical business process.

Lateral communications: Transferring data, information, etc. among peers.

Leadership: The act of inspiring a group of individuals to reach a common goal or outcome through the effective use of interpersonal skills.

Lean: A perspective that transcends siloed or narrow functional thinking to deliver value to the customer.

Lesson plan: Describes the purpose, goals, and objectives of the training as well as identifies the content.

Maintain BP plans: One of the seven BC actions, which involves keeping BP plans current and of value to stakeholders of a critical business process.

Maintenance: Updating one or more BP plans to ensure better resiliency of a critical business process.

Management by objectives: A cascading, top-down, definition and alignment of targets agreed upon by management and employees.

Maximum allowable downtime (MAD): The total time a process or dependency can be unavailable before it negatively impacts the performance of a critical business function; once the downtime reaches that specific point in time, the critical business process feels the pain of an event.

Methodology: A detailed manifestation of a framework to institute and maintain BC within an organization.

Metrics: Numeric verification of progress toward achieving a target.

Mission statement: A high-level description of the purpose and focus of an organization based upon its vision; the emphasis is on how at a high level rather than what (vision).

Muda: Japanese for waste.

Multi-tier suppliers: Several layers of vendors providing goods and services to a supplier, such as a prime contractor.

Normal operations: Also known as business as usual, it is the state of business operations prior to the occurrence of an event.

Operational level: The daily, ongoing processes, procedures, tasks, etc. to produce and deliver products and services to a customer.

Operational risk: The potential failure of procedures and controls of a critical business function.

Opportunity: A risk event that has a positive impact on a project, program, or business process.

Paradigm: A mental mindset to help understand and interpret phenomena.

Pareto charting: The display of values using bars and a cumulative line to determine the cause of a defect, for example.

PDCA cycle: Also known as the Deming cycle, it involves four phases that repeat: plan, do, check, act. Plan is determining what to address; do is addressing what; check is determining progress in addressing the what; and act is making adjustments, if necessary.

Performance measurement baseline: A plan to measure progress against an integrated scope, schedule, and cost criteria.

Policy: States the purpose and high-level goals for the BC and serves as a guideline to develop supporting processes to realize the content of the policy.

Preparedness: Continuously establishing measures and controls to ensure a greater likelihood of recovery.

Procedure: Documents written to execute the processes in normal and atypical circumstances; multiple procedures make up a process.

Process: A high-level, cross-functional view, for example, IT, human resources, finance, and manufacturing, involving multiple procedures or operations to accomplish a goal.

Process evaluation: Analyzing, evaluating, and improving BC processes, procedures, techniques, and tools to ensure more efficient and effective application across an enterprise and within a critical business process.

Process owner: An individual, usually at a senior or executive management level, responsible for the efficient and effective management and execution of a cross-functional value stream.

Project management (PM): The concepts, principles, tools, and techniques to complete a project according to its performance measurement baseline.

Project management plan: A document that contains all of the individual plans of how to plan, manage, execute, monitor, control, and close a project.

Project management staff: Members of the PM team that have been assigned leadership roles by the project manager.

Project management team: A subset of the project team, consisting of the project manager and the PM staff.

Project manager: The individual who is accountable for all aspects of the project. This person is responsible for communicating with and managing the expectations of the stakeholders.

Project portfolio management: An array of projects managed as investments to further the strategic goals and objectives of an organization.

Project team: The individuals assigned to the project to complete the work (both technical and nontechnical) of the project.

Proprietary information: Content that requires protection from competitors or from other harmful circumstances.

Protocol: A set of rules or guidelines for taking action under certain conditions.

Quality: Focusing on meeting the requirements and expectations of a customer.

Reasonable assurance: Often associated with auditing but is applicable to BC, meaning no one can guarantee 100% that something will prevent an event from happening; from a BC perspective, no plan can ensure a critical business process can be completely resilient.

Recovery: Implementing prioritized strategies and actions to recover from an event.

Recovery period: The time continuum between the occurrence of a disruptive event and the eventual return to minimum normal operations. It is recorded in the BP plan.

Recovery point objective (RPO): A point in time when it becomes necessary to restore systems and data to avoid significant data loss.

Recovery team: A group of individuals responsible for recovering a critical business process or function after a disruptive event; each BP plan should have a recovery team with specific responsibilities.

Recovery time line: A sequence of activities when recovering business process operations over a time continuum.

Recovery time objective (RTO): The point in a time continuum to recover a business process.

Relearning: Becoming reacquainted with previous knowledge or work to continue to execute a process, procedure, technique, etc.

Reliance statement: Describes why a critical process needs a specific resource for recovery; every procedure within a BP plan contains a reliance statement and one or more workarounds.

Residual risk: The part of the risk that remains after implementing a response.

Resilience: The ability of an organization and its accompanying critical business processes to respond or recover from the impact of events.

Response: Applying processes, procedures, and actions as quickly as possible to prevent, mitigate, or avoid the impact of a negative incident.

Restoration: The process, procedures, and actions taken to return a critical business process to normal operations, or business as usual. It includes response and recovery. Hence, restoration equals response plus recovery.

Resumption: The processes, procedures, and actions to restart a critical business process after a disruptive event. It entails getting a critical process back on its feet; in other words, begin the recovery after the response has adequately dealt with the incident or event.

Review cycle: A regular, ongoing approach to ensure a deliverable is up to date; from the perspective of BC, a plan is reviewed to ensure it contains the latest information.

Risk attitude: A person or organization's degree of perception about uncertainty.

Risk event: A discrete occurrence affecting a project, initiative, or program, either positively or negatively.

Risk management: The actions taken to reduce the probability and impact of uncertainty on a process, project, or organization.

Risk tolerance: A person or organization's degree of willingness to face uncertainty.

Roles, responsibilities, and authorities (RAA): The delineation of titles, tasks, and decision-making authority.

Run charting: A graphical technique displaying data over a time continuum.

Scatter diagramming: A graphical technique that displays the relationship between two numeric variables.

Scenario: A realistic yet fictitious event presenting a set of conditions and impacts challenging a recovery team when identifying, analyzing, and applying the content of their BP plan or plans. The scenario should consist of an event that occurs plus a minor but related incident that adds an unexpected challenge.

Secondary risk: A risk that arises as the direct result of implementing a response to another risk.

Set up time: The duration needed to ready a machine, procedure, system, etc. to start a task.

Showstopper: An unanticipated event that halts progress and requires a workaround.

Silo thinking: Not taking a cross-functional perspective by viewing an organization from a narrow, functional perspective.

Simulation exercise: Having recovery team members actually apply the specific content of their BP plans against a scenario; also known as a drill.

Single point of contact (SPOC): A person assigned in a process with a specific responsibility; from the perspective of BC, it involves assigning a specific individual with responsibility to maintain a plan.

Single point of failure: A specific breakdown in a sequence of activities, impacting a critical business process; a single point of failure impacts all subsequent activities downstream.

Situation-Target-Proposal: This document enables presenting information about improvements, background information concerning the existing way of doing business, the end state reflecting improvements, and the path to achieve the target.

Stakeholder: A person or organization having a direct or indirect interest in, or that can be impacted by, the outcome of a process or project.

Stand down: A response to an event no longer necessary whether for an exercise or real life event; additional action is unnecessary by the recovery team.

Standard operating procedure: A document providing direction on implementing the BC strategies according to prescribed direction.

Strategic level: The executive and senior management levels of an organization where decisions and actions provide overall direction rather than manage its daily operations.

Supply chain: A network of one or more processes that begin with the extraction of raw materials to the delivery of a product or service to a customer.

Tabletop exercise: Applying the contents of a BP plan to a scenario using discussion and not taking action, such as during a drill or simulation exercise.

Test BP plans: One of seven BC actions that involve testing of BP plans to ensure relevancy and accuracy of content.

Test plan: A document detailing the specifics of a testing exercise, such as identifying and recording who, what, when, where, why, and how.

Testing: Systematically verifying and validating the effectiveness of an organization's ability to respond to and recover from an event.

Think outside the box: A creative approach requiring coming up with unique solutions to problems or issues.

Threat: A risk event that has a negative impact to a project, program, or business process.

Time continuum: A range of intervals, such as durations, from a beginning to an ending point.

To-Be analysis: Uses the same approach as the As-Is analysis to compare before and after states of a process except it reflects areas requiring changes.

Touch point: Multiple components, objects, processes, procedures, and plans that share some degree of relationship when executed.

Unk-Unk risk: An unanticipated risk that becomes realized; translated it means unknown-unknown.

Value: Satisfying the requirements and expectations of the internal or external customer at the right time efficiently and effectively.

Value stream: A series of procedures or operations making up a process to create a product or deliver a service of value to the customer.

Vertical communications: Transferring data, information, etc. up and down the chain of command within an organization.

Vision: A high-level description of an end state from which all decisions and actions in an organization are directed.

Workaround: A set of activities to execute a procedure if a specific resource is unavailable during recovery.

Workaround procedure: Alternative activities to employ when an important critical dependency is unavailable for recovery.

Appendix A: Case Study Project Charter

Project Title: Save Our Wine Project
Project Sponsor: Roger Fitzsimmons III, CFO
Date Prepared: 10/15/xx
Project Manager: Mary Steinhauser
Project Customer: Board of Directors

PROJECT PURPOSE OR JUSTIFICATION

To identify the key processes and resources to complete the design, develop, and test a set of business preparedness (BP) plans that will ensure survivability and restoration of normal operations in the event of an anticipated or unanticipated event, incident, disaster, crisis, or catastrophe. It also requires establishing a business continuity (BC) governance infrastructure and providing education and training on BC throughout the corporation.

PROJECT DESCRIPTION

The BP plan development project will entail gathering of information from various functional and operational areas of the business, for identifying the key processes and resources required to adequately respond to various situations that could threaten the company's supply chain, final product, reputation, or its very existence. This requires thinking outside our normal operational scope to identify those events within other entities, companies, and countries that would have an impact on our operations.

HIGH-LEVEL REQUIREMENTS

- Key stakeholders must be identified (by title)
- BP plans developed must be agreed on by the key stakeholders
- BP plans must be tested through simulation or quantitative techniques
- BP plans must address threats at a high-level and must be modifiable for specific events, for example, the weather BP plan can be modified to deal with a tornado or a flood
- Response team responsibilities will be drafted, team member attributes will be identified, team members will be identified and trained
- Cost to implement a BP plan will not be included in project costs

HIGH-LEVEL RISKS

- Uncooperative stakeholders (all levels)
- Loss of executive support for the project
- Inadequate funding

PROJECT OBJECTIVES

- All six critical business processes have a BP plan
- All BP plans are tested and each one has a follow up schedule to verify corrective actions have been implemented

SUCCESS CRITERIA

- Built and approved plans for each critical business process
- Tested plans for each critical business process

SCOPE

This project requires all identified critical processes have a BP plan and be tested. It does not include maintenance and process improvement activities. Both maintenance and process improvement will be treated as separate projects.

COST

Build and test for all six critical business processes will be $250,000 (direct and indirect).

SUMMARY MILESTONES

Phase I Infrastructure and Training Development to Complete: 7/1/xx
Phase II BP Plans Built and Tested to Complete: 5/3/xx

STAKEHOLDERS AND ROLES

Stakeholders	Role
Frank Malatesta	Controller
Roger Fitzsimmons III	Chief Financial Officer and Executive Sponsor
Mary Squires	Steering Committee Member, Vice President Internal Services
Henry Maxwell	Steering Committee Member, Executive Vice President and President of Blended Red Wine Enterprises
Russ Farquar	Steering Committee Member, Senior Vice President of Information Technology and Operations
Nancy Walascom	Steering Committee Member, Executive Vice President and President of Blended White Wine Enterprises
Terry Wattsmythe	Steering Committee Member, Executive Vice President and President of Blended Rose Wine Enterprises

Jeff Lackstaff	Steering Committee Member, Senior Vice President of Domestic and International Sales and Marketing
Wanda Edwardson	Steering Committee Member, Chief Counsel and Senior Vice President
John S. Tamarson	Chairman and Chief Executive Officer
Linda Steinhauser	Senior Project Manager, Internal Services
Board of Directors	Customer

PROJECT MANAGER AUTHORITY LEVEL

Staffing Decisions

The project manager's requests for specific staff members will be given serious consideration by all functional managers. While functional managers are expected to maintain staff within their own departments to meet operational objectives, this project is a priority and must be completed by the due date listed in the milestone list. In the event of a conflict between the functional manager and the project manager, the sponsor will become involved to make the decision.

Budget Management and Variance

The project manager will identify and gather a team that will plan and estimate the project tasks to determine the cost of the project. If the planned budgeted amount exceeds the estimated budget in this document, the decision whether to proceed will be made by the sponsor. Variances of greater than 10% of the budgeted amount require immediate action by the project manager and the team.

Technical Decisions

All winery-based (operational) technical decisions will be made by the winery operations manager. Any technical-related decisions, not specifically focused on the winery operations, will be decided by the subject matter experts identified in the stakeholder register.

Conflict Resolution

Conflict will be handled in a professional and appropriate manner. The team selected for this project is expected to conduct themselves professionally. Any disagreements between team members will be handled between the conflicting team members first. In the event the conflict cannot be resolved between the team members, the issue will be brought to the attention of the project manager for resolution. In the event the project manager is unable to resolve the conflict, the functional managers of the conflicting team members will attempt resolution.

APPROVALS

-signed-	4/25/xx
CFO and Sponsor Signature	Date
-signed-	4/25/xx
Controller Signature	Date
-signed-	4/25/xx
Program Manager Signature	Date

Appendix B: Project Statement of Work

Project: Save Our Wine Project
Sponsor: Chief Financial Officer

EXECUTIVE SUMMARY

Recent national and international events have steered the executives of RWM, Inc. to implement business preparedness (BP) plans during the calendar year 20xx. A recent insurance review revealed that the corporation lacked formal plans to handle an event that could potentially disrupt normal business operations and jeopardize recovery. Therefore, this project is imperative and has the highest priority within the corporation.

This project will entail gathering of information from functional and operational areas of the business, for identifying the processes and resources required to adequately respond to situations that could threaten the company's supply chain, primary and final product, reputation, or very existence. Events that are beyond our control, such as natural and manufactured disasters, events within other organizations that either distribute our products or supply this organization with raw materials, or events beyond our nation's borders, can affect normal operations.

PROJECT DESCRIPTION

The scope of this project will include developing several BP plans, aimed at possibly occurring events, also referred to as unknown unknowns. The events considered should include, but are not limited to, weather-related events such as drought and monsoons; crop disease; workplace violence; untimely death of a key employee, for example, Wine Master, COO, CFO,

CEO, etc.); supplier and distribution chain disruption; and specifically a plan to handle a breach in the upstream dam. See the information listed later for the primary supplier and distribution chain considerations.

The BP plan for each possible event should consider the following basic process:

1. Receive the raw materials (grapes) from the grape suppliers.
2. Process the raw materials to extract the raw juice.
3. Process and filter raw juice in preparation for barreling.
4. During the fermentation process, color and taste test the product.
5. Approve the product for bottling.
6. Bottle, label, and then distribute the product.

The project work will also include the resources and time required to conduct simulations for each possible event, incident, disaster, crisis, or catastrophe.

SUPPLY CHAIN CONSIDERATIONS

BP plans should include possible events occurring within and among different suppliers. Events of this nature can include, but are not limited to, a supplier going out of business, a supplier failing to supply the correct product in the correct amounts, a supplier being purchased by one of its competitors or one of our competitors, and any other possible event affecting one of our suppliers. Specifically, a BP plan needs to be created for alternate suppliers in the event our raw material supplier has a diseased crop.

When considering possible events of our supply chain, four main suppliers may be affected:

- Raw materials, for example, grapes (Grapling Grapes, Inc.)
- Bottle supplier (Glass Container, LLC)
- Label supplier (TagIt Enterprises, Inc.)
- Barrel supplier (Roll Around, Inc.)

DISTRIBUTION CHAIN CONSIDERATIONS

BP plans should include possible events occurring within and between our different distributors, considering local, national, and international distribution supply chains. The sales manager and chief operating officer are the subject matter experts in the area of distribution. While our international distributors are important to us, the primary focus of the BP plans should be within our local and national distribution chain. The reasoning behind this philosophy is simple: Even though events that occur beyond our nation's borders are volatile, the immediate impact on our normal operations is much less.

When considering possible events of our distribution chain, look at the following four main outlets:

- Direct sales to customers here at the winery
- Grocery stores
- Restaurants
- Liquor stores

PRODUCT DESCRIPTION

Each BP plan is considered a separate product, or deliverable of the project. Ideally, each plan will be agreed on by all parties involved in implementation of the plan. In the event of disagreement on how best to handle a particular event, incident, disaster, crisis, or catastrophe, the project sponsor will intervene and make the final decision. Each plan must be designed to include a simulation of an event, incident, disaster, crisis, or catastrophe, if possible.

Once all of the plans have been completed, they must be integrated. Each plan will include all specific actions and responsibilities of key personnel in the event of an unplanned event, incident, disaster, crisis, or catastrophe. Clear definitions for the terms *event*, *incident*, *disaster*, *crisis*, or *catastrophe* will be included.

Appendix C: Draft Business Preparedness Plan

xx/xx/xx

Critical Business Process Title: Receive the raw materials from grape providers

Process Owner: Dante Ferragio

Business Preparedness Project Manager: Jorge Rodriquez

Date: xx/xx/xx

Version: 1.0 (Draft)

Background: Lessons learned from recent earthquake activity in Napa Valley in California have augmented the board of directors' (BoD) fears about being vulnerable. Fear of inaccessibility to resources and the collapse of the transportation infrastructure have shaken the BoD and they believe that the long practice of self-insurance for recovery is no longer relevant or adequate; more robust reliable action is necessary to ensure greater resiliency. As a result, the BoD decided to act by making RWM, Inc. more resilient in the face of many threats. It has decided to establish a business continuity (BC) program that emphasizes developing and testing of a series of business preparedness plans. The process covered by this business preparedness (BP) plan is one of six processes deemed critical by the BoD.

Purpose, Goals, and Objectives: The purpose of this BP plan is to guide the recovery team for this process in improving the resiliency of the company. The goals are to enhance recovery in the most efficient and effective manner possible contingent upon the impact of an event hurting the resiliency of the company. The objectives are to (1) assure the effectiveness of the call tree, (2) ensure accurate membership of the recovery team, (3) provide procedural guidance on the recovery of key resources, also known as dependencies, including the quantities required over a time continuum, (4) define the maximum allowable downtime (MAD) for the process, and (5) identify touch points with other processes to assure effective and efficient coordination.

Scope: This procedure covers only "Receive the raw materials from grape providers." Other than for touch points identified herein, all other processes are considered out of scope. Also out of scope is vineyards owned by suppliers. Exception: If a supplier's vineyard is impacted, then refer to procedure on vendors.

Authority: Decision made by the BoD on xx/xx/xx and Policy 7, "Company Resiliency."

Assumptions: (1) Resiliency will remain a high priority for the company; (2) all functional departments and operating units will cooperate in building and testing this plan in the face of other priorities; and (3) sufficient financial and labor resources will be available to complete building and testing of this plan.

Maximum Allowable Downtime: 5 days

Integration with Other Plans and Critical Business Processes: Opportunities may exist for synergy with other critical business processes and their respective plans. These integration opportunities, referred to as touch points, should serve as opportunities for greater resiliency through integration. These other critical processes, the priority deemed by the BoD, are

- Approve the product for bottling
- Bottle, label, and then distribute the product
- Process the raw materials to extract the raw juice
- Process and filter the raw juice in preparation for barreling
- During the fermentation process, color and taste the product

In the future, integration may be required with other plans for processes that are important but not critical to the recovery of the company.

Major responsibilities: The major responsibilities for this plan are: (1) establish an up-to-date call tree; (2) identify resource requirements in total and over time; (3) identify procedures and determine the appropriate strategies for recovery; (4) determine responsibility for each procedure; (5) determine recovery time objective; (6) regularly test the plan; and (7) keep the plan current.

RECOVERY TEAM

Purpose: The recovery team consists of key stakeholders deemed essential to the recovery of this critical process. These stakeholders may or may not have a direct involvement in the recovery of this process. They could be people who have important knowledge or expertise that can help stakeholders having a direct interest in the outcome of the process. These stakeholders may include subject matter experts or representatives from other processes.

Membership and Contact List:

Note: The following table should be populated with stakeholders as they are identified during the completion of this plan.

Last, First Name	Recovery Team Role	Phone (Land Line)	Phone (Cell Phone)	E-mail	Pager #
Ferragio, Dante	Team Leader	(xxx) xxx-xxxx	(xxx) xxx-xxxx	Dante.ferragio@ rwm.com	(xxx) xxx-xxxx#
Levensque, Harold	Labor	(xxx) xxx-xxxx	(xxx) xxx-xxxx	Harold.Levensque@ rwm.com	(xxx) xxx-xxxx#
TBD (to be determined)					
TBD					
TBD					
TBD					
TBD					
TBD					

Activation and Response: The recovery team should be activated when the BoD and the Emergency Operations Center (EOC) deem the location of the event is all clear. It is expected that all members of the recovery team can work from home to begin recovery. If necessary, the recovery team leader can designate where the recovery team can reassemble, if applicable, at a work location.

THREAT ASSESSMENT AND IMPACT ANALYSIS

While this plan should be threat independent, meaning it should apply to just about any event, the reality is that certain events having a substantial likelihood and impact should be considered when building this plan. The top five threats are

- Major earthquake
- Flooding

- Frost/cold temperatures
- Immigration restrictions
- Unpredictable climate change

RESOURCE (DEPENDENCY) CATEGORY REQUIREMENTS

- Labor
- Transportation
- Information technology/applications
- Equipment
- Supplies
- Documentation
- Facilities
- Vendors

Recovery Strategies for Each Resource: Labor (in work)
Responsibility: Harold Levensque
Recovery Time Objective: 3 days
Minimum Quantity Requirements (TBD):

Day	Day 1	Day 2	Day 3	Day 4	Day 5	Day 6	Day 7	Day 8	Day 9	Day 10	Minimum Quantity
Resource											
Laborers (hand pickers and drivers)	12	15	24	22	21	15	14	13	12	12	25
Wine master (viticulture specialist)	1	1	1	1	1	1	1	1	1	1	1

Strategies (workarounds and other pertinent information):

1. Determine if sufficient labor is available to perform recovery work. Note: At least one local wine master or viticulture specialist must be available to verify whether the vineyard is recoverable and to what extent.
2. If yes, determine the people with the requisite knowledge and skills to enable recovery.

3. If no, perform the following steps in order from most to least:
    a. Contact local companies specializing in providing the necessary labor.
    b. Contact other vineyards owned by RWM, Inc.
    c. Contact raw materials, for example, grapes (Grapling Grapes, Inc.) at (xxx) xxx-xxxx.
4. If resources are unavailable, contact the EOC at (xxx) xxx-xxxx or via e-mail at eocrmc@rwm.com.

Recovery Strategies for Each Resource: Vehicles
Responsibility: TBD
Recovery Time Objective: TBD
Minimum Quantity Requirements (resource requirements over time): TBD

Day	Day 1	Day 2	Day 3	Day 4	Day 5	Day 6	Day 7	Day 8	Day 9	Day 10	Minimum Quantity
Resource											
Tractor											
Netting machine											
Vine harvester											
Pickup truck											
TBD											

Strategies (workarounds and other pertinent information): TBD
Recovery Strategies for Each Resource: Information Technology/Applications
Responsibility: TBD
Recovery Time Objective: TBD
Minimum Quantity Requirements (resource requirements over time): TBD

Day	Day 1	Day 2	Day 3	Day 4	Day 5	Day 6	Day 7	Day 8	Day 9	Day 10	Minimum Quantity
Resource											
Laptop with Internet connection											
TBD											
TBD											
TBD											
TBD											

Strategies (workarounds and other pertinent information): TBD
Recovery Strategies for Each Resource: Equipment
Responsibility: TBD
Recovery Time Objective: TBD
Minimum Quantity Requirements (resource requirements over time): TBD

Day	Day 1	Day 2	Day 3	Day 4	Day 5	Day 6	Day 7	Day 8	Day 9	Day 10	Minimum Quantity
Resource											
Grape fork											
Grape shears											
Harvest lugs											
Micro bins											
Sprayers											

Strategies (workarounds and other pertinent information): TBD
Recovery Strategies for Each Resource: Supplies
Responsibility: TBD
Recovery Time Objective: TBD
Minimum Quantity Requirements (resource requirements over time): TBD

Day	Day 1	Day 2	Day 3	Day 4	Day 5	Day 6	Day 7	Day 8	Day 9	Day 10	Minimum Quantity
Resource											
Herbicides (e.g., gallons)											
Fungicides (e.g., gallons)											
Lime sulfur											
Wire											
Netting											

Strategies (workarounds and other pertinent information): TBD
Recovery Strategies for Each Resource: Documentation
Responsibility: TBD
Recovery Time Objective: TBD
Minimum Quantity Requirements (resource requirements over time):

Day	Day 1	Day 2	Day 3	Day 4	Day 5	Day 6	Day 7	Day 8	Day 9	Day 10	Minimum Quantity
Resource											
Federal											
State											
Local											
TBD											
TBD											

Strategies (workarounds and other pertinent information): TBD
Recovery Strategies for Each Resource: Facilities
Responsibility: TBD
Recovery Time Objective: TBD
Minimum Quantity Requirements (resource requirements over time): TBD

Day	Day 1	Day 2	Day 3	Day 4	Day 5	Day 6	Day 7	Day 8	Day 9	Day 10	Minimum Quantity
Resource											
Equipment storage											
Grape storage											
Temporary living quarters											
TBD											
TBD											

Strategies (workarounds and other pertinent information): TBD
Recovery Strategies for Each Resource: Vendors
Responsibility: TBD
Recovery Time Objective: TBD
Minimum Quantity Requirements (resource requirements over time): TBD

Day	Day 1	Day 2	Day 3	Day 4	Day 5	Day 6	Day 7	Day 8	Day 9	Day 10	Minimum Quantity
Resource											
TBD											
TBD											
TBD											
TBD											
TBD											

Strategies (workarounds and other pertinent information): TBD

GENERAL RESPONSE REQUIREMENTS

1. Receive direction from the EOC that response is complete.
2. Await policy directions from the executive advisory group to determine whether to proceed with recovery of the critical process.
3. Determine whether to contact the recovery team via the call tree. If so, determine whether to meet at a designated location or electronically, for example, teleconference.
4. Assess impact to the critical process, such as the sub-processes or procedures negatively impacted and to what degree.
5. Determine which resources, or dependencies, will be impacted and the corresponding procedures in the plan needing to be executed.
6. Determine the firing order of those procedures needed for recovery.
7. Execute appropriate procedures and monitor progress, keeping in mind the maximum allowable down time for the overall company and recovery time objective for the critical process.
8. Once recovery is complete, conduct a lessons learned session.

REFERENCES

- Save Our Wine Project Charter
- Statement of Work
- Company Mission Statement
- Enterprise Business Impact Analysis
- Project Master Schedule

Bibliography

Adrian, Nicole. 2008. "Incredible Journey." *Quality Progress*, June.

Aerts, Luc. 2001. "A Framework for Managing Operational Risk." *Internal Auditor*, August.

Albert, George. 2006. "Blurry Lines: Shared Services Embraces Outsourcing." *Global Services*, March.

Anderson, Shannon W., Margaret H. Christ, and Karen L. Sedatole. 2006. "Risky Business." *Internal Auditor*, December.

Anthes, Gary H. 2006. "Blind Spots." *Computerworld*, February 20.

Atkinson, William. 2006. "Managing Risk in Outsourcing." *Global Services*, December.

Balfour, Frederik, and David Kiley. 2005. "The Soft Underbelly of Offshoring." *Businessweek*, April 25.

Banham, Russ. 2007. "Chinese Checking." *CFO*, September.

Barnes, James C. 2001. *A Guide to Business Continuity.* Chichester: John Wiley & Sons.

Barrett, Paul M. 2011. "Success is Never Having to Say You're Sorry." *Bloomberg Businessweek*, July 4–10.

Barrett, Paul M., and Peter Millard. 2012. "Over a Barrel." *Bloomberg Businessweek*, May 14–20.

Barry, John M. 2005. *The Great Influenza.* New York: Penguin Books.

Basu, Indrajit. 2007. "Services in Europe's Backyard." *Global Services*, June.

Beaulieu, Bert R. 2004. "Security through the Palanterra." *GeoIntelligence*, July/August.

Begley, Sharon, and Andrew Murr. 2011. "How to Save California." *Newsweek*, March 28 and April 4.

Belk, Daniel D., and Kevin P. Corbley. 2005. "Simulation Advances Emergency Preparedness and Response." *GeoIntelligence*, July/August.

Bennis, Warren G. 2006. "Leading for the Long Run." *Harvard Business Review*, May.

Berstein, Pewter L. 1998. *Against the Odds.* New York: John Wiley & Sons.

Bhambal, Juhi. 2006. "Managing Errant Contractors." *Global Services*, April.

Black, Thomas. 2011. "The Impact on American Companies." *Bloomberg Businessweek*, March 21–27.

Blanchard, David. 2007. *Supply Chain Management Best Practices.* Hoboken, NJ: John Wiley & Sons.

Blythe, Bruce T. 2002. *Blindsided.* New York: Portfolio.

Boudway, Ira. 2011. "The Arms Race against the Pirates." *Bloomberg Businessweek*, April 25–May 1.

Bowersox, Donald J., David J. Closs, and M. Bixby Cooper. 2010. *Supply Chain Logistics Management*, 3rd ed. Boston: McGraw-Hill Irwin.

Bradley, Tony. 2005. "Warning Lights." *Information Security*, April.

Brand, Stewart. 2011. "What's Next for Nuclear Power?" *Fortune*, April 11.

Brandel, Mary. 2006. "Culture Clash." *Computerworld*, February 20.

Brandel, Mary. 2007. "Offshoring Grows Up." *Computerworld*, March 12.

Brilliant, Larry. 2006. "What to Expect from Government." *Harvard Business Review*, May.

Brinkley, Douglas. 2007. *The Great Deluge.* New York: Harper Perennial.

Brown, Ted. 2008. "RTOs, RPOs, and RTAs." *Continuity Insights*, September/October.

Bryce, Emma. 2012. "How an Outbreak Spreads." *Discover*, November.

Burkholder, Nicolas C. 2006. *Outsourcing*. Hoboken, NJ: John Wiley & Sons.
Burnson, Patrick. 2011. "Weighing the Risks of Global Sourcing." *Logistics Management*, August.
Burton, Christopher. 2010. "The Death of All Hazards Planning?" *Disaster Recovery Journal*, September.
Calder, Josh. 2006. "States of Confusion." *Wired*, April.
Campbell, Ballard C. 2008. *American Disasters*. New York: Checkmark Books.
Caralli, Richard A., Julia H. Allen, and David W. White. 2011. *CERT Resilience Management Model*. Upper Saddle River, NJ: Pearson Education, Inc.
Carey, Bjorn. 2009. "Death by the Numbers." *Popular Science*, March.
Castleden, Rodney. 2007. *Natural Disasters That Changed the World*. Edison, NJ: Chartwell Books.
Chakravarti, Nilotpal. 2006. "Globalization and Complexity." *Global Services*, April.
Champion, David. 2009. "Managing Risk in the New World." *Harvard Business Review*, October.
Christopher, Martin. 2011. *Logistics & Supply Chain Management*, 4th ed. Harlow, England: Financial Times.
Collett, Stacy. 2006. "Balancing Act." *Computerworld*, February 10.
Computerworld. 2006. "Snapshots," February 20.
Contingency Planning & Management. 2000. "The State of the Public-Private Union," CIP, C-12–C-16.
Continuity Insights. 2008. "Inside Business Continuity Consulting," September/October.
Cooper, Sherry. 2006. "A Preview of Disruption." *Harvard Business Review*, May.
Crosby, Daniel. 2011. "Risk Assessment and Why You Stink at It." *Risk Management*, September.
Crouhy, Michel, Dan Galai, and Robert Mark. 2006. *The Essentials of Risk Management*. New York: McGraw-Hill.
Cullen, Davew. 2009. *Columbine*. New York: Twelve.
Dahl, Darren. 2009. "Managing Outsourcing to Save Money?" *Inc.*, January/February.
Daley, Jason. 2012. "Japan Quakes; Nuke Power Stays Steady." *Discover*, January 2.
Daniels, John D., and Lee H. Radebaugh. 2001. *International Business*, 9th ed. Upper Saddle River, NJ: Prentice Hall.
Diacu, Florin. 2009. *MegaDisasters*. Oxford: Oxford University Press.
Diamond, Jared. 2005. *Collapse*. New York: Viking.
Di Justo, Patrick. 2009. "Apocalypse: Not." *Wired*, July.
Dobson, Wendy, and Brian R. Golden. 2006. "All Eyes on China." *Harvard Business Review*, May.
Dominguez, Linda R. 2006. *The Manager's Step-by-Step Guide to Outsourcing*. New York: McGraw-Hill.
Doughty, Ken, ed. 2001. *Business Continuity Planning*. Boca Raton, FL: Auerbach.
Dowell, Scott F., and Joseph S. Bresee. 2006. "How a Human Pandemic Could Start." *Harvard Business Review*, May.
Dreikorn, Michael. 2009. "What's on the Horizon." *Quality Progress*, November.
DRI International. 2000. *Business Continuity Planning: Accelerated Course (BCLE 2000), Book 1*. New York: DRI International.
DRI International. 2000. *Business Continuity Planning: Accelerated Course (BCLE 2000), Book 2*. New York: DRI International.
DRI International. 2000. *Professional Practices for Business Continuity Practitioners*. New York: DRI International.

Drucker, Vanessa. 2013. "Confluence of Risk." *Global Finance*, March.
Dunn, Christine. 2006. "Building a Vendor Scorecard." *Computerworld*, May 29.
Durfee, Don. 2006. "Innocents Abroad." *CFO*, June.
Dutta, Soumitra. 2010. "What's Your Personal Social Media Strategy?" *Harvard Business Review*, November.
Dwyer, Jim, and Kevin Flynn. 2005. *102 Minutes*. New York: Times Books.
Dye, Lowell. 1998. "Just What is Scenario Planning Anyway?" *PM Network*, June.
Earls, Alan R. 2005. "Offshoring Pays Off But Not as Much as You Think." *Application Development Trends*, January.
Ehrenfeld, Jon, and Charles Aaenenson. 2013. *Strengthening the Alliance*. Seattle, WA: Peace Winds America.
Engardio, Pete, and Bruce Einhorn. 2005. "Outsourcing Innovation." *Businessweek*, March 21.
FEMA. 2004. *Continuity of Operations (COOP) Plan Template Instructions*. Washington, DC: FEMA, April.
FEMA. 2010a. *ICS for Single Resource and Initial Action Incidents Student Manual (IC 200)*. Washington, DC: FEMA, August.
FEMA. 2010b. *Introduction to the Incident Command System Student Manual (ICS 100)*. Washington, DC: FEMA, August.
Fischetti, Mack. 2006. "Protecting New Orleans." *Scientific American*, February.
Fischhoff, Baruch. 2006a. "Getting Straight Talk Right." *Harvard Business Review*, May.
Fischhoff, Baruch. 2006b. "Visualizing Your Vulnerabilities." *Harvard Business Review*, May.
Fox, Geraldine, and Nigel Hughes. 2008. "7 Sins of Offshore Sourcing." *Baseline Magazine*, September.
Funston, Rick, and Bob Ruprecht. 2007. "Risk in the Strategic Planning Process." *Business Performance Management*, May.
Gale, Sarah Fister. 2011. "A Series of Unfortunate Events." *PM Network*, January.
Garcia, Andrew. 2008a. "Business Continuity Best Practices." *Eweek*, November 10.
Garcia, Andrew. 2008b. "Emergency Info Delivery." *Eweek*, November 10.
Goff, John. 2006. "Coming Distractions." *CFO*, April.
Goodden, Randall L. 2008. "Better Safe Than Sorry." *Quality Progress*, May.
Graeber, Charles. 2011. "Nothing to Do But Start Again." *Bloomberg Businessweek*, April 25–May 1.
Grant, Elaine Appleton. 2006. "Flirting with Disaster Recovery." *CFO*, May.
Greaver II, Maurice F. 1999. *Strategic Outsourcing*. New York: AMACOM.
Greeley, Brendan. 2011a. "Facing Up to Nuclear Risk." *Bloomberg Businessweek*, March 21–27.
Greeley, Brendan. 2011b. "The God Clause." *Bloomberg Businessweek*, September 5–11.
Green, Paula L. 2013. "Staying on the Attack." *Global Finance*, September.
Grose, Vernon L. 1987. *Managing Risk*. Englewood Cliffs, NJ: Prentice Hall.
Grunwald, Michael. 2010. "Katrina's a Man-Made Disaster." *Time*, December 6.
Hagg, Andy. 2000. "CIP: The History, The Hurdles Ahead." *Contingency Planning & Management*, CIP, C-9–C-11.
Hammer, Joshua. 2008. "The Oil Cowboy Blues." *Men's Journal*, January.
Harper, Rebecca. 2003. "America's Most Toxic." *Wired*, April.
Hawthorne, Christopher. 2011. "Altruism, Architecture, and Disaster." *Architecture Magazine*, September.
Heller, Peter. 2011. "Not Again." *Bloomberg Businessweek*, June 13–19.
Hill, Emma, ed. 2010. *501 Most Devastating Disasters*. London: Bounty Books.
Holbrook, Emily. 2011. "Historic Floods of the Big Muddy." *Risk Management*, July/August.
Hollins, Mary P. 2006. "Risky Business." *Washington CEO*, July.

Holmes, Nigel. 2009. "Why is Swine Flu So Worrisome?" *American History*, December.

Honore, Russell L. 2009. *Survival.* New York: Atria Books.

Hughes, Greg. 2008. "The Future of Risk." *Global Services*, February.

Hulme, George V. 2008. "Global Risk: The Balancing Act." *Smart Enterprise Magazine.*

Hult, Tomas, and David Closs. 2014. *Global Supply Chain Management.* New York: McGraw-Hill.

Hunsberger, Kelley. 2011. "The Risks of Outsourcing." *PM Network*, November.

Ito, Aki, Keiko Ujikane, and Mayumi Otsuma. 2011. "Financing the Reconstruction." *Bloomberg Businessweek*, March 21–March 27.

Johnson, Sarah. 2011. "Very Big, Yet Hard to See." *CFO*, November.

Journal of Accountancy. 2007. "News Digest," January.

Kapadia, Reshma, and Elizabeth O'Brien. 2010. "The Case for Going Global." *Smart Money*, August.

Katz, David M. 2011. "All in the Timing." *CFO*, June.

Keller, Glenn R. 2007. *Modern Corporate Risk Management.* Ft. Lauderdale, FL: J. Ross Publishing, Inc.

Kendrick, Tom. 2003. *Identifying and Managing Project Risk.* New York: AMACOM.

Kerney, Gary, Bill Churney, and Jim Loveland. 2010. "Managing Risk with Advanced Modeling Techniques." *Disaster Recovery Journal*, Summer.

Keys, David. 2012. "The Growth of a Deadly Virus." *BBC History Magazine*, July 20.

Khan, Imrana. 2008a. "5 Most Popular Outsourcing Risks." *Global Services*, June.

Khan, Imrana. 2008b. "The Uncertain Global Economy." *Global Services*, November.

Kildow, Betty A. 2011. *A Supply Chain Management Guide to Business Continuity.* New York: AMACOM.

Kirvan, Paul. 2003. "Protecting your Critical Infrastructure." *Contingency Planning & Management*, January/February.

Kliem, Ralph L. 1992. *The People Side of Project Management.* Aldershot, England: Gower.

Kliem, Ralph L. 1997a. *Project Management Methodology: A Practical Guide for the Next Millennium.* New York: Marcel Dekker.

Kliem, Ralph L. 1997b. *Reducing Project Risk.* Aldershot, England: Gower.

Kliem, Ralph L. 2003. *The Project Manager's Emergency Kit.* Boca Raton, FL: St. Lucie Press.

Kliem, Ralph L. 2004. *Leading High Performance Projects.* Boca Raton, FL: J. Ross Publishing.

Kliem, Ralph L. 2008. *Effective Communications for Project Management.* Boca Raton, FL: Auerbach.

Kliem, Ralph L. 2011. *Managing Projects in Trouble.* Boca Raton, FL: CRC Press.

Ko, Ryan K. L., Stephen S. G. Lee, and Veerappa Rajan. 2012. "Understanding Cloud Failures." *IEEE Spectrum*, December.

Krell, Eric. 2011. "Manufacturing 2.0." *Consulting*, January/February.

Krzykowski, Brett. 2008. "K'Nex Success." *Quality Progress*, May.

Kunreuther, Howard, and Michael Useem. 2010. *Learning from Catastrophe.* Upper Saddle River, NJ: Wharton School Publishing.

Light, Joe. 2009. "Global Opportunities … and Risks." *Money*, June.

Lubben, Richard T. 1988. *Just-in-Time Manufacturing.* New York: McGraw-Hill Book Company.

Lunt, Penny. 2005. "A Watertight Plan." *IT Architect*, September.

MacVittie, Lori. 2005. "Chain Strain." *Network Computing*, December 8.

Margulius, David L. 2005. "10 Ways to Get Offshoring Right." *Infoworld*, August 29.

Matlack, Carol. 2010. "The Growing Peril of a Connected World." *Bloomberg Businessweek*, December 6–12.

McAdams, Jennifer. 2006. "Casting Call." *Computerworld*, February 20.

McDougall, Paul. 2005. "Small Scale Offshoring." *Information Week*, July 25.

McHugh, Josh. 2008. "Fear Factors." *Wired*, July.

McNair-Huff, Rob, and Natalie McNair-Huff. 2006. *Washington Disasters*. Guilford, CT: Morris Book Publishing, LLC.

McNamee, David, and Georges Selim. 1999. "The Next Step in Risk Management." *Internal Auditor*, June.

McQuaid, John, and Mark Schleifstein. 2006. *Path of Destruction*. New York: Little, Brown and Company.

Mearian, Lucas. 2009. "Swine Flu Emergency Should Put IT on Alert." *Computerworld*, November 2.

Mileti, Dennis S. 1999. *Disaster by Design*. Washington, DC: National Academy of Sciences.

Mitchell, Robert L. 2007. "On the Edge of Disaster." *Computerworld*, April 30.

Mitchell, Robert L. 2011. "The Grill." *Computerworld*, March 21.

Mitchell, Robert L. 2012. "Predictive Analytics Go to Work." *Computerworld*, October 8.

Moyle, Ed. 2006. "Business Survival 101." *Information Security*, November.

Mudge, Kenneth, Skip Skivington, and Cheryl LaTouche. 2010. "When Suppliers Go Out-of-Business." *Disaster Recovery Journal*, Summer.

Myers, Kenneth L. 1999. *Manager's Guide to Contingency Planning for Disasters*. New York: John Wiley & Sons.

Myser, Michael. 2005. "The World of Terror." *Wired*, June.

Nohria, Nitin. 2006. "Survival of Adaptive." *Harvard Business Review*, May.

Osterland, Andrew. 2014. "Rising Tides of Risk." *Global Finance*, January.

Overby, Stephanie. 2004. "The Inner Cost of Outsourcing." *CIO*, November 1.

Overby, Stephanie. 2006. "Big Deals, Big Savings, Big Problems." *CIO*, February 1.

Palmer, Katie. 2012. "The Year's Worst Natural Disasters." *Discover*, January 2.

Patton, Susannah. 2006. "Captain Contingency." *CIO*, March 1.

Pesek, William. 2011. "The Cataclysm this Time." *Bloomberg Businessweek*, March 27.

Peters, C. J., and Mark Olshaker. 1997. *Virus Hunter*. New York: Anchor Books.

Pickford, James, ed. 2001. *Mastering Risk*, Volume 1. London: Pearson Education Limited.

Popular Mechanics. 2006. "Now What?," March.

Popular Mechanics. 2010. "The Men Who Saw It Coming," April.

Pratt, Mary K. 2005. "Redefining Disaster." *Computerworld*, June 20.

Pratt, Mary K. 2006. "Global Gotchas." *Computerworld*, February 20.

Price, Tom, and T. J. Aulds. 2005. "The Texas City Oil Refinery." *Popular Mechanics*, July.

Pritchard, Carl L. 2005. *Risk Management*, 3rd ed. Arlington, VA: ESI International.

Quality Progress. 2010. "Survey: Many Unhappy with Outsourcing Providers," December.

Rae-Dupree, Janet. 2004. "Offshore Winds." *CIO Insight*, 4th Quarter.

Rash, Wayne. 2008. "10 Things You Should Know about Business Continuity." *Eweek*, January 7.

Risk Management. 2011. "Hindsight," July/August.

Roetzheim, William H. 2005. "Disaster Prevention." *Software Development*, February.

Rohmeyer, Paul. 2007. "Inviting Risk." *Information Security*, May.

Ryan, Vincent. 2011. "A World of Risk." *CFO*, June.

Schwartz, Karen D. 2006. "Managing Subcontractors." *Global Services*, July.

Scigliano, Eric. 2002. "10 Technology Disasters." *Technology Review*, June.

Scott, Steven. 2009. "A Matter of Choice." *Contingent Workforce Strategies*, November/December.

Seal, Vivek. 2006. "Outsourcing IT: Not the Best Solution." *Global Services*, April.

Shapiro, Jeremy F. 2001. *Modeling the Supply Chain*. Pacific Grove, CA: Duxbury.

Sheffi, Yossi. 2005. *The Resilient Enterprise*. Cambridge, MA: The MIT Press.

Shelburne, Elizabeth Chiles. 2009. "The Next Breadbasket?" *The Atlantic*, September.
Sherbinin, Alex de, Koko Warner, and Charles Ehrhart. 2011. "Casualties of Climate Change." *Scientific American*, January.
Simchi-Levi, David, Philip Kaminsky, and Edith Simchi-Levi. 2003. *Designing and Managing the Supply Chain*, 2nd ed. Boston: McGraw-Hill Irwin.
Sipress, Alan. 2009. *The Fatal Strain*. New York: Penguin Books.
Slone, Reuben E., John T. Mentzer, and J. Paul Dittman. 2007. "Are You the Weakest Link in Your Supply Chain?" *Harvard Business Review*, September.
Spandanuta, Laura. 2012. "Planning for Disaster." *Security Management*, March.
Spotts, Pete. 2013. "Can We Arrest Global Warming?" *The Christian Science Monitor Weekly*, April 22–29.
Staples, Jeffrey. 2006. "A New Type of Threat." *Harvard Business Review*, May.
Stuart, Alix. 2011. "Making the Leap." *CFO*, June.
Sullivan, William L. 2008. *Oregon's Greatest Natural Disasters*. Eugene, OR: Navillus Press.
Susser, Peter. 2006. "Limiting Exposure—Of the Legal Kind." *Harvard Business Review*, May.
Svoboda, Elizabeth. 2006. "Forecasting Hurricanes." *Popular Science*, July.
Taleb, Nassim. 2010. *The Black Swan*. London: Penguin Books.
Taleb, Nassim N., Daniel G. Goldstein, and Mark W. Spitznagel. 2009. "The Six Mistakes Executives Make in Risk Management." *Harvard Business Review*, October.
The Committee of Sponsoring Organizations (COSO). 2004a. *Enterprise Risk Management—Integrated Framework: Application Techniques*. Jersey City, NJ: COSO.
The Committee of Sponsoring Organizations (COSO). 2004b. *Enterprise Risk Management—Integrated Framework: Executive Summary Framework*. Jersey City, NJ: COSO.
The Economist. 2009. "Fixing a Broken World," January 31.
Thompson, Kalee. 2011. "When the First Responder is You." *Popular Mechanics*, June.
Thorton, Emily. 2009. "Managing through a Crisis." *Businessweek*, January 19.
Thorton, Grant. 2009. "International Sourcing: Offshore or Near-shore?" *World Trade*, May.
Thurman, Mathias. 2013. "Plans are Made to Be Revised." *Computerworld*, May 6.
Tirone, Jonathan. 2011. "Searching for Clues along the Ring of Fire." *Bloomberg Businessweek*, March 21–27.
Ursano, Robert J., Ann E. Norwood, and Carol S. Fullerton. 2005. *BioTerrorism*. Cambridge: Cambridge University Press.
US Dept. of Homeland Security. 2009. *National Incident Management System: An Introduction (IS-700.A)*, January. Washington, DC: US Government.
Useem, Michael. 2007. "Decisions under Pressure." *CIO*, February 15.
Vashistha, Avinash. 2007. "Top 50 Emerging Outsourcing Cities." *Global Services*, October.
Vashistha, Avinash, and Imrana Khan. 2008. "The 50 Emerging Global Outsourcing Cities." *Global Services*, October.
Violino, Bob. 2006. "Offshore R&D Takes Off." *Global Services*, March.
Wade, Jade. 2011. "Benchmarking Risk Management." *Risk Management*, September.
Webster, John S. 2006. "Safety Zone." *Computerworld*, February 20.
Weier, Mary Hayes. 2007. "Get a Grip." *Information Week*, November 5.
White, Debra Alligood. 2006. "What to Do When Things Fall Apart?" *Global Services*, April.
Wohlsen, Marcus. 2013. "Faster Than Overnight." *Wired*, April.
Wold, Geoffrey. 2010. "How to Survive a BCM Audit." *Disaster Recovery Journal*, Summer.
Worthen, Ben. 2007. "Extreme Outsourcing." *CIO*, May 15.
Zappier, Alicia. 2008. "New Emergency Operations Center Converted from Bomb Shelter." *Government Video*, September.
Zolli, Andrew, and Ann Marie Healy. 2012. *Resilience*. New York: Free Press.

Index

Page numbers followed by f indicate figures.

B

F

L

U